ROGER FEDERER

THE GREATEST

CHRIS BOWERS

JOHN BLAKE

Published by John Blake Publishing Ltd,
3 Bramber Court, 2 Bramber Road,
London W14 9PB, England

www.johnblakepublishing.co.uk

Parts of this book have previously been published in
Fantastic Federer and Roger Federer – Spirit of
a Champion by Chris Bowers

This edition published in paperback in 2010

ISBN: 978 1 84454 956 6

British Library Cataloguing-in-Publication Data:

A catalogue record for this book is available from the British Library.

Design by www.envydesign.co.uk

Printed in Great Britain by CPI Bookmarque, Croydon, CR0 4TD

1 3 5 7 9 10 8 6 4 2

Papers used by John Blake Publishing are natural, recyclable products made
from wood grown in sustainable forests. The manufacturing processes conform
to the environmental regulations of the country of origin.

'He is a highly intelligent lad, who has the right feeling for the right moment, and there are very few people who in the right moment find the right thing to do. He is one of them. He's no academic, but his word is bond, a deal is a deal.'

—*ROGER BRENNWALD, SWISS TENNIS IMPRESARIO*

'I heard something on television about two weeks ago saying Tiger Woods is going to pass Michael Jordan as the best athlete of our time. I think that's a joke. I'd make a case for Roger Federer being the best athlete of our time. Not tennis player, athlete. No offence to Tiger, he's an incredible golfer, but his record in matchplay events, the events where you're out if you have a bad day, isn't particularly impressive. We tennis players have that every single week. Roger wins every Grand Slam title except the French Open, and he wins every Masters Series tournament. That means he can't allow himself a single bad day. That's incredible.'

—*JAMES BLAKE, AMERICAN TENNIS PLAYER*
(US OPEN, 2006)

'I was out there with the best player I ever saw – Roger.'

—*RAFAEL NADAL, SPANISH TENNIS PLAYER*
(AUSTRALIAN OPEN, 2009)

'You are the most popular tennis player in China because you have a nice smile and a big nose.'

—*A CHINESE JOURNALIST PREFACING A QUESTION TO FEDERER*
AT THE 2002 TENNIS MASTERS CUP IN SHANGHAI

'Who plays tennis on a ship? Jolly Roger Federer.'

—*A JOKE COMPILED BY THE AUTHOR'S SIX-YEAR-OLD DAUGHTER*

ABOUT THE AUTHOR

CHRIS BOWERS is a freelance writer and broadcaster who has covered the global tennis circuit since 1992. After graduating in German with History, Linguistics and Music in 1983, he trained as a newspaper journalist, before moving into radio in 1986. Over the next two years, he spent 22 months working for Switzerland's overseas service Swiss Radio International in Bern. During that time he played a year's Swiss league tennis for the Flamingo tennis club owned by Frantisek Kratochvil, whose son Michel became a touring professional; his doubles partner in that season was Severin Lüthi, who is now captain of the Swiss Davis Cup team and a close confidant of Roger Federer. After working for an environmental organisation for two years, he went full time on the global tennis tour in 1992, working for newspapers, magazines, radio, television and internet media. He is best known as a commentator for Eurosport and BBC Radio, but is a reporter on radio networks throughout the world. As a writer, he has reported for various newspapers, magazines and websites and this is his eighth book about tennis. He also works in the environmental field, and is a councillor in English local government. He is forty-nine years old, and lives with his partner and daughter in East Sussex, England.

CONTENTS

NOTE

Much reference is made in this book to 'Masters' and 'Masters Series' tournaments, the group of nine elite tour events that form the biggest men's tournaments below the four Grand Slams. In 2009, the ATP officially changed the name of these events to '1000' tournaments, a name based on the amount of ranking points the winner receives. But because the nine were branded moderately successfully over the preceding decade as the 'Masters Series', the name 'Masters' has stuck, with the term 'Masters-1000' evolving as a halfway house between the common and the official names. This book sticks largely to 'Masters Series', with occasional references to 'Masters' and 'Masters-1000'.

AUTHOR'S INTRODUCTION

Who is the greatest? It's a question asked by children in the school playground, by people discussing legends over a drink in the bar, by journalists trying to assess the relative merits of a body of work, and by countless others. They all want to know who the greatest in a certain discipline is.

The question is asked slightly differently in this book. Since winning the French Open and Wimbledon in 2009, the tennis world is pretty much united in its recognition of Roger Federer as the greatest tennis player of all time. But who is he? Where does he come from? How has his route to greatness shaped him? And what lessons from the Federer legend are there for others to learn, especially parents who may have equally gifted offspring and aren't sure entirely how to help them?

This book is both a work in its own right and a development of three earlier books. In 2005-06, I wrote *Fantastic Federer*, which was updated in 2007. At that time, Federer was still in his mid-twenties, so the book was very much a profile of him and a speculation of what he might go on to achieve. As his greatness came more to the fore, a third book appeared in 2009, *Roger Federer – Spirit of a Champion*. But what Federer achieved in the six weeks in the middle of 2009 marks a watershed between the part of his career characterised by potential, and the period in which he has been truly acknowledged as the greatest in his discipline. The Roger Federer story is by no means finished, as he continues to play on the tour and is still among the frontline favourites for every tournament he enters. But the time has now been reached where the body of work that is his career can be seen in some context, superseding the years when we had to wait to see what else he would achieve before we could safely assess his legend.

This book builds on the three earlier books. His childhood and early career have not changed since 2006, but the way we view him as a person and a champion has. And some events that seemed quite important a few years ago have been eclipsed by bigger achievements since then. As such, readers who come to this book without having read the other three will be as at home with this biography of Roger Federer as those who have read every word of the others.

Yet however comprehensive this book tries to be, it is only part of the Federer story. When the man himself comes to write his own autobiography – or authorised biography – there will be more meat on the bones. In many ways it is odd that he has not yet published a work about his life. Most sports stars have published at least one autobiography by the time they reach their twenty-eighth birthday, in some cases more. Inevitably, some of these works are more enlightening than others – those that offer information about what makes a person tick are invariably more interesting than those which serve little more of a purpose than commercial aggrandisement.

But Roger Federer is different. Since he won his first

Wimbledon title in July 2003, he and his advisers have been inundated with requests from publishers and journalists for him to write his autobiography, or to cooperate on an authorised biography. He has always turned such requests down. The reason he gives is that he doesn't yet want to invest the time necessary to do a proper job on his own story. While that reason rings true, he is also known to be keeping a diary of his own thoughts and reflections so that one day – probably when his playing career is over or drawing to a close – he will be able to write his own account of his career. Until then, he is very relaxed about others writing about him, as long as no book claims to be in any way authorised.

This book is therefore an 'unauthorised' biography, although I prefer the word 'independent' as 'unauthorised' is often taken to mean inherently hostile. The lack of authorisation gave me a degree of freedom to write about Federer without constraints about what he or his advisers might have wanted me to write. I was able to speak freely with many of the people who have helped to shape him, and paint a picture of him both as a person and a tennis player. The picture that emerges is still one of a thoroughly decent bloke, albeit one whose naturally amenable character has come under increased bombardment from a cocktail of fawning and financial inducements that would test the moral fibre of a saint.

Yet even when Federer comes to write his own book and reveal more of what went on in his mind and in Team Federer during his time at the top, it will not be the definitive work on its own. Federer's career is made up as much of the impact it has had on others and the way his personality has evolved through his various successes and setbacks, as it is through the man's own thought processes and recollections. As such, the tales and memories of those who have shaped him and travelled the journey with him are also a valid part of the story. As with *Fantastic Federer* and *Spirit of a Champion*, this book pulls together my own research and draws on published material in English, German and French.

I am fortunate to be in a pretty much ideal situation to write about Roger. I've known him since he was sixteen – I first interviewed him after he'd won the boys' singles at Wimbledon in 1998 – and the fact that I have lived in Switzerland, speak German and French (even the Swiss German dialects that baffle many citizens of Germany), and know several people with whom he grew up puts me in a unique position among international tennis writers to write his biography.

Obviously, I'm indebted to a number of people who have borne witness to Roger's development and have given me the benefit of their experience, including (in alphabetical order): Yves Allegro, Madeleine Bärlocher, Roger Brennwald, Beat Caspar, Marco Chiudinelli, Ashley Fisher, Roger Jaunin, Seppli Kacovski, Marco Mordasini, Francesco Ricci Bitti, Niki von Vary, Freddy Widmer and Thomas Wirz. I am also grateful, for various bits of important help, to: Faye Andrews, Nicola Arzani, Tim Curry, Richard Eaton, Tony Godsick, Mark Hodgkinson, Frank Hofen, Mitzi Ingram Evans, Annie Hammerton, Severin Lüthi, Ian McDermott, Konrad Meyer, Peter Miles, Jack Milner, Helen Mittwoch, Daniel Monnin, Claudia Moser, Andrew Rigby, Neil Robinson, Barbara Travers, Jürg Vogel and Paul Zimmer. I'd also like to thank Lynette Federer and Tony Godsick for their help in discussing the original concept and for their willingness to help subsequently within the constraints set by Roger.

And particular thanks go to John Blake and Michelle Signore of John Blake Publishing for having the original belief in me and the book, and for investing in this latest version of the Federer story following Roger's triumphs of 2009.

The aim of this book is to give greater understanding of the personality and – with all due caveats to what he might yet go on to achieve – chart the body of work that has made this remarkable sportsman and inspirational person the greatest in tennis. If it achieves any of that, it will have served its purpose.

Chris Bowers
April 2010

THE YOUTH OF A CHAMPION

1

1

THE STORY OF ROGER FEDERER is no 'Williams story'. In fact, to those who hanker after an egalitarian tennis world where the economic circumstances of a child's background are no obstacle to them making it to the very top of the game, this will offer no supporting evidence. While Venus and Serena Williams were genuine products of the ghetto community of Los Angeles, and Jimmy Connors grew up in a blue-collar area of Illinois, encouraged to despise the rich kids who populated the established tennis clubs, Federer is a product of the affluent middle classes.

He is the second child of a modestly well-to-do but unremarkable family from Basel. He's certainly not had to defy social obstacles to reach the top, he's not even a middle-class rebel without a cause like John McEnroe was. He has never felt the need to turn his anger into on-court intensity, the way Connors, Lleyton Hewitt and even Pete Sampras could turn their opponents into deeply hated enemies, at least

3

for the duration of a match. Nor has he ever resorted to the snide tactics of a McEnroe, Ion Tiriac or Ilie Nastase to derail an opponent's concentration. He's a well-spoken and well-behaved child without an apparent chip on his shoulder.

Yet the drive that underlies the phenomenal body of work he has created cannot be assembled without a steely determination. Perhaps the lesson for tennis sociologists from the Roger Federer story is that such determination is classless – that it can burn as brightly in someone for whom everything was laid on, as it can in someone who has had to fight for everything. Having said that, a little money to oil the wheels of junior coaching and a willing parental taxi service clearly helped, and Federer benefited considerably from both.

Roger Federer was born on 8 August 1981 in Switzerland's second-largest city, Basel, the second child and first son of Lynette and Robert Federer, who had lived there since their marriage in 1973.

Though hardly a destination for the trendy international jetsetter, Basel's location on the Rhine river at the junction of three countries – Switzerland, Germany and France – makes it a highly appropriate place of origin for a global sporting icon. In fact, the city's location at an international crossroads had something of a role in Federer today being conversant in three languages – or four, if you consider the fiercely independent guttural Swiss-German dialects as a language in their own right. Five languages are regularly visible in everyday life in Basel: the four Swiss languages – German, French, Italian, the original pure Swiss language of Romansch (now spoken only in the east but still in use on banknotes and some official signs) and English. The city's airport, sited on French territory, was for years known as Basel–Mulhouse but is today known as Euro-Airport, which cities in Germany, Switzerland and France all claim as their own.

As the most European city in a country whose inhabitants are still very sceptical about joining the European Union, Basel has a mildly un-Swiss character and a sense of humour all of its own. It has its own variation of the German carnival called the *Morgestraich* (literally, 'morning roam through the streets'), a pagan procession held on the Monday after Ash Wednesday at 4am, at which time all the lights in the city go off to enhance the effect of a stream of candlelit torches. It's also one of Europe's oldest university cities and a centre of the European pharmaceuticals industry. It was in Basel in 1943 that a chemist, Professor Albert Hofmann, tested on himself a molecule he had devised and named LSD-25 – when he began having hallucinations, it became clear he had become the first man to experience the effects of the drug commonly known today as LSD.

Roger Federer's story begins in the Basel pharmaceuticals industry, though somewhat less prosaically. His father, Robert, was a laboratory assistant with the Basel-based chemicals giant Ciba-Geigy. As the 1960s ended, he decided to travel, threw in his job, and landed in South Africa, as much because it was easy to get into than for any other reason. Ironically, he then got a job with Ciba's main plant in South Africa, which was based in Isando, an industrial suburb on the east rand of Johannesburg. There in 1970 he met an 18-year-old secretary, Lynette Durand, who worked at Ciba and had lived all her life in the affluent nearby suburb of Kempton Park. They got to know each other outside work; he introduced her to tennis, she loved it, they played a lot, and began a romance, which led to marriage in 1973.

Robert Federer was born in 1946. The son of a textile worker, he grew up in eastern Switzerland near the town of Altstätten, and played tennis for fun, but never aspired to doing it particularly well. Lynette is six years his junior, born in 1952 to a family whose first language was Afrikaans. She went on to play tennis to a much higher level than her husband – according to Beat Caspar, the former sports editor of Basel's daily newspaper, the *Basler Zeitung*, 'She had a good sense of co-ordination, much better than Robert' – but, despite having a fair amount of ambition, she too never aspired to make a career of it.

In 1973, the couple moved to Switzerland – leaving Lynette 8,400 kilometres (5,200 miles) from 'home' – and settled in Riehen, a suburb of Basel near the German border. (The English-speaking world is still not entirely sure how it wants to spell and pronounce Switzerland's second biggest city. 'Basel', pronounced *Barsl*, is the Swiss German name and, as it is a Swiss German city, that is the local name. It's also the spelling and pronunciation used on the tennis circuit for the Swiss Indoors tournament that takes place there every October. But there is an old English version 'Basle', pronounced *Barl*, derived from the city's French name 'Bâle', pronounced as in the English word *balcony*, which dates from the days when most major European cities had an English spelling and is still used by some British newspapers. This book uses the local spelling of 'Basel'.)

Robert went on to become a sales executive for Ciba while Lynette also secured a posting with the company in her new home city, and the two played tennis at the firm's multi-sports club, which had a handful of courts shaded by mature trees in the Basel suburb of Allschwil. Company sports and leisure grounds were a very cheap way for employees to practise their recreation, in fact some companies allowed their staff and their families to use the firm's facilities for free. That was fine for the bank balance but for anyone with a bit of ambition, the social nature and lack of competitive structure could become frustrating.

After a few years living in Basel, Lynette joined the 'Old Boys' Tennis Club, one of Basel's top two tennis clubs (the other being the equally Swiss-sounding 'Basel Lawn Tennis Club'), mainly to play competitive matches, and in 1995 she was a member of the Old Boys' women's team that became Swiss national inter-club champions in the 'Young Veterans' age group. She also actively supported local and regional tennis, serving on the board of the Basel regional subsection of the Swiss Tennis Association and taking on responsibility for developing young natural talent. For many years, she also worked at Basel's ATP tournament, the Swiss Indoors. Today she plays virtually no tennis, instead preferring golf, at which she currently boasts a handicap of around fifteen.

The remarkable thing is that both Robbie and Lynette are very short. Neither is more than 1.7m (5ft 7in), and for a while it was feared that any offspring of theirs couldn't possibly grow tall enough to become a force on the tennis circuit. Yet, out of some genetic inheritance, Roger Federer has grown to 1.85m (6ft 1in).

In late 1979, Lynette and Robbie's first child, Diana, was born. A much quieter person than her younger brother, she has quite deliberately kept out of the limelight, and has pursued her own career as a psychiatric nurse, working outside but not far from Basel.

Diana's childhood was inevitably strongly affected by

Roger's exploits, but the Federers appear to have largely avoided the classic trap of having a gifted child whose interest needs to be serviced to such an extent that other offspring suffer. 'The family was always relatively harmonious,' says Thomas Wirz, a Basel journalist and tennis coach who on several occasions carried out interviews in the Federer family home. 'I have sometimes wondered what Diana did while Roger was being ferried from tournament to tournament, and she may well have certain misgivings about the tennis world, but she has always seemed very independent, pretty sure of herself and very polite. There certainly never seemed to be any sense of resentment.'

Diana, who enjoys skiing and snowboarding, was often approached by the *Basler Zeitung* for quotes. 'She never wanted to have an article about herself in the newspaper,' says Beat Caspar. 'I often asked her. I told her the people would be interested in her, especially when they see her sitting courtside watching Roger's matches, but she always said no. Lynette constantly made it clear that Diana wasn't to get the short straw from Roger's tennis. She always told Diana that she shouldn't be in any way bothered by the fact that people were always asking about Roger. And Diana has always kept her distance from tennis and the media, and has never wanted to talk publicly about her brother.'

Twenty months after Diana's birth, after the family had moved across the Rhine to Münchenstein, a suburb closer to Basel city centre, Roger was born. With no middle name, the birth register simply bears the entry: 'Roger Federer'. Because he's Swiss, and because French is the second language in Switzerland, many assume that his first name is pronounced the French way (eg as in *Roget's Thesaurus*), but, as he has often had to point out, it is pronounced the English way, and most French-speaking people who know this have developed their own pronunciation (as if written 'Roj-air'). The correct pronunciation of 'Federer' has the emphasis on the first syllable, with the vowel sound somewhere between the vowel in the English words 'fair' and 'fay' and the first 'r' flipped. The English-speaking world has settled into a pronunciation that resembles the English word 'federal', a pronunciation that Federer accepts as legitimate.

What was he like as a boy? Everyone who remembers him from that time talks about a happy and cheerful boy with seemingly limitless amounts of energy and a burning need to play sport, especially ball sports. In an interview in 2005, Lynette said, 'He wasn't a straightforward child. He was very, very lively, full of energy, and he was always trying out the boundaries with his parents – and, later, with his teachers – in sport, in school. He was always a bundle of energy and very emotional, not easy to be with. For a while, I was constantly worried about his concentration, but he later worked on that.'

The Swiss education system offers each Swiss canton (administrative district) a fair bit of freedom in its educational set-up. In Basel, then as now, children went to kindergarten at five, primary school at seven, secondary school at eleven or twelve and then on to various forms of further education at fifteen or sixteen, once the compulsory years were over.

Roger followed his sister Diana into the Neuewelt School, a state-run primary school in a quiet leafy and affluent corner of Münchenstein – the name 'Neuewelt' literally means 'new world' but it is just the name of an area in Münchenstein and doesn't indicate any wider idealistic project. Although they could have afforded to send their children to private schools, Robbie and Lynette's decision to send Diana and Roger to the local state primary wasn't unusual, as that was very much what one did in Switzerland. There was little demand for private schools, especially in moderately well-off areas where facilities were good, and it was felt that parental support encouraged high standards of education. The Neuewelt School had both a kindergarten and a primary school, and both Diana and Roger went there from five to twelve.

Data-protection legislation and other privacy safeguards prevent Roger's teachers from saying too much about his schooling, but Theresa Fischbacher, who was head teacher for part of the time Roger was in his primary-school years, remembers him more from his time outside the classroom than in it. 'I was convinced he would become a footballer,' she recalls. 'You hardly ever saw him without a football at his feet, and he used to say, "I want to become a footballer!" For a long time, I had no idea he played tennis and, when I eventually found out, I assumed it had to be very much a secondary activity because of his passion for football. I have to admit that he was very good, and it wouldn't have surprised me to see him make it as a football player.'

A few years before Roger arrived at the Neuewelt School, two of its alumni, the brothers Murat and Hakan Yakin, had been as enthusiastic footballers in their primary-school days as Federer and went on to become local icons for FC Basel, each playing more than fifty games for the Swiss national team. Their success created a culture at the school that it was cool to play football, and, with tennis at that time still a very limited sport in a country whose primary sporting passions were football, skiing and ice hockey, young Roger might well have felt more comfortable with the big ball at his feet than the small ball on his racket strings.

Fischbacher remembers one other thing about him: 'He was always moving. He was happy, had a lovely nature and was well brought up, in terms of his manners, but he had this constant need to be on the move. He was a fidget.' Yet she denies that this restlessness in any way made him a bad pupil. 'He was clearly bright, and I've known many restless, fidgety kids who were very bright.'

Federer himself says of his primary-school days, 'I loved playing with balls, whatever sport they were from: ping-pong, tennis, basketball, football. I was always trying something.'

At twelve, he left to attend the Progymnasium, a form of secondary school specifically for children expected to go on to the full Gymnasium (literally 'grammar school', although not really comparable to the English grammar schools) at the age of fifteen. Although he never went on to the full Gymnasium, never excelled in academic pursuits and finished his schooling at Switzerland's National Tennis Centre, he wouldn't have been allowed into the Progymnasium if he hadn't been at least moderately bright.

One might expect there to be pictures of such inspirational alumni as the Yakin brothers and Roger Federer adorning the corridors of the Neuewelt School. In some countries, there might even have been a plaque, 'ROGER FEDERER WENT TO SCHOOL HERE, 1988–93'. But no. Switzerland just isn't that sort of country. For today's pupils, parents and staff at the school, Federer is just someone who went there a couple of decades ago. Perhaps this lack of ostentatious admiration provides a part-explanation for Federer's phenomenal normality and humanity in the face of the global admiration he enjoys today.

The Federers often holidayed in South Africa, but these trips largely dried up when both Roger and Diana were at school. In an interview with the South African *Sunday Times*, Lynette recalled, 'When the children were still young we used to come to South Africa more often, but when they went to school we couldn't return as often because the European summer holidays are in South Africa's winter, which isn't so appealing. But my kids love South Africa very, very much, especially the Garden Route [a popular tourist stretch of the south coast of South Africa between Cape Town and Port Elizabeth]. When Roger was still in his teens, we spent a holiday on the south coast. He loves the game and the wildlife.'

One of the bibles of the global tennis circuit is what used to be known as the annual Media Guide, now re-termed *The Official Guide to Professional Tennis*, brought out by the ATP (originally the Association of Tennis Professionals) and the WTA Tour (originally Women's Tennis Association). It's a guide to the global tennis circus, but the meat of it is the biographies of leading tennis players, including their results, vital statistics, general career summary and a few personal details. Each of the ten editions of the guide in which Federer has featured since 2000 – including the 2007, 2008 and 2009 issues which have come out since the first edition of *Fantastic Federer* was published – has recorded that he started to play tennis at the age of eight. That figure is out by five years, and it seems somewhat astonishing that someone hasn't thought to tell the ATP that its usually reliable guide has such an oft-repeated error (either that or

Federer is happy to have the world think he started playing at eight). It is true that he didn't start to take tennis seriously until he was eight, but he first picked up a racket not long after his third birthday. There's even a picture of him holding a wooden racket by the throat (it being too heavy for a three-year-old to wield by holding the grip), taken at the Ciba Club, his father's works club, in late 1984. Roger's story is like that of many players who go on to make it as professionals: his parents played as a hobby and at weekends took him along to their club, where he picked up a racket and was soon hooked. 'He loved the sport from the beginning,' his mother has said.

When he wasn't seeking out youngsters at the Ciba Club to mess around with, Federer would take his racket and hit ball after ball against the garage door of the family home. 'I remember always loving to play against the garage door,' he said in an interview in 2005, 'or even against the cupboard doors inside, with any kind of ball. My mum got fed up because it was bang, bang, bang, all day.'

He was taken to a handful of tennis clinics, and at the age of six or seven he attended a training course organised in the Basel suburb of Allschwil by the VBTU, the regional association of tennis clubs in greater Basel. The course involved a dozen under-tens receiving coaching on three full-length courts. It was there he met Marco Chiudinelli, a boy just thirty-three days his junior, who went on to become one of his best friends and who would one day deputise for and play with him in the Swiss Davis Cup team.

By the time his eighth birthday came around, Federer was still playing at the Ciba Club. He had no rating, so by default was R9 (the lowest category in the system by which players are classified in Switzerland). His mother continued to play to a higher level at the TC Old Boys, but she was becoming aware of her son's talent, and also that her club had a framework in which Roger could prosper, one more suited to him than the Ciba Club's. One day, she approached Madeleine Bärlocher, who had taken over the dilapidated Old Boys' junior programme in 1980 and put some new life into it, and said, 'I have a son who plays tennis to a good level. You have a good junior programme. I would like you to take my son into your junior set-up.'

With that, Roger Federer became the new boy at Old Boys, and took the step that brought him into contact with the people who taught him how to play tennis.

2

THE TENNIS ENVIRONMENT into which Roger Federer was thrust at the age of eight was ready-made for a promising young talent. Madeleine Bärlocher, a secretary who had played in the Wimbledon juniors in 1959 in the days long before tennis was ever likely to offer career prospects, had a recipe that was hardly revolutionary – she just set in train fixed squads with a regime of private one-to-one coaching and group training, all at fixed times every week, some of it funded by money from youth sports foundations. And it worked. She brought in appropriate coaches and within a short time had vindicated her belief that, if you can attract one or two good people, a lot more good people will follow.

Although set in the affluent leafy suburbs of Binningen to the west of Basel city centre, the TC Old Boys was hardly a magnet for the rich. Founded in 1927, it was – and is – an outdoor club with just seven clay courts and a modest clapperboard clubhouse. The only indoor facilities it has to this day are two courts covered by an inflatable bubble, and then only during the winter. If members want to play indoors during the winter months, they generally have to rely on the club's arrangement with the *Paradies* indoor tennis centre, owned by Roger Brennwald, the Basel sports impresario who owns and runs the Swiss Indoors ATP tournament every October in the city's premier indoor arena, the St Jakobshalle.

In the 1980s, tennis was still very much a fringe sport in Switzerland. The country's main passions were football and winter sports. Advertising hoardings featuring sports stars were largely the preserve of Pirmin Zurbriggen, Maria Walliser and Vreni Schneider, a photogenic trio who headed a golden age in Swiss skiing, which itself followed on the heels of an earlier golden age headed by Bernhard Russi and Erika Hess.

In 1987, the tennis fraternity was boosted when Switzerland finally qualified for the Davis Cup world group with a team featuring Jakob Hlasek, Claudio Mezzadri and the veteran doubles specialist Heinz Günthardt, who had won a Wimbledon doubles title in 1985. The Swiss chose to play their first world group tie in Basel in the St Jakobshalle, losing in February 1988 to the French team of Yannick Noah, Henri Leconte and Guy Forget. Hlasek had broken his wrist in a car accident a couple of months earlier and couldn't play, but he came back to post his best year on the tour, finishing in the top ten and finally putting Switzerland on the map as a tennis-playing nation.

In the mid-1990s, Old Boys had a promising player in Emmanuel Marmillod, a naturally gifted left-hander who might have blazed a trail for Federer to follow, but it was not to be. There are those who believe Marmillod was also partly undone by a general lack of ambition in Swiss tennis. 'When a promising player came along,' recalls Bärlocher, 'we tended to think of them as being potentially nationally ranked but never really world ranked. That was also the case when Roger arrived: we just didn't think in big terms because we had never had anyone who had reached those heights.'

Old Boys' connection with world tennis came via two channels: the annual Swiss Indoors tournament at Basel's St Jakobshalle and the presence of a few professionals in the Swiss national inter-club league. There was a tradition of each of the top league clubs enlisting the services of one touring professional – usually in the twilight of his or her career – to come and play a few matches a year in the summer months. This arrangement gave the clubs the scope to make their team more attractive and increase their chances of winning, even though they were prevented from paying the players anything more than their expenses (at least officially).

Old Boys had a national A-League team, and in the late 1970s they recruited the British player John Feaver, who reached ninety-eighth in the world rankings back in 1973, to play three seasons between 1979 and 1981. Feaver was so enamoured of the camaraderie and opportunities presented by inter-club leagues such as Switzerland's that he started a national league in Britain. 'The reasons we played were that you could get good, competitive clay-court matches,' he recalls. 'That was particularly attractive for the British players, as there were limited clay courts and no inter-club in the UK – and it was also really good fun. You had a nice evening after the match – a steak, a few beers. Sometimes they'd even ring the church bells. For some matches, we had a couple of hundred spectators, especially when you had teams each with a touring professional, so the singles match in which the two number ones played each other could be quite attractive. It was a great breeding ground for young players to get some good experience.'

Another touring pro who landed in Basel was Peter Carter, a shy Australian in his mid-twenties. And perhaps the single most beneficial thing Bärlocher did for Federer was to persuade Carter to do some junior-squad coaching.

Carter was a touring professional from Nuriootpa in the Barossa Valley, north of Adelaide, who reached 173rd in the ATP rankings in the 1980s. He was coached in his teens by Peter Smith, an Australian who played a part in the formative years of many Australian tennis players, including John Fitzgerald, Darren Cahill, Broderick Dyke and Lleyton Hewitt. Cahill and Carter were the same age, and Smith later said Carter was arguably the better of the two. But, by 1989, Carter was approaching twenty-five, dogged by injury and sliding down the rankings, so he accepted an offer to play a year's league tennis for Old Boys in the Swiss national A-League. He proved a hit there and enjoyed the experience, so he stayed for another year.

That second year, Madeleine Bärlocher asked him if he was willing to take a junior-squad coaching session. Carter was taken aback and had to fight off his initial instinct to say no. After giving the matter some thought, he agreed to try it. Despite having very little German, he found a way of communicating easily with the juniors, proved a natural at coaching and settled into a role looking after the club's squads that was to last until 1997. 'He had a sunny boy image,' recalls the Basel journalist and tennis coach Thomas

Wirz about Carter, 'but underneath he was very serious. That combination really works for Roger. And he also played a very similar style to Roger: very classical strokes, especially the one-handed backhand.'

So when, in 1989, the eight-year-old Roger Federer arrived at Old Boys, he found not only a structure in place to meet all his needs but also an understated but highly disciplined character from the English-speaking southern hemisphere to guide him through squad training. Even though they didn't work together for a year or so, Federer had met one of the people who was to shape his career most profoundly. One night, a couple of years later, the Australian phoned home and told his dad, 'Oh, have I got a young boy here who looks promising. He's only about twelve or thirteen, but I think he's going to go places.'

But Federer also needed someone who could teach him to play tennis. He'd clearly demonstrated an aptitude for the sport at the Ciba Club and against his garage wall, but he needed someone to hone his strokes, to teach him footwork and general movement, and to give him the weapons that would one day conquer the world. That man was Seppli Kacovski.

Adolf Kacovski – 'Seppli' is a nickname he picked up in Switzerland – is a Czech who had the good fortune to be coaching in Tunisia when Soviet tanks rolled into Prague in August 1968 to crush what was known as the 'Prague Spring'. Once Alexander Dubcek, the Czechoslovak leader who had tried to practise what he called 'communism with a human face', had been deposed, it was virtually impossible for Czechoslovak citizens to travel abroad, a situation that lasted until the Velvet Revolution of 1989 swept away Soviet-controlled rule. Had he been at home, Kacovski might never have escaped the country and the Roger Federer story would have been somewhat different. But in 1969, Kacovski – by then an asylum seeker – was enticed to Basel to become the principal coach at the Old Boys club and given the priority of 'furthering the juniors and young talent in general'.

Kacovski, whose motto translates as 'we're going further', introduced a number of features to Old Boys. His main innovation was the introduction of a 'godfather' system of having a more experienced player assigned to youngsters as sparring partner and mentor. He also brought with him a strong sense of ambition.

When Federer arrived at Old Boys in 1989, it was Kacovski's job to give him one-to-one coaching. Of all the people who knew Federer there, Kacovski is the only one who claims to have seen the boy's potential from the start. 'When he came to me, after one or two days I knew this was a massive talent,' he recalls. 'I've been a tennis coach for more than forty years, and in that time you get to know who's got talent and who hasn't. After two days, I knew Roger was born with a racket in his hand. Everything about him suggested his talent: his speed off the mark, his footwork, his willingness to work hard – everything.'

Kacovski also recognised something else about Federer with which he personally identified: the fact that he was only half Swiss. 'I come from the East,' he says, 'and I have a very different attitude to sport. I'm much more ambitious, and at one stage I had to tone down my coaching because the Swiss weren't happy. Some of them complained that I was too ambitious for them. I believe Roger is more ambitious because he isn't one hundred per cent Swiss. His father is very Swiss, and the calmness that Roger has comes from his father, but the ambition and willpower come from his mother, who's not Swiss.'

Kacovski's theory is supported by others, including Niki von Vary, a teammate of Federer's in the 1990s and now president of the Old Boys club. 'Here in Switzerland, sport isn't as accepted as it is in many other countries as a profession to go into,' he says. 'We're pretty keen on the security of a learned apprenticeship, and in that context sport is viewed somewhat suspiciously as a way to make your living.'

And Köbi Kuhn, the highly regarded former coach of the Swiss national football team, has said his job was made easier by the influx of Swiss players with dual nationality, especially those whose second nationality is from countries – many from south-eastern Europe – where football has a much higher priority than it does in Switzerland. He says it has made more of his team keener to succeed than the all-Swiss national teams Kuhn himself was part of in his playing days.

Sadly, the story of the man who taught Roger Federer to play tennis had a somewhat messy ending. At the start of 2006, with Kacovsky approaching his 65th birthday, the Old Boys committee told him they would have to end his employment when he reached 65; this was largely for reasons of insurance. In March 2006, the club offered to throw a party to thank Kacovsky for his 37 years of service, but Kacovsky declined, and settled for a small, low-key send-off. The following day he disappeared. For several weeks no-one in Basel knew where he was, including his wife and daughter. Then it emerged he had returned to the Czech Republic where he still lives now (his wife has remained in Basel). It should really have been a triumphant homecoming for one of the victims of 1968, especially one who went on to play a crucial role in shaping the playing style of the world's best tennis player. Instead, it was all rather shabby, and Kacovski remains a rather sad figure in the country of his birth, largely detached from the scene of his greatest work.

For six years – from the ages of eight to fourteen – Seppli Kacovski and Peter Carter were Roger Federer's coaches. Kacovski, an ardent fan of the one-handed backhand, did the one-to-one work, Carter looked after squad coaching and refined some elements of Federer's game, and Madeleine Bärlocher ran the Old Boys' junior team for inter-club matches. Roger also had input from two other coaches, Haiggi Abt and Daniel Gerber, through the squads run by the VBTU, the regional association of tennis clubs in greater Basel, one of a dozen regional subsections of the national tennis association. It was a perfect environment for a talented, quick-to-learn and ambitious young tennis player.

But such ambition was not always his own. Bärlocher recalls an early practice session in which the young Roger wanted to play with his friends, even if they weren't the best players. 'His mother asked me to put him with the best,' she says, 'so I did, but his friends weren't the best, so Roger came to me and said, "I told you I wanted to play with my friends." He didn't have any fear of playing against the best, but it was more important to him to play with the people he liked. But his mother insisted I put him with the best, and that's where he ended up.'

Federer is sometimes asked by fan magazines and other publications who his idols were when he was growing up. The name he gives most often is Boris Becker, but Stefan Edberg and Pete Sampras also crop up. He admits that the fact that all three play with one-handed backhands was part of the attraction – although Federer always played his backhand the traditional way; Edberg and Sampras learned with two hands and switched to the one-hander in their teens. And Federer also stresses that admiration for a given player did not make him want to copy them – his playing style is his own.

Many of those who remember Federer from that time describe him as a *Lausbub*, a Swiss-German word that best translates as a fun-loving rascal or rogue. There is certainly nothing malicious meant, and he clearly had a strong sense of fun. On one occasion, for example, at a team match at another Basel club, there weren't enough courts for everyone to play concurrently, so Federer had to wait his turn. Then, when a court finally became free, no one could find him – he had climbed a tree overlooking the club to observe what was going on, and to see how long it would take for people to find him.

Much of his sense of fun came as part of a double act with his friend Marco Chiudinelli, who proved something of a late developer and was knocking on the door of the world's top fifty by the start of 2010. Both boys lived in the Basel suburb of Münchenstein, the Federers in Im Wasserhaus, the Chiudinellis 200m around the corner in Poppelweg, and they frequently met up on their bikes and cycled to Old Boys, where they practised together before cycling home together again. 'We played a lot of sports,' recalls Chiudinelli. 'We were always pretty much on the same level, except for tennis which he always won. We also used to play squash together on the squash court with tennis rackets and a squash ball. It was pretty dangerous – certainly for the rackets!'

Another person who uses the term *Lausbub* to describe

Federer is Niki von Vary, who says, 'It was never boring with him around. He and Marco Chiudinelli were best friends – they're the same age and grew up with us at the club – and when those two were together, then we knew the crazy gang was around and the calm of the tennis club disappeared.'

Practice sessions were particularly difficult. 'We used to mess around in practice,' says Chiudinelli. 'We lost interest very quickly and used to talk a lot. There was a lot of unrest. Rackets used to fly around in all directions, which was probably the most dangerous thing that happened. We were frequently sent on training runs or just sent home. Peter Carter didn't have an easy time with us.'

While Marco and Roger engaged in typical boys' posturing, Bärlocher picked up on something that proved to be prophetic: 'Whenever Roger was messing around with his friends, he'd always say, "I'm going to be number one." He'd hit a great smash, and then he'd stop and say, "That's the shot I'm going to win Wimbledon with." It was obviously a joke – all boys do that – but that's what he used to say.'

The less agreeable side to the fun-loving personality was his temper, a far cry from the calm and composed figure Federer cuts on court today. One of his coaches even referred to him as 'a little Satan' on court. He would throw his racket, scream and swear, and had great difficulty accepting defeat.

There was one notorious match when Federer was eleven. Whenever he played locally, he always seemed to come up against Dany Schnyder, the younger brother of Patty Schnyder, who went on to be ranked in the women's top ten. Dany was Roger's first nemesis. One year, the two played in the final of the Basel Junior Championships, Schnyder the

Swiss number one and Federer the Swiss number two in the under-twelves age group. Thomas Wirz recalls, 'They played that match and threw their rackets and swore, and both of them got a warning from the supervisor. It was horrific, but also quite amusing.'

Madeleine Bärlocher says Federer could never stand it when an opponent played a really nice point against him. 'He'd often say, "Lucky!", and a couple of times I had to say to him, "Hang on. There are others who can play good tennis as well, you know." The fact is that he never liked to lose, and you see that today in his attitude towards players who have regularly beaten him, like Agassi, Hewitt and Nalbandian.'

On one occasion after a defeat in an inter-club match, he was so angry that he cried his eyes out and hid under the umpire's chair, whereupon Bärlocher, his team supervisor, had a hard time persuading him to come out. Years later, she asked Federer if he remembered that scene. Federer said no. But he did remember another incident that also gives an insight into the youngster's character.

In one of his first Basel League inter-club matches, Old Boys were playing away at a club with only two courts and not a great reputation. At ten, Federer was the youngest and the smallest in the six-member team, and with a format of six singles and three doubles there was a lot of waiting around for matches to finish and courts to become free. Federer wasn't in one of the first two matches to go on court, and during the first matches it became clear that there was one player from the other team who kept screaming from the side, trying to influence line calls. Bärlocher intervened and some angry words were exchanged. Aware of the bad blood developing between the teams, she decided not to play Federer in the singles. 'He was the youngest, he would have been up against someone who wasn't playing fair on line calls, and I was worried that something would happen,' she recounts. 'And he was so angry with me because I wouldn't let him play singles, only doubles. He remembers that! I was concerned that they'd look at him and say, "Oh, that little kid. We can have some fun with him. We can call lines our way and he won't stand up to us." I knew that Roger was very fixated on the truth. He had a very powerful sense of fairness. He never took a call for himself that he felt wasn't absolutely right but, if someone on the other side of the net made a call that Roger knew was wrong, he'd be so angry that he'd start throwing his racket. That's why I didn't want to risk him. I wanted to protect him, but he was mad with me.'

Tears of frustration and ambition were a regular feature of Federer's junior matches, but he also had a charitable side to his nature. Marco Chiudinelli tells a story from the first time he played Federer in an official match. 'We were about eight or nine. He wasn't very good at losing, and I wasn't either. After about six games he'd opened up a considerable lead and I began to cry, so he came up to me at the change of ends and started consoling me, said, "It'll get better" – and it did. About five games later, I'd taken the lead, and then he began to cry, so I went up to him and said, "Take it easy," and he came back to win. In retrospect, it was a beautiful moment, because you can see that we were friends.'

Federer has admitted that there were times when he would be aware of his parents watching him from the Old Boys' terrace while he was losing his temper on court. Occasionally, they would call out for him to be quiet, and on one such occasion he shot back, 'Go and have a drink and leave me alone.' Federer said that the family would then drive home 'in a quiet car with no one speaking; I would carry on like an idiot.'

In general, the tightly wound bundle of emotion on the court was very polite and well mannered off it. Local journalists who dealt with him at that time speak of a happy and helpful boy, and Federer clearly recognised convincing authority figures when he saw them. Bärlocher says he seldom threw his racket when she was in charge, although his language could be colourful, which caused concern with his parents. 'I once had Lynette coming up to me, asking me to say something about his cursing,' she recalls, 'but I thought it was pretty harmless, and he always behaved pretty well with me. I had a lot of kids who behaved a lot worse than Roger. I was keen to enforce good standards of behaviour because I knew that anything bad [would reflect poorly] on the club.'

Seppli Kacovski noticed something else about Federer's on-court tantrums. 'I've known enough players who play a bad match,' he says. 'They scream at themselves, can't accept a defeat and say, "I'm giving up. I'm not playing tennis any more." Roger never said that. He got angry, he had difficulty accepting defeats, but he never once said, "I'm giving up."'

When Federer beat Gaston Gaudio 6–0, 6–0 in the semi-finals of the 2005 Tennis Masters Cup in Shanghai, he was asked whether it was true that he'd never until then won a match with that score. 'Yes, it is,' he said, before adding, 'I have lost one 6–0, 6–0, but that was in juniors.'

It was actually his first official match. Two weeks after his tenth birthday, the Basel regional championships took place. This was at the Grüssenhölzli tennis facility in Pratteln, an industrial area right by the motorway that takes traffic out of Basel towards Bern and Zurich. As the rules state that you can play in an age group as long as you are below that age at the start of the year, Federer was eligible for the under-tens, but there were too few entrants, so he was put in the under-twelves event. In the first round he came up against Reto Schmidli, a powerfully built boy more than two years and eight months older than Federer. At that age, nearly three years can make a massive difference, and with Federer one of the smaller boys in his year at that stage, it did. He didn't win a single game.

Asked about the defeat many years later, he replied, 'It's the only 6–0, 6–0 loss I've ever had, and I didn't play that badly!' Schmidli is today a police officer in the Basel region, and since the first edition of this book revealed his name, he has become something of an occasional celebrity. 'I knew I'd beaten him 6–0, 6–0,' he says, 'but I had no idea I was the only one. Of course I was a bit lucky – I was so much stronger than him at that time, but given what he has done since, I'm proud of what I did.'

At eleven, Federer was ranked number two in his age group in Switzerland, and on 13 July 1992 he made his first few column centimetres in the local daily, the *Basler Zeitung*. He had lost in the final of a national under-twelves event for lower-rated players to the Geneva-based Japanese player Jun Kato, who later went on to play one Davis Cup match for Japan. A year later, however, Federer won the Swiss under-twelves national championship. But could anyone at that stage truly have said that this was a champion in the making?

To their credit, most people who remember him say no. 'There are plenty of people who like to think they saw it coming,' says Niki von Vary, 'but, as far as I can remember, no one ever seriously expected Roger to go as far as he's gone. Certainly not when he was eleven or twelve.'

Thomas Wirz remembers watching the twelve-year-old Federer at the time he won the national under-twelves championship, but he also remembers thinking the youngster's on-court temper tantrums might hold him back. 'You could see very early what good hands he had, but he'd play two or three good points and then do something wild, and he often threw his racket. He wasn't that disciplined, so it's hard to say that he was headed for greatness.'

Even in 1992, the year Marc Rosset won the gold medal for Switzerland at the Barcelona Summer Olympics and he and Jakob Hlasek steered the Swiss to their first Davis Cup final, there was still a lack of ambition in the Swiss ranks. 'At that time the Swiss level wasn't that high, so we didn't look that high,' says Madeleine Bärlocher. 'As a result, I can't say I or any of us ever thought Roger would go as far as he has. I always said to him, "Rogi, whatever it is you want to achieve in tennis, you have to decide for yourself. We can help you, but in principle you have to know what you want to achieve." We had a lot of good juniors, and he was always the youngest, so we knew he was good, but potentially world number one? I'd have to say no.'

What about those who knew him on court? 'I thought he'd make it on to the tour,' says Marco Chiudinelli, 'because from an early age he saw off his Swiss competition and did seem to have something special, but I don't think anyone at that time could have suggested he'd achieve what he's done.'

The only member of the Basel contingent in direct contact with Federer in the early 1990s who claims to have seen the potential for greatness is Seppli Kacovski, the man who taught him his strokes. Interviewed for this book before his inglorious flight from Basel, Kacovski came across as a strict yet immensely likeable sexagenarian who oozed an enthusiasm for tennis that he managed to communicate to the youngsters he was coaching. It's easy to imagine him getting excited about the fluent strokes of a youngster, but he says it was Federer's ability to learn and bounce back from defeats that gave him such hope for the lad. 'The learning process went so quickly with him, and I never had to repeat anything. He had an enormous ability to grasp what I was telling him. I always say it's a long cable between the head and the racket to describe how long it takes most people to grasp what I'm coaching them, but Roger just got it straight away. I saw it; the coaches saw it; the club saw it.'

Kacovski also noticed that Federer's willingness to learn matched his ability to learn. 'Even back then he hated losing, but he had the ability to draw the conclusion that, "If I don't want to lose, I have to put in the work." If he won 6–1, 6–1, he'd often wonder how he could have won 6–0, 6–0. I was pretty hard with him, though in a friendly way. He was quite small – certainly smaller and physically less robust than everyone else – but then he played with such great technique, and that allowed him to win a lot of matches where he was physically inferior. But then, his father isn't tall, so we weren't sure how tall he'd end up.

'And he never had enough coaching,' Kacovski adds. 'We'd have a long coaching session, he'd work very hard, and then, when it was all over, he'd go to hit against the wall or seek out a sparring partner to hit some more. And he always used to say, "I'm going to be number one!" No one believed him. We could see that he had the potential to be a big star in

Swiss tennis, but he was saying he was going to be *world* number one. He's not the only thirteen- or fourteen-year-old to have said that, but he had it in his head, and he worked towards achieving it.'

All of which may be true, but the *Basler Zeitung*'s former sports editor, Beat Caspar, remembers Kacovski having problems with Federer at the beginning. 'He might well have recognised his talent, but he also had to remove Federer from training sessions because Federer was, at times, impossible. For a long time he wasn't allowed to practise with the best because his head was always stuffed full of silly ideas.'

But there was a distraction: football. Federer's love of all sports, especially ball games, had made him a highly proficient footballer. He joined the club Concordia Basel and played as a striker. 'I'm personally convinced that, if he'd chosen football, he'd have made it to the Swiss national team,' recalls Seppli Kacovski. 'I only saw him twice, but he scored three goals in those two matches, and in one of them he took the ball in his own half, dribbled 60m with it and scored. He just had it.'

Federer admits today that he thought he was 'pretty good, pretty skilful' at football, and he played the game with the same passion and competitiveness that he gave to tennis. His friend Marco Chiudinelli also played, having joined the FC Basel youth team, and on a few occasions the two came up against each other. 'We were both so determined to win,' Marco says. 'When we won, he cried. And when Concordia won, I cried. It meant a lot to us.'

Part of the Federer folklore is the claim that he was offered junior terms with FC Basel. This is almost certainly a myth, and he himself denies ever having received such an offer. Although it's true that today football clubs are showing an increasing interest in pre-teenage talent, in the early 1990s FC Basel had its own youth team, and Federer played for another club. (When asked about it now, Federer says, 'I wish I had had an offer!') Since he's become famous as a tennis player, there have been offers for him to train with the FC Basel squad, but, while he's been happy to be photographed with the club's players, he has always turned down any chance to train with them, no doubt through fear of suffering an injury that could harm his tennis.

Once he'd become national under-twelves champion in tennis, the question of which sport he should concentrate on became increasingly urgent. 'I was practising tennis and soccer in the week,' he says, 'but I was tending to favour tennis over soccer, so I couldn't attend all the soccer practice sessions. The coach eventually told me that if I didn't attend all the sessions he couldn't really put me in the team for matches at the weekend. And I couldn't make all the matches anyway because I was also trying to play tennis tournaments, even though I felt I was in one of the best soccer teams and playing in an age group above my own age. But I knew that I couldn't do both soccer and tennis until I die, that I would have had to improve my left foot – which was never a strength of mine back then – so I eventually made the decision to go for tennis.'

The fact that his parents were both into tennis – his mother seriously so – probably helped sway the decision and, although he occasionally wonders what would have happened had he opted for football, it's not a decision he's ever regretted. 'I like tennis more, and I like to be in control. In tennis, it's up to me – I can't blame defeats on goalies or something like that. So I'm happy I chose tennis. In the end, it wasn't a difficult decision.'

Having honed the strokes that Seppli Kacovski taught him, Federer by twelve was finding it was Peter Carter who was having a growing influence on his game. Although Carter was never Federer's personal coach at Old Boys (his main role was that of group trainer), his growing assurance as a coach brought on the games of many of those in his squads. 'If you had to define the attribute of calmness in a person, in whatever context, then Peter Carter was your perfect example,' says the Swiss journalist Marco Mordasini. 'He formed [Roger]. He took this bundle of energy, took the components and put them together, almost like taking a rough diamond and polishing it up.'

And Madeleine Bärlocher, who had brought Carter into the Old Boys' squad-coaching set-up, remembers, 'The training with Peter Carter was perfect, both in tennis terms and on a human level. Peter was very personable but very restrained; he never pushed himself into the foreground. If a youngster had problems, he'd always take them aside and talk with them. He could talk very well with the juniors, but, if someone behaved badly, he threw them out. Sometimes he sent Roger home.'

Marco Chiudinelli feels Carter had the great attribute of being able to tell each of his charges what they needed to do to improve. 'It was a great time with Peter Carter,' he says. 'There are three periods in my career when I was really able to raise my level, and the first of them was when I came to Old Boys and worked with Peter. I think Roger had the same thing, because, while Seppli was a very good teacher, Roger needed Peter to take him to the next level.'

There was still the unresolved issue of Federer's on-court outbursts. He would frequently go out on court, settle into a nice rhythm and then start having fun and lose his concentration. He later admitted, 'When I was ten, twelve, fourteen, I was definitely at my worst. It was horrible, even funny sometimes – a lot of throwing rackets, making comments on every shot, because I just couldn't accept to lose. I was very talented and I thought, How can it be that I'm not playing well?'

His mother, Lynette, later recalled in a newspaper interview, 'I used to say to Roger, "When you have these outbursts like this, you're just telling your opponent that you're ready for him to beat you. You're sending out invitations. Is that what you want?"' And on another occasion she said, 'This stage was part of his growing up but, when his behaviour was bad, we told him it was bad and that it upset us. We used to say, "Come on, Roger. Get control of yourself. Pull yourself together. Is it such a catastrophe if you lose a match?"'

There were some people at Old Boys who were concerned that their talented youngster might squander his talent in a whirl of joking around and losing his cool, but the combination of Peter Carter and Roger's parents was a very powerful one. While Carter kept Federer moving forwards in his game, Lynette and Robbie gave him a frame of reference for his behaviour. The Swiss tennis impresario Roger Brennwald, who met Federer for the first time when the boy was twelve, says, 'He has an awful lot to be grateful to his family for. He has parents who grew up with certain ideals and values, and he has been able to overcome the crises he has gone through, including the crisis he had with his results in 2008, because of those values.'

Federer had one other bit of exposure to top-level tennis: as a ballboy. In 1994, he and Marco Chiudinelli were ballboys at the

Swiss Indoors ATP event, which gave them the opportunity to rub shoulders with some of the biggest names in the sport. Federer was also asked to ballboy at Old Boys for a women's satellite tournament the club staged every year until 2002. That was 1994, when the two finalists were Martina Hingis and Patty Schnyder, who along with Federer himself went on to become three of the six most successful Swiss tennis players ever.

By the spring of 1995, Federer was classified R2 in the Swiss ratings scheme (effectively on the second tier at regional level), which wasn't bad for a thirteen-year-old but still a long way short of the national ratings to which he aspired. That year, he reached the quarter-finals of the Basel Championships, and was making steady progress. But there were worrying signs.

A note from an official Swiss tennis publication from the mid-1990s expresses concern about how the country's most promising youngsters were being handled. Referring to the Old Boys club's greatest prodigy pre-Federer, it reads, 'Emanuel Marmillod is a glowing example of the lack of forward planning. Although the Basler has massive talent and was able to make his way easily to the age of eighteen, he has now suddenly become aware that without the necessary work he won't get anywhere, nationally or internationally.' Meanwhile, another note lists a group of youngsters (including Federer, ironically) and describes them as 'all talents who are prevented from unleashing their potential because the school system or society is not yet willing to accept this working together of education and top-level sport. Something has to happen!'

While Lynette Federer no doubt saw these notes, there's no

evidence that the Federer family was in any way influenced by them. They were aware, however, that the 'Tennis Études' programme run at the Swiss National Tennis Centre in Ecublens, on the outskirts of Lausanne, offered a potential next step for the thirteen-year-old Roger. It offered the option of continuing his education in a tennis environment. For someone not keen on going to school, like Roger, it was certainly a possibility.

In March 1995, Roger took the three-day entry test and passed with flying colours, clearly giving the coaches the impression that he really wanted to enrol on the programme. But going to Ecublens would have meant leaving the tutelage of Peter Carter and, more importantly, leaving his family in Basel to live for at least five days a week in a different part of the country where he hardly spoke the language. And he had always professed himself as being very close to his family. He was chugging along nicely at Old Boys, so there was no need to uproot, was there?

His parents were happy to show him the tennis centre and investigate other possibilities for furthering his career, but Roger seemed set on staying in Basel. In the car on the way home from the entry test at the centre, he said to his parents, 'I'm never setting foot inside Ecublens again.'

3

FEDERER ARRIVED AT Ecublens just a few days after his fourteenth birthday and just a few months after vowing never to set foot in the Swiss National Tennis Centre. While his decision to enrol on the Tennis Études programme seems to have developed a momentum of its own, it was probably a lot more intentional than that. Shortly after passing the entry test, he was asked by a journalist from the Swiss tennis magazine *Smash* whether he was thinking of taking up a place at Ecublens. 'Perhaps,' he replied, 'you never know.' That quote made it into print. On reading it, his parents – somewhat nonplussed after hearing his views in the car after first visiting the centre – questioned him about it, to which Roger replied, 'Well, it's written there, so I'm going.'

Lynette Federer says there was no parental pressure on him either way. She told the British newspaper the *Daily Telegraph*, 'We're a close family, but Roger took the decision at a very early age that he wanted to play tennis away from home. His father and I saw our role as supporting his project, to help him develop his own confidence, and to help him if things didn't turn out quite the way he would have wished. As a result, we never forced him to do anything; we let him develop on his own. He made a lot of important decisions himself when he was younger, and that was key to his success. He learned to be very independent.'

By 1995, the Swiss National Tennis Centre was in something of an interim state. In 1992, the national association Swiss Tennis (the English name 'Swiss Tennis' has been used since the 1980s as a single brand to avoid the need to write the German, French and Italian versions of 'Swiss Tennis Association' on every official document) suffered a major internal schism over how best to structure the development of the country's top talent. The upshot was that, the following year, the four regional tennis centres were merged into one in Ecublens, a picturesque town on the shores of Lake Geneva, just west of Lausanne, which would serve as a temporary arrangement until the organisation's brand-new purpose-built centre opened in Biel in 1997. Even the choice of Biel was politically sensitive; although its bid to host the new administrative and performance centre had its merits, part of the reason it was picked was its geographical location, right on the linguistic border between German- and French-speaking Switzerland (hence its frequent representation on maps as 'Biel/Bienne', 'Bienne' being its Francophone name).

The Tennis Études programme was inaugurated in 1993 and was intended to provide the most promising tennis players with the chance to make the most of their talent without neglecting their schooling. When Federer went there, his school lessons went down from thirty hours a week to twenty. The programme was set up by one of the most experienced coaches in European tennis, Georges Déniau, but he fell victim to the Swiss Tennis eruptions of 1992, and, by the time Federer arrived, the centre was being run by Déniau's deputy, Christophe Freyss (responsible for the coaching), and Pierre Paganini (in charge of the fitness programme). After a troubled first year at Ecublens, the centre's reputation quickly grew among the Swiss tennis-playing community to the point where, in its third year, sixty young hopefuls applied for just four places. Those sixty were whittled down to sixteen who were allowed to take the entry test. This consisted of running, a fitness assessment course, demonstration of various strokes and a test match in which an applicant's technique and competitive temperament were analysed.

During his test, Federer so impressed the two heads of the programme that he was offered a place on the spot. Freyss said of him, 'He shows a natural talent as well as a basic technique that has no significant weaknesses, but he will have to work hard physically in the next few months. But it was also an important criterion for selection that Roger left us with the impression that he really wants to come to Ecublens.' So much for never setting foot there again!

When Federer moved to Ecublens in 1995, the centre had a dozen or so youngsters (boys and girls). They couldn't accommodate more than about 15 because the centre had access to only four indoor hard courts, four outdoor clay courts and a small gymnasium, all rented by Swiss Tennis. The students also had part-time use of a football pitch and a running track 100 metres from the tennis facilities. They had their own accommodation, generally in a studio or shared apartment for the older ones or lodgings with a family for those also attending a local school.

The average day for those based at the centre would begin with a wake-up call at something like 6.30, with school starting at 7.45 and lessons for those on the Tennis Études programme finishing no later than 1pm. The students would then head to the tennis centre for a two-hour practice session, followed by an hour's physical training, before going home for a quick dinner. At weekends, the centre was empty, the occupants either having gone home or – more often – participating in tournaments elsewhere in Switzerland, so any homework had to be done in the evenings during the week.

There were other coaches working at the centre besides Freyss and Paganini – Alexis Bernhard was one who worked with Federer – but Freyss had overall control not just of the programme but also of each player's tournament schedule. With one coach for every three or four players, when the students went to play tournaments, one coach would look after a handful of players. Everything at Ecublens was in the French language, not just the schooling and relations with host families, but French was also the house language of the tennis centre. So, while the handful of kids from the German-speaking part of Switzerland could speak German among themselves, they had to speak French to their coaches and officials.

In an article written by Thomas Wirz that appeared in the *Basler Zeitung* in March 1995 proudly announcing Federer as the first player from Basel to be accepted by the Tennis Études programme, his father Robbie made it clear that the school element was not to be neglected. 'Roger isn't the most hard-working in school,' he said, 'but thanks to the fact that he'll have access to one-to-one advice, and the centre has Annemarie Rüegg looking after the educational side of things, we're not expecting this to be a major problem.' Wirz then ends the article with an interesting observation: 'Federer has now secured his place in the Tennis Études team, and after the summer holidays he will embark on the second stage of the apprenticeship that might soon lead to his becoming a very good tennis player.'

That Federer survived the first few months was something of an achievement. He had only limited French, was frequently homesick, and admits to being close on several occasions to packing his things and returning home. 'For me, the first half-year was very tough,' he has said in several interviews. 'I wanted to go home. I was not happy. I used to cry when I had to leave on Sunday nights to go back.' He told the Swiss journalist Roger Jaunin, 'I was the Swiss German who everyone liked to make fun of. People were mean to me and it was hard to leave for Ecublens on Sunday nights. Very hard.'

Piecing together tales emanating from that time, he was clearly the butt of numerous practical jokes, including frequent occasions when he entered his name on the massage list only to turn up for his appointment to find it had been erased by an older boy who then took his place. In short, it was bullying.

Federer found release for his frustration on court. Even so, while he was able to express himself through impressive forehands and backhands, the off-court stress hardly made him behave any better, and he became notorious for his racket-throwing. He had gone from being a big fish in a small pond – he had won the Swiss national under-fourteens title just a month before going to Ecublens – to being a small fish in a much bigger pond; 'small' in both size and standing.

One of the more senior players already at the centre when Federer arrived was Yves Allegro, a player three years older who went on to make it into the world's top fifty in doubles and partner Federer in the Davis Cup and the Olympic tennis event of 2004. He remembers Federer frequently reduced to tears of frustration at the difficulty of coming to terms with it all, phoning home at regular intervals and generally 'having a tough time'. Yet, through that difficult time, he developed a cussed will to stick it out and, while it might be a little far-fetched to attribute his determination to come back from seemingly hopeless match situations to those first few weeks in Ecublens, there's no doubt he learned several lessons which made him a stronger person for the somewhat strange life that was to follow on the global tennis circuit. His mother told the British journalist Mark Hodgkinson, 'It was a great lesson in life for him – that things don't always go your own way, and that you don't get anywhere in life with talent alone. You have to work at things. I know it wasn't always fun and games for Roger there, and that many days he wasn't that happy, but those struggles were good for him. Overcoming those ups and downs were a challenge, and it helped him develop as a person.'

Two things clearly helped Federer get through those first few weeks at Ecublens: tennis and his lodgings. However difficult he found speaking French, and however much he longed for his family and his friends in Basel, he could at least express himself on the court, and some of his former associates at Old Boys believe that the determination that Peter Carter had helped him unearth was instrumental in seeing him through the initial weeks. He also had a temporary family to go home to in the evenings, who clearly tried to make him feel like one of their own. While Allegro had his own studio apartment, Federer was housed with Cornelia and Jean-François Christinet, who had three children – Vanessa, Nicolas and Vincent. By August 1995, Vanessa and Nicolas had left home, and the Christinets agreed to take in a Tennis Études student, partly for the fourteen-year-old Vincent to have some domestic company of his own age. He and Federer became *de facto* brothers, and remain good friends to this day. 'Most evenings we used to mess about – fighting or playing basketball or table tennis,' Vincent later told Roger Jaunin. 'I remember his coaches reproaching him for his lack of punctuality, and he had no excuse. Even on the days when he had exams at school, you had to shake him three times to get him out of bed.'

The role of Federer's parents at this stage was particularly crucial, and could stand as a lesson for all parents of talented youngsters. In his book, *Das Tennisgenie* (*The Tennis Genius*), the leading Swiss tennis journalist, René Stauffer, says Lynette is convinced that what got Roger through those first five months was the fact that he had made the decision to go to Ecublens himself and hadn't been pressured into it by his parents. 'He had made the decision himself,' says the mother who spent about an hour a night on the phone to her son in those early months, 'and only became aware later of all the things that the decision brought with it. But because he wanted it himself, he was willing to battle through.'

Eventually, Roger settled down and became happy at the centre, but, until his tournament schedule became too heavy, he would come home every weekend to spend time with his family and his friend Marco Chiudinelli. 'We played very little tennis after he went to Ecublens, but we still used to hang out together,' Chiudinelli says. 'We'd play a lot of computer games, both at home and in arcades in the city. We both had a strong sense of competition, we both wanted to win. I look back on it as a wonderful time, and Roger was a big part of it.'

Federer also continued to be a part of the Old Boys set-up, turning up for inter-club matches until he became world junior champion at the end of 1998. The work he'd done at Ecublens became clear to his old sparring partners. 'There was one occasion,' recalls Niki von Vary, 'when he was fourteen. He'd just gone to Ecublens and had a national rating. Then he came back to play with us and I was up against him in practice for inter-club matches. He'd really improved, and we could see that he was going to be good. Even so, as good as he's turned out, no one could have seen it at that time.'

Von Vary was also a witness to Federer and Chiudinelli's continuing demon double act. 'On one occasion, Old Boys staged the Basel championship,' he says, 'and during the event Roger, Marco, Reto Staubli [one of Roger's closest friends who still sometimes travels with him on the tour] and I were playing cards in the club restaurant. Roger and Marco were so loud that the tournament director stomped in and said that they were making so much noise that the players on the centre court couldn't concentrate. There are other stories about them, but that sums up who they were: spirited, funny and loud, yes, but never malicious. And you had to be on your guard, because they were always up for a prank or a practical joke.'

Looking back, Federer only really began seriously working on his tennis when he went to Ecublens, and again the question arises: were people aware at that time that they had a potential world-beater in their midst? Probably not, because by general standards Federer was something of a late developer. 'Up to the age of fourteen, he was what you might call a normally talented youngster, doing well in junior tournaments, winning some, but realistically not much more,' says the Basel journalist and coach Thomas Wirz. 'For example, at fourteen he lost in the quarter-finals of the Basel junior championships – a regional tournament – which isn't bad but doesn't indicate someone headed for the very top. He was a junior with a good game – no more, no less. Otherwise, he would have been more dominant. His biggest spurt, in terms of results and achievement, came between autumn 1996 and spring 1997, when he was fifteen.'

It was in 1996 that the first signs that people were getting excited about him began to emerge. In September that year, he made his international debut, representing Switzerland in the World Youth Cup, a team tournament organised by the International Tennis Federation, held that year in Zurich on outdoor clay. When Switzerland were drawn to play Australia, a number of media people showed up for the battle of the number ones: Federer against an exciting young Australian, Lleyton Hewitt.

It was a fascinating encounter in more ways than one. Hewitt was somewhat better known, having made more progress as a junior than Federer, and just four months later he was to announce his presence by winning the full ATP

Tour title in Adelaide at just sixteen. Although Federer wasn't working officially with Peter Carter at that time, he was in regular contact with him so was well aware that Hewitt was being coached by Darren Cahill, Carter's former stablemate from Peter Smith's set-up in Adelaide. There was a sense that this could be a meeting of players who would go on to great things, and the match lived up to the billing, Federer winning 4–6, 7–6(3), 6–4 after saving a match point, although Australia went on to win the tie on a deciding doubles.

The following year proved to be a pivotal one in Swiss tennis. In January, Martina Hingis became the first Swiss of either gender to win a Grand Slam singles title when she won the Australian Open. By the end of March, she was world number one, and she went on to win three of that year's four major singles titles, adding the Wimbledon and US Open trophies to her Australian success, and narrowly missing out on the French Open when she was beaten by Iva Majoli of Croatia in the final.

1997 was also the year Swiss Tennis opened up its new performance and administrative centre in Biel. Finally, the political infighting of five years earlier could be laid to rest (well, partly; it's never far from the surface in Swiss Tennis) and the small Alpine country had a base devoted to training its top tennis talent, both juniors and touring professionals. With the opening of the new facility and Hingis's elevation to the status of sporting icon, tennis in Switzerland was appearing increasingly attractive, and soon a number of highly respected names were attracted to Biel, among them the Dutch coach Sven Groeneveld and the Swede Peter Lundgren, who was appointed 'National Trainer' there.

Another coach to arrive at Biel was Peter Carter, who had been lured away from the Old Boys club by Swiss Tennis in the summer of 1997, largely because of his links with Federer, who was being increasingly recognised as a prospect worth nurturing. After his eight years of service in Basel, the club held a large farewell party for him, and the collection raised for him went into four figures – a sign of how well liked and respected he was there.

Things were looking up for Federer, too. After two years at Ecublens, he could base himself much closer to home, having mastered French and overcome his other demons. And he had his most trusted coach back with him, with funding from Swiss Tennis. But where was he to live? He didn't want to lodge with another family, but at sixteen he wasn't ready to have his own place.

Enter Yves Allegro. Although he had finished his own schooling in Ecublens, when he turned professional Allegro decided to base himself in Biel and had taken an apartment there. When the Federer family heard about this, they asked him if Roger could share with him. Allegro agreed and the pair became flatmates for two years. 'We had a lot of fun,' Allegro says today. 'We became very close friends. He was close to turning pro, so it wasn't very easy for him sometimes because he wasn't great at waking up at eight o'clock to go to practice and he was late a lot. He used to love playing PlayStation in the evening, and sometimes I had to stop him and say, "Come on, it's time to go to bed now." I was kind of like an elder brother to him.'

Given all the hassles with French that had plagued Federer when he first went to Ecublens, it may have been psychologically valuable for him to have developed a friendship in which the default language was French. 'We always speak French,' says Allegro, 'which is quite strange because by that point my Swiss German wasn't bad. Even today we speak more French than Swiss German together, although now we mix three languages: French, Swiss German and English.'

But what was Federer like to live with? Did he do his share of the washing-up? 'He was all right,' says his former flatmate. 'We weren't too bad. If I told him to do something, he did it. He probably wouldn't have done it by himself but, if I told him, he always did it.

'To be honest, we were away so much at tournaments that we weren't at home together very much, but in general, I cooked and he played PlayStation. He was pretty lazy about clearing up and such things, and if he ever tidied his room, within a couple of days it was as untidy as it was before. But he's always been someone who, when he decided to do something, he did it properly, and tidying up wasn't that important to him.'

Allegro also noted something else that everyone who had observed the young Roger had noticed – he was so much better a player in matches than he ever was in practice. Most players, at all levels of tennis, can play some wonderful tennis in practice, but the moment they're in an official match, their level drops a little because of the pressure and the formality of the situation. With Federer it was the reverse. Many of his Old Boys friends can claim victories over him on the practice courts, but when it became official, Federer's level rose. 'He was frequently late for practice,' recalls Allegro of their time in Biel, 'but then he was always more of a match player, and practice often bored him.'

Allegro carved out a moderately successful career for himself as a doubles player on the ATP tour. He had a succession of semi-regular partners, and for a while he enjoyed occasional high-profile appearances as Federer's doubles partner in Davis Cup ties, a few tournaments and the 2004 Olympics. So does he find it strange to be the former 'older brother' who became the junior on-court partner to one of the biggest names in world sport? 'No, it's not strange. In fact, I think it's a nice story. I'm not jealous at all. I'm very happy about what Roger's doing. I'm doing my stuff and he's doing his stuff. It was nice to win two titles with him, and it's nice to play in the Davis Cup with him, just because it's a nice story.' Stanislas Wawrinka's rise to prominence as a singles and doubles player effectively ended Allegro's appearances alongside Federer.

1997 was also the year Federer gave up on his schooling. 'I told my parents, "I'm not in the mood to go to school any more and I want to focus on tennis,"' he said in an interview in 2004. 'They understood, but they said that if, in the next few years, I didn't have any results, I'd have to go back to school. It was a pretty big risk for me to stop school at sixteen because I didn't have an ATP ranking at that time. Maybe I was 800th or something, and in the juniors I was, like, 60th or something. But somehow I felt that school was disturbing me from being one hundred per cent focused on tennis. That's why I quit school, and then tennis went much better.'

Robbie Federer, who in 1997 turned down a plumb job in Australia because he and Lynette felt it might hinder Roger's chances of becoming a top tennis player, later told the Swiss tennis journalist René Stauffer, 'Everyone kept telling us how talented Roger was, but we wanted to see deeds.' And Stauffer quotes Lynette as adding, 'We made it clear to Roger that we couldn't support him financially for ten years just so he could be ranked around 400 in the world.' She even increased her working hours to ensure the family remained financially secure, no doubt a sensible move at the time but one that, with hindsight, seems ludicrously overcautious.

By the time he left school, he had notched up his first tournament success. In January 1997, he became the Swiss under-eighteens junior champion while still only fifteen. Then in May he won the international junior title in Prato, Italy, winning six matches in straight sets against some of the best juniors of the time. But that was to be the only title he won that year, and he still hadn't played in a junior Grand Slam.

So what kind of a player was Federer at sixteen? He has said his graceful style came naturally and didn't really emerge until his late teens, but under the guidance of Alexis Bernhard, Christophe Freyss and Peter Carter he was clearly enhancing the efficiency of the smooth stroke-making Seppli Kacovski had taught him at Old Boys. Thomas Wirz recalls of that time, 'I always had a little concern about his playing style. He always played a high-risk game, hitting very flat, clearing the net by very little, and that made me think at the time that he would never win the French Open. He's added some spin that allows him to play better on clay, but his game still isn't well suited to slow courts. But then, he's always had a very economical style, so he doesn't need the degree of musculature that some players need. He's a bit like Michael Stich in that respect, very efficient.'

And still the volatile temperament was there to haunt him. 'I was throwing around my racket like you can't imagine,' he said in an interview quoted by the website tennis-x.com. 'Helicopters were flying all over. I mean, I was getting kicked out of practice sessions when I was sixteen. I used to talk much more, too, and scream on court.'

His parents tell the story of driving home from a tournament through an Alpine pass. Federer was angry at the way he had played, and was becoming very hot-tempered in the car. His father tried ignoring him, but that didn't work, so he stopped the car, dragged Roger out and rubbed his head in the snow as a symbolic way of cooling him down. 'Roger never heard a bad word from us just because he had lost,' his mother said in an interview with Freddy Widmer of the *Basler Zeitung*, 'but when he misbehaved or when he just didn't make an effort, we weren't going to let that go.'

Lynette is convinced her son gained strength from his bad experiences because of her and her husband's attitude towards him. 'Our son was always allowed to be a bit wild, but he always had to take responsibility for the consequences. If he dug himself into a hole, he had to dig himself out of it.'

This same philosophy was adopted by the Swiss Tennis centre in Biel, where his temper soon landed him a punishment from hell. The new 'House of Tennis', as the centre was called, was newly fitted out, and one of its fittings was an expensive anti-noise drape. All players were warned that it had cost a lot of money, and if anyone damaged it, they would have to clean the toilets for a week. Federer later admitted he thought the drape was so thick you couldn't possibly damage it. But he was wrong. After missing a shot, he spun his racket out of his hand, it hit the drape and put a significant slit in it. 'He had to be in at seven in the morning to clean the toilets for a week,' says

Allegro. 'For him it was the worst possible punishment. It was the middle of winter, so very cold, and he was hopeless at getting up even at eight o'clock, so getting up early enough to be at the courts by seven was a real nightmare for him.'

Yves Allegro certainly remembers the tantrums. 'He'd get pissed off very easily and throw rackets all over the place,' he recalls. 'Not very bad, but often. I think he was even worse in practice than in matches. He was very competitive in matches.' But Allegro also recognises that it was around that time, towards the end of 1997, that Federer began to make the most progress in his game. And, as the new year dawned, he was set to take the junior world by storm.

There are mixed opinions as to how to regard the official world junior champion. For some, the achievement is a stepping-stone to greatness, while for others it can be the opening chapter in a tale of unfulfilled promise. Since the first world junior champions were crowned in 1978, a number have gone on to top the rankings – Ivan Lendl, Stefan Edberg, Andy Roddick, Martina Hingis and Amélie Mauresmo, for instance – while others such as Brian Dunn, Federico Browne, Zdenka Malkova and Nino Louarsabishvili have disappeared with little trace. They might be the best in the world at under-eighteens level, but, if they're born in a year of few top players or many late developers, the honour might be of little ultimate meaning. The same goes for the Grand Slam junior championships: while they give young players a chance to rub shoulders with great players in the locker rooms and play on the courts they've recently vacated, winning a junior Grand Slam title doesn't always offer the greatest indication of likely champions of the future.

In 1998, Federer played a full year of the top junior events, which include the four Grand Slams and a series of colourfully named tournaments including the Coffee Bowl, the Banana Bowl and the culmination of the year: the Orange Bowl. He won the Victoria Junior Championships in Australia the week before the Australian Open, and then went on to reach the semi-finals at what was then still called Flinders Park (now Melbourne Park).

Playing his first Grand Slam event brought him into contact with the kind of regular media presence that would accompany him for the rest of his playing career. Marco Mordasini is a Swiss radio journalist, who was earning most of his money at the 1998 Australian Open reporting on Martina Hingis and Patty Schnyder, but – like most reporters – was keeping an eye out for any new home-grown talent in the junior events. He spoke to Federer several times during that tournament, most notably after the Swiss had lost a very close match in the semi-finals to Sweden's Andreas Vinciguerra 4–6, 7–5, 7–5.

'I'd asked to speak to him,' Mordasini recalls, 'so, a while after his match had finished, Mitzi Ingram Evans, the player liaison officer for the juniors, brought him into the radio room. At that moment, Hingis or Schnyder had just won and I had to go on air to give the result, so I asked Roger if he could wait a couple of minutes – I explained why – and he said yes. So I sat him down next to me and, as I was waiting to go on air, I heard a snuffling sound. I looked over and there he was, crying his eyes out. He cried for what seemed like about ten minutes about losing this match. I asked him what was up. As I'd seen it, he'd played a superb match; the other guy just happened to be one notch better. Roger explained that he wasn't sad because he'd lost but because he knew then that he'd had the chance to win and hadn't used his chances. He could see what he should have done differently, and it hit him hard. It was a powerful moment.'

Mordasini says Federer was easy to deal with on a personal level, although he needed some coaxing. 'He seemed shy,' said the journalist, 'at times very shy, but always very well mannered, said "Sie" [the more formal or deferential of the German pronouns for 'you'] to me, unlike most teenagers. He was very calm; he didn't speak in torrents. You had to encourage him to come out of himself a bit. It was like there were two people: one on the tennis court, where he knew what he was doing, and the other in the media area, where he was a bit restrained. I told him the rules of my game – that I'd cut out anything he said which didn't come out right – and I think that encouraged him to develop something of a sense of trust with the media – at least with me. Over the years, he's genuinely come out of himself. It's not a PR act that he's learned.'

A third junior title, and the second of the year, came in the springtime in Florence, which helped to raise his profile in Switzerland. One of the many people who took note of his performance was Köbi Hermenjat, the tournament director in Gstaad whose Swiss Open clay court event used to take place the week after Wimbledon. Hermenjat judged that, if this young Swiss boy – still only sixteen – could win a junior title on clay, he was worth a wildcard. (The field for a professional tennis tournament is made up mostly of players who are the highest-ranked applicants, plus a handful of 'qualifiers' and 'wildcards'. A pre-tournament competition is held to work out who wins through 'qualifying', and a tournament director has a couple of invitations – 'wildcards' – to give to players who wouldn't qualify as of ranking but who would enhance the appeal of the tournament, eg local players or star names on a comeback after injury. Qualifying tournaments also have wildcards, and Federer was given one for the tournament in Toulouse.)

Hermenjat offered Federer his wildcard, and Federer jumped at the chance. His opening on to the full ATP Tour had finally arrived, a milestone that helped him to decide that 1998 would be his last year on the junior circuit (even though he'd still be eligible in 1999). But, before the Gstaad tournament came round, he had another milestone to reach.

Although he bombed at Roland Garros, losing 6–4, 5–7, 9–7 to the Czech Jaroslav Levinsky, he found his feet on the grass in London. First, he reached the semi-finals at Roehampton, losing to Taylor Dent in three sets, and then went on to Wimbledon, where with barely a volley in sight he won the junior event, beating the Georgian Irakli Labadze 6–4, 6–4 in the final. Then he and the Belgian Olivier Rochus won the doubles title, beating Michaël Llodra and Andy Ram, also in a 6–4, 6–4 final. After all the fun in practice sessions at Old Boys in which he'd said, 'With this shot I'll win Wimbledon,' Federer was finally a Wimbledon champion, albeit in the junior events.

Permit me a personal recollection here. The day he won his Wimbledon junior title was the day I met him for the first time. During the 1990s, I talked to a lot of juniors. Some were cocky, some were shy, some were fiercely ambitious and some were coy about saying how far they could go. What struck me about Federer was a remarkable mixture of charm and ambition. He made instant connections with people, he certainly made me feel he was pleased to have chatted with me (and I know I'm not the only one to have felt this), and he had an arrogance that was in no way offensive. There's always quite a media interest surrounding junior Grand Slam champions – largely as an investment for the future, just in case they prove to be any good – and the clichéd question is always: do you think you'll win the full title one day? I regret I succumbed to the cliché; in response, Federer flashed his cheeky smile and said, 'Why not?'

I'd love to say that I saw there and then that he was destined for greatness, but I can't. I'd talked to too many juniors who saw their destiny in the world's top ten, if not beyond. What I can honestly say is that he made a bigger impression on me as a human being than any of the others did.

Federer's two Wimbledon titles earned him an invitation to the black-tie Wimbledon champions' dinner at London's Savoy hotel, where he would have been fêted alongside the full singles champions that year, Pete Sampras and Jana Novotna. But he turned it down, after his coach Peter Carter persuaded him that concentrating on his ATP debut in Gstaad was more important than a social event in London.

Federer's ATP debut turned into a third successive 6-4, 6-4 match, but this time with him on the losing side. On a damp, overcast day, he was scheduled to face the German Tommy Haas, but, when Haas pulled out with a stomach upset, in stepped the Argentinian clay specialist Lucas Arnold. Arnold has one or two claims to fame, notably a courageous – and so far successful – battle against testicular cancer; on his return to the tour he added his mother's name, Ker, to his own in recognition of her role in his healing process. But his biggest claim is that he beat Roger Federer in Federer's first match at tour level, Arnold proving just too streetwise for the tour debutant. And yet Federer's reaction to his defeat wasn't one of disappointment but of excitement; he was buoyed up by the knowledge that he'd created enough opportunities and possessed the weapons to have perhaps even won the match. His confidence was building.

By now, like many other juniors embarking on the transition to the adult tennis scene, Federer was playing on two circuits: the junior and the lower ranks of the full tour. He was given a wildcard into the Geneva Challenger at the end of August, where again he lost in the first round, this time to Orlin Stanoytchev of Bulgaria, 6–4, 7–6.

In the first week of September, it was off to the US Open, where he had the chance to go to the top of the junior rankings. He went to New York ranked fourth, and reached the final with wins over his doubles partner Olivier Rochus and the powerful Dane Kristian Pless, who had beaten three seeds en route to the semis: Aisam Qureshi, Taylor Dent and Fernando Gonzalez – all players who have since gone on to enjoy varying degrees of success as professionals. If he'd beaten David Nalbandian in the final, Federer would have gone to number one, but the sixteen-year-old Nalbandian – a year younger than Federer, which can make quite a difference at that age – worked out how to play the Swiss and beat him 6–3, 7–5.

Federer felt he was too negative in the whole tournament, saying after the final, 'I didn't play my best tennis, I didn't take enough chances.' Having shown his mastery of the useful but meaningless tennis player's answer, he gave a bigger indication of his determined mindset when asked what he could still improve in his game. 'I could improve everything,' he replied.

The Nalbandian defeat was one of the losses which Federer says taught him so much. 'I always learned more from losses, not wins, and losing the US Open junior final was one that made me wake up. I thought, "I've got to work harder," but it was only a few months after the US Open that I really decided to put in the work, and it paid off in results.'

The next pay-off came just a couple of weeks after his trip to New York. Offered a wildcard into the qualifying tournament for the ATP event in Toulouse, he came through three matches to make it to the main draw. A 6–2, 6–2 first-round win over the veteran Frenchman Guillaume Raoux meant Federer had opened his account on the full tour, and another straight-sets win over the Australian Richard Fromberg took him to the quarter-finals, where he was beaten by the eventual champion, Jan Siemerink. He had served notice that he had nothing to fear on the full tour.

Three days later, Federer was in his third ATP event and the one that really meant something to him: the Swiss Indoors, held at Basel's St Jakobshalle. The line-up for the event is normally impressive, and 1998 was no exception; the field featured four Grand Slam champions: Pete Sampras, Andre Agassi, Patrick Rafter and Yevgeny Kafelnikov. When the draw threw Federer into a first-round meeting with Agassi, the former ballboy was set up for his first encounter with one of the true greats of the sport. In front of a near-capacity 8,000 spectators on the first day of the event, he lost 6–3, 6–2, but he knew he'd arrived. 'The road is long,' he said after the match, 'but I've learned a lot in these past few months.' But, as he found out the following week, there was still plenty to learn.

After playing to the packed seats of one of the tour's most prestigious arenas, Federer went to Küblis, a picturesque resort near Klosters in eastern Switzerland, which was hosting the first event in a four-week autumn Swiss satellite tournament series. The town of Küblis was home to around 500 souls, and very few of them showed up to watch a few journeymen and budding tennis professionals plying their trade in the local indoor tennis centre, whose four carpet courts were out of bounds for the week. Such is the largely unseen reality of the supposedly glamorous pro tennis tour.

After his fêting in Basel, Federer struggled for motivation at Küblis. In the first round he came up against a lowly ranked Swiss, Armando Brunold, and, instead of using the confidence of the Agassi match and his five Toulouse wins to sail through, he lost the first set on a tiebreak. When he went a break down early in the second set, he began just belting the ball, teeing off on everything and missing most. He also threw in several listless double faults. This came to the attention of the tournament's referee, Claudio Grether, who came out to watch the last few games of Brunold's 7–6, 6–2 win. Grether judged Federer not to be giving his 'best efforts', as required by the tennis players' code of conduct, and fined the embryonic Swiss hero $100, $13 more than the first round losers' prize money of $87.

The following day, Switzerland's mass-circulation daily *Blick* had a field day, printing large and colourful headlines to depict the shame of the boy who only the previous week had been portrayed as the future of Swiss tennis. 'It was tough,' says Yves Allegro, who played doubles and shared a room with Federer over the four-week series. 'It wasn't that he wasn't trying, but after Basel he lost the motivation a little. The next day he was in the paper, and he felt really bad about it.'

Yet you can't keep a good man down for long. Federer took his punishment on the chin, he and Allegro won the doubles in Küblis, and then Federer won the next singles tournament and reached the final in the one after that, finishing first – ahead of Allegro in second – in the satellite standings after the four weeks.

All that time, Federer had put on hold his unfinished business in juniors: the quest to finish the year as world junior champion. But he had three tournaments left, two of them with singles ranking points to collect. It started badly when he lost in the third round of the Eddie Herr Championships, but he then won his two matches in the Sunshine Cup team event (the first against Juan Carlos Ferrero, another junior who was to beat Federer to the top of the tree), and then went to the Orange Bowl in Miami, the most prestigious junior event outside the four Grand Slam junior tournaments.

On that trip, Federer did something that shocked his parents and many others who knew him: he dyed his hair blond. He says today of the decision, 'Actually, I wanted to change my hair colour many more times, but I just kept it to blond one time. I was on the point of colouring it red once, but that didn't go down too well with my parents. The next thing I wanted was long hair. I guess that's a little bit rebellious.'

Winning the Orange Bowl not only helped Federer to become world junior champion for 1998, but it was a significant psychological boost in helping him realise he could win when the odds were stacked against him. After his first match, he injured his foot while messing about in the gym, and feared he might have to withdraw. But he followed the medical advice he was given to the letter, and by the time he faced Nalbandian in the semi-finals, he was moving without hindrance. He then gained revenge for his US Open defeat, and went on to defeat Nalbandian's roommate Guillermo Coria, 7-5, 6-3, in the final for one of the most satisfying wins of his burgeoning career. The champion's photos, which are somewhat comic anyway as the winner has to hoist a bowl of oranges overhead, testify to the glory (or horror, depending on your taste in hairstyles) of the blond rinse.

More importantly, Federer was guaranteed the year-end number-one ranking and with it the tag of world junior champion. His invitation to another black-tie dinner – the ITF world champions' dinner, during the second week of the following year's French Open – was guaranteed, but his passage into the higher echelons of the full ATP Tour was not. He'd made an impressive start, but with his junior career now over, the question was: would he join the ranks of Lendl, Edberg and Hingis to graduate from junior champion to world number one, or would he join Dunn, Browne and a host of other talented hopefuls who failed to make an impression as touring professionals? It was a question that took another four and a half years to answer.

TRANSITION TO THE TOUR

2

4

OBSERVING WHAT MAKES someone successful is both easy and difficult. On the one hand, everything they do contributes in some way to their success, while on the other it's often hard to pinpoint exactly what makes the difference between the top dog and the rest of the pack. And yet it's hard to ignore the little changes Federer made as he left the junior circuit to join the ranks of the big boys.

In his last days as a junior, he enlisted the help of a sports psychologist, Chris Marcolli, a former professional footballer. Although somewhat diffident today about recalling the help he sought and received, he said in one interview, 'I was getting too upset, so I needed some help on how to think about different things and how to get rid of the feelings of anger. That's why I worked with the psychologist. I think I've always been told the right things from the people around me – things like how to behave, how hard to work, what to do, what not to do – but in the end it's yourself who has to react and want to put in the effort, and thank God I realised that – probably a little bit late, but in time to change some things. So, after working with the psychologist, I kind of worked on it myself.'

Yves Allegro, Federer's flatmate at the time he was seeing Marcolli, recalls, 'He didn't do it within Swiss Tennis; he went outside and found his own person and worked with him for a few months. I think it helped his tennis, certainly a little.'

Another thing that changed was a tiny gesture, but obviously a significant one. While playing at junior level, Federer had had a remarkable little routine before every point on his own serve, a routine the Swiss radio journalist Marco Mordasini remembers disappeared overnight. 'He would pick up the ball,' says Mordasini, 'take it with his left hand, throw it from behind his back, from back left to front right, then play it back with his racket between his legs before catching it behind his back, all with an amazing speed and precision. It became one of his trademarks, yet around that time it just stopped. When I asked him why, he just said, "That was junior time. This is now." He used to do it before every point, sometimes even while walking to the service line, and with a perfection that was incredible. But he obviously dropped it as part of a change in attitude, probably begun by Peter Carter and certainly continued by Peter Lundgren.'

With his tennis becoming increasingly disciplined, he needed an outlet for his sense of teenage fun, and that outlet seemed to be his hair. Having done the blond rinse on the Orange Bowl trip, he let that grow out and decided to go for the long look, growing it long enough to tie in a short ponytail, supplemented with a bandanna. That became the trademark Federer look, and he kept it until the second half of 2004. Often in the early days, he was asked why he was growing it long, to which he tended to reply, 'I like it this way. Why should I have it cut?'

Most players coming into their rookie professional year end up playing a number of satellite events on tour, effectively the third level of tournaments below the full ATP (or WTA for the women) and Challenger circuits. But Federer played just one Challenger event, in Heilbronn, before graduating straight to the lower level of the full ATP tour, where, thanks to a wildcard, he got into the main draw in Marseille, one of the full tour events on the short European indoor swing in February and early March. In the first round there, he beat Carlos Moya, who was only six weeks away from being world number one. Then, having qualified for the main draw in Rotterdam, he reached his second successive quarter-final.

Such was the reputation he was creating on the tour that he was given another wildcard, this time into the Ericsson Open in Key Biscayne, his first Masters Series event (the Masters Series was still known at that time as the 'Super Nine'). Although he lost in the first round, he was knocking on the door of the world's top 100 just four months into his first full year on the tour.

Then, in April 1999, Federer made his Davis Cup debut. Normally, a seventeen-year-old playing his first Davis Cup tie will attract some attention but is by and large viewed as one to watch for the future. Not so with Federer's debut. Switzerland were at home to the previous year's runner-up, Italy, in a first-round tie played in Neuchâtel. The current International Tennis Federation president Francesco Ricci Bitti – then president of the Italian Tennis Association –

recalls, 'I saw the line-up and thought, "Oh dear, we're in trouble." His results didn't surprise me, because he had amazing talent, but from 1999 to 2003 he was a guy lacking in concentration. It was so easy for him to play that he didn't work on his concentration. He was really up and down, except in the Davis Cup, when he played wonderfully well, because the responsibility for the country gave him more reason to concentrate.'

By April 1999, Italy were in trouble, and for reasons other than having to face the young Roger Federer. The nation that had won the Davis Cup in 1976, at the height of the career of the charismatic Adriano Panatta, had never been outside the competition's sixteen-nation world group, but by the late 1990s they were in serious decline in world tennis. They seemed to use up all their luck in getting to the 1998 final, which they lost heavily at home to Sweden, and by the following April they'd lost two of their mainstays, Andrea Gaudenzi and Diego Nargiso. Nonetheless, they still paraded as their top player the experienced Davide Sanguinetti, who Federer had to face after Marc Rosset had won the opening rubber against Gianluca Pozzi.

In Federer's first best-of-five-sets match, he despatched the greying Italian 6–4, 6–7, 6–3, 6–4 in a remarkable display of maturity that backed up what Ricci Bitti had feared. 'I was nervous at the start,' Federer said later. 'It was just so different. You're not playing for ranking points but for your country.'

With Rosset and Lorenzo Manta beating Italy's Stefano Pescosolido and Laurence Tieleman in the doubles to seal Switzerland's passage inside two days, Federer suddenly found himself part of a team fancied to go a long way.

With the veteran Rosset, the increasingly confident doubles specialist Manta, who in June 1999 reached the fourth round of the Wimbledon singles, and the emerging talents of Federer and George Bastl, Switzerland had the makings of a useful team. Suddenly, an away quarter-final against Belgium two weeks after Wimbledon seemed not only winnable but a passport to a home semi-final against France.

With Rosset recovering from a viral infection, Federer was promoted to number-one Swiss player for the quarter-final at the Primrose Club in Brussels, with Manta playing second singles. The Belgians themselves had a rising star in Xavier Malisse, who took Manta apart in the opening match. In the second, Federer was favoured to beat Christophe van Garsse, but van Garsse was one of those lowly ranked players who seem to find at least two extra gears when playing for their country. A left-hander with a somewhat unorthodox playing style, he'd previously posted a handful of ranking-defying results in the Davis Cup, and added another five-set victory on 16 July 1999 against the still seventeen-year-old Federer. In the fourth set, with Federer leading by two sets to one, van Garsse needed treatment for cramps, but then Federer also ended up by cramping as Belgium took a 2–0 lead.

Aware that the Belgians had a tradition of being chronically unable to win doubles matches, the Swiss knew they still had a chance, and they took the doubles to narrow the deficit to 1–2. But all hope rested on the Federer–Malisse match that Sunday. As the American journalist Christopher Clarey wrote of the match, 'Though it is undeniably risky, in this era of egalitarianism and injuries, to predict the future in men's tennis, it was tempting to view the match as the first of many between these two in the game's major events.' As it has turned out, that view – shared by many others at the time – has not borne fruit, for, while Federer has gone on to great things, Malisse has been unable to capitalise on his unquestioned talent, having just one Wimbledon semi-final to post alongside Federer's growing tally of Grand Slam titles. But on that summer Sunday on the clay of Brussels, Malisse had the edge and won 4–6, 6–3, 7–5, 7–6, to end Swiss involvement in the Davis Cup in the twentieth century.

Although the Swiss team had performed creditably, the fallout from their defeat was bitter. Always a patchwork of linguistic and political factions, the Swiss tennis scene can at times have a vulnerability to descend into internecine fighting, and the result in Belgium unleashed a period of infighting that took a good two years to work through. In the debriefings that followed, it was noted that Rosset's viral infection – which some clearly didn't feel was that debilitating – had probably cost Switzerland a home semi-final against France. Rosset's devotion to the national cause suggests he would only have refused to play if he really was physically unable to, and suggestions that he might not have been as ill as he made out say more about the infighting in the Swiss camp than about Rosset himself. The captain, Claudio Mezzadri, came in for criticism – he had only come in as captain for the tie against Italy three months before, after his predecessor, Stéphane Oberer, had been forced to resign because Rosset had fired him as his personal coach. In November 1999, Mezzadri was himself fired, only to be replaced by his former Davis Cup teammate Jakob Hlasek, a man hardly likely to usher in harmony. Hlasek was on record as saying he couldn't see a reconciliation between himself and Marc Rosset. In other words, the Swiss national tennis association had picked a captain whose relationship with the country's top player was decidedly rocky.

Worse still, the association hadn't consulted the players. In sports with large teams, such as football or rugby, a national governing body would find it impractical – and probably unfair – to consult the leading players formally about their preferred choice of coach. But in tennis, where two players – or one outstanding player and a doubles partner – can take a team a long way, failing to speak with the leading players before deciding on a captain can be suicidal. In fact, in most teams, the captain is *in situ* by the grace of the players.

Swiss Tennis's announcement provoked a display of solidarity among the players and elicited the threat of a strike over Switzerland's first Davis Cup tie of 2000 against the newly crowned champions, Australia. That match in February 2000 was first scheduled to take place at Geneva's Palexpo Arena, a venue that can hold over 10,000 spectators. Through fears that no noteworthy players would end up playing for Switzerland, the venue was switched to Zürich's Saalsporthalle, a venue that can just about clear 4,000.

As it happened, the tie against the Australians proved to be a superb spectacle. Federer found himself forced to play, despite his solidarity with those who were threatening to strike, because he was under contract to Swiss Tennis and was receiving financial help from them. As expected, Hlasek opted not to pick Rosset, which upset Federer, who made it clear he wasn't happy with the choice of Hlasek as captain. Hlasek managed to persuade Bastl and Manta to play, but Manta made it clear he was playing under protest. Not a happy team!

And yet, on the opening day of the tie, Federer beat Mark Philippoussis in four sets to cancel out Lleyton Hewitt's win over George Bastl. Then, when he and Manta beat Wayne Arthurs and Sandon Stolle in the doubles, the feuding nation was on the point of bundling out the champions just two months after the Aussies had triumphed in the 1999 final in Nice. But Hewitt – no doubt mindful of his World Youth Cup defeat to Federer in that same city four years earlier – stormed back to beat his former junior rival in four sets in the first reverse singles, and Bastl couldn't quite overcome Philippoussis, the Australian winning the fifth rubber 6–4 in the fifth set.

To have come so close to victory amid such unrest must have given the Swiss hope, but it was a blow to Hlasek's already under-fire captaincy and sowed the seeds for further trouble fourteen months later.

Back on the tour, Federer's rapid rise of early 1999 came to a bit of a standstill for a few months. Six successive tour events all ended in first-round defeats, including his main draw debut at Roland Garros and Wimbledon. He lost at the French to Patrick Rafter, and at Wimbledon to Byron Black. His best results had come in indoor tournaments, and when the circuit allowed him to play indoors again, he picked up his rise. He beat Cedric Pioline – a top ten player that year – in Tashkent in September and Rainer Schüttler in Toulouse the following week. Those results took him from being a player knocking on the door of the top 100 to breaking into it.

He closed 1999 by returning to the Challenger circuit, winning his first and only Challenger title in Brest, ending the year ranked sixty-fourth, a rise of 238 places from his start-of-year position of 302.

At the start of 2000, winning two rounds at the Australian

Open boosted Federer's ranking further, and he reached his first tour final in Marseille in mid-February, the week after the politically charged Davis Cup tie against Australia. And who should he meet in that final but the man he'd sided with throughout the tussles: Marc Rosset. It was a highly respectful final, decided in Rosset's favour on a 7–5 third-set tiebreak. Whether Federer wasn't quite ready for his first title is open to question; the chances are that, had he been facing someone he was less close to than Rosset, his will to win might have been a little sharper. Rosset later joked to the Swiss journalist Roger Jaunin that he'd thanked Federer for letting him win, which clearly hadn't been the case, although Federer was particularly pleased that Rosset had won another tournament, the fourteenth of his career and his third in Marseille.

If any period marks Federer's coming-of-age, it has to be the early part of 2000, as he took several decisions then that defined his independence. He finished with the sports psychologist Chris Marcolli after working with him for over a year. Late in 2002, Marcolli told the Swiss newspaper, *Neue Zürcher Zeitung*, that the sports psychologist's job is 'to offer the client help so he can help himself', and that by the early part of 2000, Federer had reached the necessary state of autonomy so there was no need to continue working together. Then in April, he announced he would be leaving Swiss Tennis later in the year.

A successful feature of many national tennis programmes is the help offered to players in their first couple of post-junior years. The Swedes in the 1970s and the Germans in the 1980s learned that many a promising junior career was wrecked because of insufficient help to ease the transition from the junior ranks to the full tour. So, while Federer had turned professional in 1998, he had remained under contract to Swiss Tennis, a situation that enabled him to practise at the new performance centre in Biel and receive financial assistance from the organisation. But it also gave Swiss Tennis the final say on who coached him, and meant he'd had to play in the Davis Cup even though he'd objected to the association's choice of captain. While he might have left under his own steam, the fact that he was obligated to the national association in the Australia Davis Cup tie probably focused his mind.

Deciding to leave Swiss Tennis was one thing, but who would then coach him? Peter Carter had been lured to the national performance centre in Biel largely because of his links with Federer from Old Boys Basel, but little by little the National Trainer Peter Lundgren came to share the job of coaching Federer with Carter. The arrangement worked perfectly well but, with Federer now breaking free, he wanted someone to travel with him, and it came down to the option of one Peter or the other.

Biblically, the name Peter comes from the Hebrew for 'rock', and Federer was certainly caught between a rock and a hard place. It was a difficult decision for him because, while Carter was reluctant to travel full-time, having a fiancée who was battling against cancer, he was also reluctant to let Federer go. Besides, the bond between Federer and Carter was much stronger – having been built up over ten years – than the three-year-old bond between Federer and Lundgren.

'It was a decision where everyone was sure he was going to take Carter,' recalls Yves Allegro, 'and then he decided to take Lundgren. I was surprised too. It was a tough decision for Roger, and tough for Peter Carter to take.'

Federer says he made the decision on the basis of 'feeling'. Much was said about Carter not wanting to travel, and that was certainly a silver lining for the Australian, who needed to be at his fiancée's bedside over the next year and a half. Nevertheless, he was very disappointed by his protégé's decision. Once it was made, Carter withdrew, although he was to have a future role in Federer's career as Davis Cup supremo in 2002. And the fact that Federer had chosen against him when he left Swiss Tennis added an element to Federer's grief when Carter was killed in August 2002.

Lundgren wasn't everybody's embodiment of a typical coach. He'd enjoyed modest success as a player, reaching twenty-fifth in the world rankings at the age of twenty and making it to the fourth round at Wimbledon and the Australian Open doubles final. But he'd earned his reputation more as the player who always toured with a guitar and who loved his hard rock as much as his soft backhand. After his playing days ended in the early 1990s, Lundgren filled out to take on the shape of someone not normally associated with top-level sport, and with his long hair and goatee beard he looked like someone more at home on the Australian beaches than coaching a tennis player aspiring to be the best in the world.

Nevertheless, Lundgren was of great value for Federer, just as he had been for Marcelo Rios and would be for Marat Safin. It's impossible to say exactly what a coach should be – every player needs something different, and only the players themselves know if they're getting what they need from their coach. But Federer clearly felt good in the laidback company of Lundgren; Lundgren had the tactical acumen to allow his charge to construct game plans, and he helped him to work on what still lingered of his volatile temperament. With Federer's hair down to his shoulders by early 2000, he and Lundgren frequently gave the impression of being, if not quite elder and younger brothers, then certainly some kind of soul mates.

By the end of 2000, there was a third 'rock' in the picture. Pierre Paganini had been at the Swiss Tennis national centre since before Federer went there in 1995. Mindful of the rigours of the global tennis tour, Federer appointed Paganini as his personal fitness trainer, working with a physio-therapist, initially Thierry Marcante and subsequently several others – the need to tour with Federer means most of his physios last about eighteen months before returning to their families or day jobs.

Born in 1957, Paganini is a shaven-headed fitness fanatic who doesn't go in for shouting from the sidelines but instead enjoys sweating with his charges. He and Christophe Freyss ran the Tennis Études programme that Federer joined as a fourteen-year-old, so it was a natural progression for Paganini to become Federer's personal fitness guru, working with him about 100 days a year. Paganini made it clear he had to be involved in planning Federer's tournament schedule as well as his diet and physical training. Out of this has arisen a structure to Federer's year, still in force today, that includes three three-week blocks of physical work – one in December, one in the early part of the year and one in July – with shorter, more intensive blocks worked in between. This gives a general cycle of tournaments followed by recovery, followed by fitness training, then tennis training, and then back to tournaments, recovery etc. The physical work is based around a five-point plan Paganini has worked out for Federer. It involves general fitness training (gym work to improve stamina, strength, speed and agility), specific fitness work (a mixture of gym work and on-court work concentrating on specific aspects, one at a time), integrated fitness work (various on-court exercises based on general fitness and tennis work), specific fitness training (tennis-playing with clear physical goals) and preventative training (involving physiotherapeutic exercises designed to prevent injuries). Over the years, Paganini has made a few alterations to the routine, but the regime has stayed largely the same since 2000.

Paganini, a former footballer and decathlete, later told the Swiss tennis journalist René Stauffer, 'Roger was lagging behind in his athleticism, especially his footwork and his general strength ... his problem was his extreme talent, as that allowed him to compensate for physical shortcomings.' Paganini said his aim was not to turn Federer into a bodybuilder. 'A tennis player is not a sprinter, nor a marathon runner, nor a shot putter,' he said, 'but he must have a bit of everything, and be able to call on all those qualities in the course of a match.'

The fitness guru also recognised that physical training wasn't near the top of Federer's wishlist of activities, so always had to make the work fun. Federer himself admits he doesn't like gym work, and has never spent more than three hours in the gym at any one time, whereas he has spent much longer than that on the practice court. But he adds, 'I've actually got quite a lot of joy out of practising tennis or fitness in the last years, because I really see the benefit of doing the tough, long hours. I like it because I know I can enjoy it even more when I'm on court. I don't want to lose any matches because of fitness or lack of practice.'

In an interview in 2005 for a book published by the *Basler Zeitung*, Paganini said, 'It's an absolute privilege to be able to work with Roger Federer. In the course of a sports trainer's career, you only have such good fortune once. No, normally you don't have the good fortune at all, so I really am very lucky.'

With Lundgren as his personal coach and Paganini as his fitness trainer, Federer had the team in place for his assault on the top level of professional tennis.

5

IT'S EASY TO MAKE the mistake of thinking that, because Federer went on to win more Grand Slam titles than any other man, his transition from junior player to tour professional was a rapid one. It was, in fact, a more measured learning process, and because his Wimbledon junior victory at sixteen had raised expectations and made him something of a marked man, it meant that many of the lessons he had to learn as part of his professional apprenticeship were learned in the full glare of publicity.

In fact, the four-and-a-half years between him abandoning the junior circuit and winning his first Grand Slam title were characterised by slow but inexorable progress. The new Lundgren-Paganini regime took a few weeks to bring results, and he lost some matches that seem baffling in retrospect. For example, by June 2000, Michael Chang was a spent force in men's tennis and had never been at his best on grass, but the veteran American still contrived to beat Federer on the grass of Halle. And another grass-court defeat came in Nottingham at the hands of Richard Fromberg, another veteran whose best surface was clay. Perhaps the defeat at this time that hit Federer the hardest came in September 2000 at the Sydney Olympics.

The Olympic format allows all four semi-finalists two bites at a medal, with the losers playing off for the bronze. Federer sailed into the last four without dropping a set, but then lost his semi-final 6–3, 6–2 to Tommy Haas. He hadn't shown his best tennis but certainly hadn't disgraced himself, and he was strongly favoured to beat Arnaud di Pasquale in the bronze-medal play-off.

Di Pasquale was Federer's predecessor as world junior champion, but the two couldn't have been more contrasting. A flamboyant player, the Frenchman was let down by flawed technique and a body that wouldn't stand up to the rigours of life on the modern tennis tour. He'd beaten three seeded players to reach the last four, but had been stopped by Yevgeny Kafelnikov in the semis and came into the play-off with Federer with several niggling injuries and little gas left in the tank.

Somehow, di Pasquale eked out the first set on a 7–5 tiebreak, yet still Federer seemed to be in charge. He sailed close to the wind in the second set, but, once he'd levelled on a second tiebreak, the medal seemed to be his. Yet he was broken early in the final set, and di Pasquale claimed the bronze – and the biggest smile on the podium – with a 7–6, 6–7, 6–3 win. The International Tennis Federation's president Francesco Ricci Bitti, an unashamed Federer fan despite the requirement of his position for a semblance of neutrality, said, 'It was one of the most frustrating matches as a Federer fan.

He was the better player and di Pasquale was injured, but Federer still somehow managed to lose.' The frustration Ricci Bitti felt was to be magnified three years later as Federer seemed to many to be on the verge of squandering his immense talent, and it was to take another eight years for Federer to get his hands on an Olympic medal.

Yet it would be wrong to say Federer came away from the Sydney Olympics empty-handed. An open-minded citizen of the world, he thrives in the Olympic environment and enjoys meeting other athletes. And yet it was a member of the Swiss tennis team who made the greatest impression on him.

Miroslava Vavrinec, known for short as 'Mirka', had more of a history resembling Martina Hingis than Roger Federer. Born in the Slovak part of Czechoslovakia in 1978, she had moved to Switzerland when she was two. She tells the story of how she got into tennis, saying that at the age of nine she was taken to the women's indoor tournament in Filderstadt, near Stuttgart, and met Martina Navratilova, by then thirty-three but still the second-best woman player in the world behind Steffi Graf. Navratilova apparently asked Vavrinec whether she played tennis. Vavrinec said no, that ballet was more her thing, at which Navratilova suggested she had the right body for tennis and offered to activate certain contacts in Switzerland to help get the girl started. By fifteen, Vavrinec was the Swiss national under-eighteen champion, and by 2000 she had bounced back from a serious ankle injury to be included in the Swiss squad for the Sydney Olympics.

Roger and Mirka had first met at Biel, shortly after the 'House of Tennis' opened in 1997, so they already knew each other a little when they met again in Sydney. While Federer was powering to the semi-finals, Vavrinec lost two first round matches; in the women's singles, she went out 6–1, 6–1 to the eventual silver medallist Elena Dementieva, and partnering Emanuelle Gagliardi, she crashed out of the women's doubles 6–2, 7–5 to the Venezuelan pairing Milagros Sequera and Maria Vento. Vavrinec lost something else in Sydney as well: her heart.

It seems Federer did most of the chasing. 'I couldn't work out why he wanted to talk to me so much,' Vavrinec said later, 'and then, near the end of the Games, he kissed me.'

Just before the end of the Olympics, Federer ran into Mitzi Ingram Evans, an International Tennis Federation player-media liaison officer who had been in charge of liaising between the juniors and the media when Federer was a junior. Federer said, 'Mitzi, wait there, I have someone very special to introduce to you.' He disappeared, and returned a few minutes later with delight and pride. 'This is Mirka,' he said.

The Sydney Olympics signalled the start of a relationship that has been of both personal and practical nourishment for Federer, and that culminated in marriage on 11 April 2009, as the couple were expecting their first child.

Vavrinec wasn't his first love (he'd had a steady girlfriend earlier in his teens), but it soon became clear that this was more than a fleeting romance. She went on to become his diary secretary and the force behind the development of his RF fragrance, but she insisted that the two of them knew the difference between personal and commercial matters. For a while, they had an understanding with the Swiss media that they were not to be photographed together. That was inevitably broken, yet the Swiss media have generally recognised that the public's right to know stops at the front door of the flat they used to share in the affluent Basel suburb of Oberwil, and the spacious house they now share in Wollerau on the banks of the Zurich Lake in central Switzerland. 'We now allow ourselves to be photographed together,' Vavrinec told the Swiss journalist Roger Jaunin in 2004, 'but you will never read in a newspaper or magazine what goes on in our house.'

The Swiss Indoors event in Basel is one of the regular features on the global tennis calendar. First staged in 1970, making it older than most events on today's tour, it used to mark the opening of the European autumn indoor season. In 2000 it was given a less-than-lucrative slot, sandwiched between the second-last and last Masters Series tournaments of the year, but it continued to survive as a prestigious and financially healthy event. That prestige was rewarded in 2009 when it was granted '500' status, making it just one level below Masters or '1000' level, with a much better slot, still the week before the Paris-Bercy tournament but a full fortnight after the previous Masters-1000 event in Shanghai.

For the past two decades it has been the baby of Roger Brennwald, a Basel tennis impresario whose first experience with Roger Federer came when Federer was twelve and Brennwald had to present him with the Most Talented Young Player in Switzerland award. Before the ceremony, Brennwald learned that he should pronounce the boy's first name the English way, not the French way as he does with his own name. Brennwald has built the Swiss Indoors into an event that is so established that the loss of Federer in 2004 and 2005 did not dent its economic viability. 'Because our event is a social event as well as a tennis tournament, Roger Federer is a bonus,' says Brennwald. 'It's a massive privilege to have him, but unfortunately we can't make the most of him because we only have 9,000 seats in the hall, and we were filling them thirty years ago. So he's a bonus rather than a foundation stone of the tournament.'

Though admirable in economic terms, there are some in the Basel tennis scene who feel it is perhaps too much of a social event, with the well-dressed, cigar-smoking visitors appearing to outnumber the genuine tennis aficionados. While there is some truth in that, there is barely a tournament on the planet which doesn't have this problem to some degree.

The Swiss Indoors was Federer's introduction to tour tennis. At fourteen he was a ballboy there, and rubbed shoulders in the locker room with some of the great names of tennis, such as Jim Courier and Boris Becker. In addition, his mother Lynette used to staff a stand there in the days before he became famous. By the time he was a professional, Basel was one of just two Swiss cities to have a tour-level men's tournament. The other was Gstaad, one of the most picturesque venues on the global tennis circuit nestling in the Bernese Oberland, where Federer had made his tour debut. Both events had special meaning for Federer, but Basel more so, given that it was his home city.

On the morning of 29 October 2000, everything seemed set for the Swiss Indoors to be the first title in Federer's portfolio. In one of his best performances as a professional, he'd beaten Lleyton Hewitt the previous day to reach the Basel final, a result which seemed to be another small turning point in his career. Strange, then, that it took another six years for him to lift his home trophy, despite his domination of world tennis.

Above: A table tennis bat proved easier to hold than a tennis racket at two years old.

Below: First steps – playing at the Ciba Club in late 1984, aged three.

Above: International appearance – an eleven-year-old Roger represented the Old Boys Basel club at the Preussen Adler Cup in Duisburg, Germany, in 1993.

Below: Ballboy to the stars – the team of ballboys for the final of the women's tournament at Old Boys in 1994 (Federer is second from left, his friend Marco Chiudinelli is third from right). They are pictured with future stars Martina Hingis and Patty Schnyder.

Above: Grand Slam Junior Champion – Federer won both the singles and doubles at the 1998 Wimbledon Junior Championships. He is pictured here with his doubles partner Olivier Rochus.

Below: Blond on the beach – Federer dyed his hair blond for his successful trip to the Orange Bowl, December 1998.

Made it at last! The smile that accompanied Federer's first Grand Slam title, Wimbledon 2003.

Above: Title defended – despite a poor start, Federer beat Andy Roddick in four sets in the 2004 Wimbledon final.

Below: Feted as champion – the 2004 Wimbledon champions, Maria Sharapova and Roger Federer, at the Champions' Dinner at London's Savoy Hotel.

Federer cites carrying the Swiss flag in the opening ceremony of the 2004 Olympics as one of the proudest moments of his life, but when he got on court, he was beaten in the second round by the teenaged Czech, Thomas Berdych.

Simply the best – at the World Champions' dinner in May 2005, Federer was crowned World Champion for 2004, receiving his award from the ITF president Francesco Ricci Bitti. Two days later he lost a rain-delayed semi-final at Roland Garros to Rafael Nadal. It was to be another four years before he won the French Open title.

The best ever? Federer beat Andre Agassi in the 2005 US Open final, after which Agassi said Federer was the greatest player he had ever competed against.

Federer's semi-final win against Hewitt in 2000 was one of the outstanding matches of his early professional career. Just five and a half months separate the two players in age, they had played against each other in juniors, they were both spurred on by coaches from Hewitt's home city of Adelaide, and both were very much standard-bearers for their generation. Had Hewitt not matured vastly more quickly than Federer, it's possible he would never have got to number one in the world rankings. But, by the time they met in Basel, Hewitt had won all three of their post-juniors matches, including the four-sets Davis Cup win earlier that year which had helped Australia to beat Switzerland by the narrowest of margins.

That allowed everyone in Basel to build up the Hewitt–Federer semi-final into the match of the week – and it was, a classic clash of the home underdog, ranked thirty-second, against the visiting celebrity favourite, ranked seventh. The two players played an outstanding match, which Federer won 6–4, 5–7, 7–6 (8–6 in the tiebreak). The Saturday faithful in the St Jakobshalle stood in admiration of both men, especially their local hero, who had vanquished his opponent.

But the effort nearly broke him. The following day, Federer turned out for a best-of-five-sets final against the Swede Thomas Enqvist, who was in the twilight of his career but still ranked ninth and still very much able to grind out victories against opponents not steady enough to match his relentlessness. Federer dug deep, and took the match to five sets, but he lost 6–2, 4–6, 7–6, 1–6, 6–1.

By the end of his third full year on the tour, he had broken into the top thirty – he finished 2000 ranked twenty-ninth –

thanks to the ranking points gleaned from reaching the Marseille and Basel finals and the Olympic semi-finals.

If timing is everything in terms of tennis stroke-making, the timing of Federer's rise to prominence during Switzerland's tennis adolescence was also perfect. A country with a reluctance to embrace sports that don't thrive on its own territory, it was forced to sit up and take notice when Martina Hingis became world number one in 1997. But Hingis wasn't Swiss-born and, while her immigration at the age of seven came early enough for her to speak fluent Swiss German, she never spoke in a way that made her sound born-and-bred Swiss, and the man and woman in the Swiss street seemed to find it hard to truly embrace her. One of the country's most experienced tennis journalists, Jürg Vogel of the *Neue Zürcher Zeitung*, once described her as 'the somewhat different Swiss'.

There was no such reservation about the Basel-born Federer. Just a week after Hingis lost in the Australian Open final to Jennifer Capriati, narrowly failing to add to her five Grand Slam titles, Federer finally won a tour title. The milestone came in Milan, when he beat Julien Boutter in the final to become an ATP champion. Boutter was hardly a player to instil fear into a still teenaged Federer, but the real work had been done in the previous two rounds. In the quarter-finals, he beat Goran Ivanisevic (who would win Wimbledon later that year) 6–4, 6–4, and in the semis he saw off the former world number one Yevgeny Kafelnikov 6–2, 6–7, 6–3.

And what better place to celebrate than in Basel, where just five days later the Swiss team played the USA in the Davis Cup.

That year, the Americans were a team in transition. Patrick McEnroe had picked up the captaincy after his elder brother, John, had given up the job after one eventful year in which he'd enticed Pete Sampras and Andre Agassi back into the Davis Cup fold, only for both to cry off from a semi-final in Spain that the Americans went on to lose 5–0. The American recovery, which was to culminate in winning the Davis Cup in 2007, began in Basel.

That weekend in February 2001 was to be Federer's. With his surging confidence, he made short work of the always brittle but immensely loyal Todd Martin – by then thirty and with creaking joints, yet still dangerous on his day – who he beat in four sets before wrapping up Switzerland's victory with another four-set victory over Jan-Michael Gambill. Sandwiched between the two singles was a win in the doubles with Lorenzo Manto over Gambill and Justin Gimelstob, a makeshift pairing who played so badly that it probably represented the nadir of US Davis Cup doubles fortunes. Perhaps symbolically, it took five minutes for the Swiss team to get the cork out of the celebratory champagne, and it was Federer who eventually prised it from the bottle.

With Switzerland 3–1 up in the five-match tie, Patrick McEnroe gave a Davis Cup debut in the dead rubber to Andy Roddick, who was clearly enthused about competing in the Davis Cup – something that couldn't be said for the good burghers of Basel. The stadium was nowhere near sold out for the weekend, despite the distinct possibility that McEnroe might pick his illustrious forty-one-year-old brother to play in the doubles. The empty seats created a lacklustre atmosphere, and no Davis Cup tie has been staged in Basel since 2001 (although in fairness this has been partly due to the unavailability of the St Jakobshalle). It seemed that, while Federer might have won the admiration of his home folk, he hadn't entirely won their willingness to support him.

The next Davis Cup tie – a home quarter-final in Neuchâtel against the French in April 2001 – proved a significant moment in Federer's emotional development. 'That was the first time that Federer showed that he wasn't everybody's darling,' recalls the Swiss radio journalist Marco Mordasini. 'After his first match on the Friday, he stood before the press – it was nearly midnight – and said, "I will not, I cannot play Davis Cup as long as Jakob Hlasek continues in the captain's chair."'

Like many disputes, the background of the falling out between Federer and Hlasek is somewhat complicated, but the fact is that the player never got on with the captain. Why this should be so is unclear. Although both are very different characters and players – Hlasek achieved what he did through discipline and sheer hard work while Federer can rely much more on natural talent – they have a lot more in common in terms of mentality and approach to life than Federer does with Marc Rosset, with whom he got on fairly well. Whatever the reason, it was hard going for both parties, as well as those around them. Hlasek brought Peter Lundgren into the Swiss entourage in the hope of understanding Federer better, and by the time they got to Neuchâtel he said Lundgren had indeed been a great help.

Hlasek had also made some sort of peace – more of a ceasefire, really – with Rosset, and both tried to put their differences behind them. When the team gathered for the week, everything seemed to be happy in the Swiss camp – but, as Roger Jaunin wrote in his 2004 work *Roger Federer*, signs of discontent were visible to the sharp eye: 'A team photo was taken in front of the hotel they were all staying at and, while almost everyone had broad smiles, Federer's face wore a very sombre expression. Was he just tired, or was it the sign of a deeper malaise? Behind the scenes, the talk was of Hlasek and Federer no longer getting on – in fact, not getting on at all. The tension was palpable, and the smiles were fake.'

As with the tie in Zurich fourteen months earlier, the unrest bubbling within the Swiss camp contributed to a truly magnificent sporting spectacle. The tie not only went to a live fifth rubber but in total had twenty-three sets featuring 275 games in twenty-one hours and two minutes of play. On the opening day, France's Arnaud Clément beat Rosset 15–13 in the fifth set of a match that lasted five hours and forty-six minutes. Rosset saved eight match points but succumbed on the ninth.

Federer then stepped up against Nicolas Escudé before a packed house in the Littoral Arena. The crowd might have been behind him, but he played probably the worst Davis Cup match of his career. By then, the sight of Hlasek repelled Federer; photos from the match show Federer staring into the distance as Hlasek spoke to him at changes of ends. Although Escudé was to become the Davis Cup's player of the year – going unbeaten in five singles and a doubles, and winning the cup for France on a live fifth rubber in the final in Melbourne – and had beaten Federer in the Rotterdam final six weeks earlier, the match was decided by Federer's disappointing showing. Escudé won 6–4, 6–7, 6–3, 6–4, leaving Federer facing the media at around midnight with eyes betraying the signs of recently shed tears.

If Federer feels he can't do a task properly, he doesn't want to do it at all. That explains his statement, 'I can't go on like this. I've been saying for months that I have no pleasure at all in playing while *he* [Hlasek] is there. To lose a match like this, and to lose it in the way I did, is destroying me. It's my career that's on the line here.'

To those within the Swiss Tennis orbit, the situation became known as 'die Kuba Krise' (the Cuba Crisis) – Hlasek was known as 'Kuba', a modification of his first name 'Jakob', which also happens to be the German word for the central American state.

Was Federer trying to test his power, to gauge the boundaries of Swiss Tennis's growing dependence on him? It's a question many people asked themselves after that weekend. The answer is almost certainly no; his feelings about Hlasek were well documented, and Federer is a man for whom the right ambience is important – indeed, some feel it's the main reason he plays Davis Cup ties. 'I have never thought he was trying to exercise any power,' says Marco Mordasini, who witnessed it all first hand.

Whatever Federer's motivation, something had to give, and Hlasek – a pioneer of Swiss tennis who put Switzerland on the map by reaching the top ten in 1988 and steering his country to the 1992 Davis Cup final – was always going to be the casualty. He fell on his sword in the aftermath of what, despite Switzerland's 0–2 deficit after that first day, still proved to be a highly dramatic quarter-final.

That night, Rosset and Federer had a fervent discussion in the team hotel. Rosset was physically exhausted after his marathon match, but both he and Federer decided that they had to play on for the sake of the fans and their teammates.

Dealing with Hlasek could come later. For now, they resolved to embark on a salvage operation, one that was to come within one point of being spectacularly successful.

Despite having had little sleep, Federer partnered Lorenzo Manta in the doubles on the Saturday afternoon. No doubt pleased to have Federer alongside him after the fireworks of Friday night, Manta played one of his best ever Davis Cup matches. The Swiss pair lost the first set against Cedric Pioline and Fabrice Santoro, but they bounced back to win the second and third sets, only to concede the fourth on a second tiebreak. Federer later admitted that he wasn't sure how the Neuchâtel crowd would greet him after his poor showing the previous day, but they were totally behind him. And their support made a big difference in a 9–7 final set that took the match time to four hours and thirty-one minutes.

When Federer beat Arnaud Clément 6–4, 3–6, 7–6, 6–4 to level the match at 2–2, a phenomenal Swiss comeback was a real possibility. However, the talismanic Rosset was still too battered from his match on the Friday, so George Bastl, who had lost his only previous live fifth rubber 6–4 in the fifth to Mark Philippoussis at the start of Hlasek's reign fourteen months earlier, was thrown in again. He raced through the first set, and then took a 2–1 lead on a third-set tiebreak. Escudé took the fourth, and suddenly the tie that had looked so one-sided on Friday night was into a deciding fifth set.

Bastl had the advantage of serving first. When it got to 4–4, he held serve to put the pressure on Escudé – the Frenchman had to hold to stay in the match. He did. At 5–5, Bastl held again for 6–5. Escudé again served to stay in it.

At 30–40, Bastl had match point. A rally developed. Escudé went for a big forehand that ended up landing close to the baseline. Someone shouted, 'Out!' and Bastl began to raise his arms in triumph – but then realised it might not have been the line umpire who'd called. He played the shot but had been knocked off balance by the call and spooned his forehand over Escudé's baseline. Deuce.

Whether that 'call' beat Bastl will never be known, but Escudé won the next two points to hold serve, and in the next game Bastl was broken. Although he had a stab at getting the break back, Escudé was never going to lose his serve, and France were triumphant.

After the match, the disappointment in the Swiss camp was obviously great, though tempered by the fact that they had salvaged some pride from the horrors of Friday. They just needed the turmoil to end.

It would be wrong to say that weekend drained Federer; a week later, he won three matches in Monte Carlo, and then two more in Rome in early May. Given his early results (he'd followed up the title in Milan with a run to the semi-finals in Marseille, the final in Rotterdam and the quarter-finals in Miami), he had now joined the ranks of the world's top ten. But for all his talent, he still hadn't found the right way to channel his nervous energy and, as he went to Hamburg for the final Masters Series tournament before the French Open, the safety valve that was keeping his on-court emotions under control was reaching bursting point.

6

IT WOULD BE WRONG to view any single event in Roger Federer's career as the defining moment. His rise to prominence was a gradual one, and there are several highs from the peak years. But what happened in Hamburg on 14 May 2001 was one of the most significant stepping stones in his entire career.

The record reads that Franco Squillari beat Roger Federer 6–3, 6–4 in the first round of the Hamburg Masters. But it was what happened at the end of the match – and the lessons that Federer drew from it – which had the most profound effect.

Hamburg's Rothenbaum is a tennis venue that oozes prestige and tradition. Set amid the imposing architecture of the grand Rothenbaumchausee boulevard, it is the venerable home of German tennis, where one of the oldest tournaments in the world is played. Until 2009, it was known as the Hamburg Masters, but then lost its Masters Series status when Madrid's megabucks proved mightier than Teutonic tradition. In 2001, neither Federer nor Squillari were names that cut a lot of ice with either German fans or global television broadcasters, so their first-round match took place on the Rothenbaum's Court 1, a concrete-laden mini-arena in the shadow of the main stadium. Its location in something of a wind tunnel means it always seems to attract the worst of the Hamburg weather, and as a result, few people witnessed the conclusion of the match.

The match summed up where Federer was in his career. He was clearly the more talented player, but he delivered a patchy performance in a match that was always finely balanced but forever tipping Squillari's way. At 5–4 in the second set, Squillari worked his way to match point. In the ensuing rally, Federer pushed the wily Argentinian left-hander back well behind his baseline and rushed to the net. It should have been an easy volley for him. Squillari played the ball with as much topspin as he could in an attempt to force Federer to play a low volley. Federer lost sight of the ball, and suddenly realised it was jammed between his racket and the heavy clay. In the background, the umpire called, 'Game, set and match Squillari, 6–3, 6–4.'

Federer shook Squillari's hand at the net, acknowledged the umpire, and then smashed his racket in a rage under the umpire's chair.

That smashed racket was perhaps one of the most valuable he has ever played with. The reaction to his defeat made him take a long, hard look at himself. 'What made me upset was not just losing the match but my attitude,' he said several years later. 'I said there that I needed an attitude change. I remember thinking, "I never smash my racket after matches, only during matches." And then I said, "That's it, I'm not getting pissed off any more. I'm acting too bad."'

And he was as good as his word. The attitude did change, almost too much at first. His on-court composure was almost Buddhist-like in the next handful of tournaments – he would hit great shots or make horrendous errors and show absolutely no reaction, merely stroll into position for the next point. 'I almost had a problem with being too quiet,' he remembers. 'I had motivation and fire, but I couldn't express it any more, so I was struggling with my behaviour. Maybe I lost some time but, looking back now, it was probably very important for me.'

It was important, but so was the fact that his new attitude was rewarded with results. Within seven weeks of his rattle-throwing in Hamburg, he had reached his first two Grand Slam quarter-finals, thanks to the result that really announced his potential to the tennis world at large.

The four victories that took him to the quarter-finals of the French Open restored some confidence and then, on the grass of Halle, he looked supremely confident for two rounds before falling to one of the top grass-court players of the time, Patrick Rafter, in the quarter-finals. Wanting more practice on grass, he opted to play the Dutch event in 's-Hertogenbosch, notching up three wins there before running into his old nemesis Lleyton Hewitt in the semi-finals.

While Federer was in the Netherlands, the Wimbledon draw was made, with the name P Sampras at the top. There was nothing unusual in this, Sampras had won seven of the previous eight men's singles titles, but by June 2001 the grandmaster of Wimbledon had been looking increasingly vulnerable. He hadn't won a tournament all year after losing to Todd Martin in the fourth round at the Australian Open and to Hewitt in the semi-finals of his favourite grass-court warm-up event, the Stella Artois Championships at London's Queen's Club. In fact, Sampras's last title had been won on the final day of Wimbledon 2000, when he'd come back from a poor start to beat Pat Rafter in four sets in the last vestiges of daylight. It seemed he was ready to be toppled.

That year, the British were too fixated on Tim Henman to look seriously in anyone else's direction. With Sampras on the wane, it seemed that the great hope of British tennis might finally have found his moment. The projected quarter-final between Sampras and Henman was the talk of the Wimbledon build-up, and the flames were only fanned by Sampras's unimpressive showing in his second-round match, during which he dropped two sets against the unfancied British player Barry Cowan, whose ultimate defeat in five sets proved the high-water mark of his career.

Then, when Henman beat Sjeng Schalken and Sampras beat Sargis Sargsian to reach the fourth round, the Sampras–Henman clash was still on. But, unbeknown to anyone at the time, Sargsian, a likeable Armenian who had come through the American college system to carve out a living on the professional tennis tour, was to be the last man to lose to Sampras at Wimbledon that year, and the second-last ever.

On an overcast Monday on which all remaining singles players of both genders were in action, Federer walked out on to Wimbledon's Centre Court for the first time. As well as preparing to face Sampras, he'd had to become acquainted with certain Centre Court traditions, including bowing to the Royal Box if a member of the British royal family was seated there (a practice since abolished). As the fifteenth seed, he was still thought by most tennis watchers to be too much of a work in progress to beat the reigning champion, and it was generally felt this would be a match he'd end up having to chalk up to experience. After all, to most British watchers the contest was just a stepping-stone to a Sampras v Henman quarter-final.

Yet enough people close to Federer had expressed their faith in the nineteen-year-old's ability to beat Sampras, and after taking a first-set tiebreak with some good fortune (a dubious serve was called in his favour, and he profited from a lucky net cord) his confidence began to grow. Federer could have been two sets up but missed six break points in the second set, which Sampras took 7–5. A poor smash from Sampras gave Federer the third set, but Sampras stormed through the fourth-set tiebreak to make it two sets all. The fifth set went with serve until the twelfth game, when Federer had Sampras at 15–40. The Swiss guessed that Sampras would serve wide to his forehand side – and he was right. Federer struck a winning forehand return and promptly fell to the ground. After three hours and forty-one minutes, he'd won 7–6, 5–7, 6–4, 6–7, 7–5 to end the great man's run of thirty-one successive Wimbledon wins, dating back to the start of the 1997 event. It was to prove the only time Federer and Sampras ever played each other in an official match.

Ever the conservative statesman, Sampras paid tribute to a man he recognised as having many of the attributes that had taken himself so far. 'There are a lot of young guys coming up, but Roger is a bit extra-special,' he observed. 'He has a great all-round game, like me doesn't get too emotional, and is a great athlete.'

The last person to have beaten Sampras at Wimbledon –

Richard Krajicek in 1996 – had gone on to win the title, and on that Monday night of 2 July 2001 there were many who were tipping Federer. But the British had got it right – this was the best year for Henman to win. With Sampras out of the way, Henman played one of his best ever matches to bundle Federer out in the quarter-finals 7–5, 7–6, 2–6, 7–6. The win over Sampras had taken its toll on the young Swiss. Although he refused to use it as an excuse, nor even mention it at his post-match press conference, Federer had strained an adductor muscle in his third-round match against Jonas Björkman, an injury that had got worse in his match with Sampras. That kind of injury needs a few days to heal. At some Wimbledons, the rain gives players that kind of time, but not Federer in 2001. He played on – understandably given that it was Wimbledon – but the muscle strain hampered him in his match against Henman and later caused him to miss several weeks of the American hard-court season.

All the same, by beating Sampras at Wimbledon, Federer had announced his presence to the wider tennis world, and although Henman had beaten him, the message for the British was clear: if Henman doesn't win Wimbledon this year, it might be too late for him, because the interregnum between the Sampras and Federer eras looked like being very short.

And so it proved. 2001 was Henman's best chance, but he lost to the astonishingly revitalised Goran Ivanisevic in the semi-finals in a five-set match played over three days.

After winning the third set 6–0, Henman had one foot in the final, but then several interruptions due to rain allowed Ivanisevic to regroup, and one break in the final set allowed the Croat to shatter British dreams. Ivanisevic's win over Rafter in a raucous Monday final is one of the great romantic tales in modern tennis folklore, so it was perhaps a good year for Federer to garner useful experience, rather than win the title that would have created expectations he was probably not yet ready to handle.

Such was Federer's loyalty to the tournament in Gstaad – the first that ever gave him a wildcard – that he opted not to rest the groin strain he sustained at Wimbledon but instead to play on the clay there a week later. It proved the wrong decision; he won just three games against the tall Croat Ivan Ljubicic, and then found he had to take six weeks off to let the strain fully heal.

At least his enforced period of recuperation gave him time to assess the progress he'd made since his realisation in Hamburg two months earlier. Apart from the emotional gesture of falling to the turf of Wimbledon's Centre Court after beating Sampras, he had been a model of calmness, demonstrating almost robotic unflappability in all his subsequent matches. Yet this wasn't something he was particularly comfortable with. 'I felt like I was walking on a tightrope,' he said in an interview that appeared in Melbourne's daily newspaper *The Age* in January 2004. 'When I was getting upset, I was right away called "the bad boy", and then when I wasn't showing anything I was "the guy tanking" ['to tank' is a verb used in tennis to denote the supposedly non-existent practice of a player deliberately losing a match while giving the impression of trying to win it]. So I really had to watch what I was doing, and... I had to find the way I wanted to be and feel on the court. Maybe I can still show more emotions or still show less, but the right balance will come in the next few years.'

The adductor injury meant the only tournament he played

on the American summer hard-court circuit in 2001 was the US Open. As the guy who had beaten Sampras at Wimbledon, Federer was suddenly a marked man. He cruised through his first three matches, winning all in straight sets, and then came up against Andre Agassi in the fourth round. Both had played themselves into an illustrious quarter of the draw; it meant the winner of the match would play the winner of another last-sixteen match between Pete Sampras and Patrick Rafter.

The Sampras–Rafter match consumed most of the public and media's interest, as Rafter had announced this would be his final Grand Slam tournament before 'an extended break', which everyone took to mean – and ultimately did mean – retirement. Sampras won the match to end Rafter's Grand Slam career, so by the time Agassi and Federer took to the court, they were playing for the right to face Sampras in the quarter-finals. And there was no question that the New York crowd much preferred the prospect of Agassi–Sampras to a repeat of the Sampras–Federer encounter at Wimbledon.

Federer was eventually to get the better of Agassi, but, in their fourth-round clash at the 2001 US Open, Agassi gave a masterclass, showing some of the best form of his career, making Federer pay for every small error and eventually crushing him 6–1, 6–2, 6–4. Agassi won the first five games, took the first set in just twenty minutes and continued his dominance throughout the rest of the match. At one stage, he had the crowd purring with a dropshot dripping with so much backspin that the ball bounced back to his side of the net, leaving Federer stranded.

Agassi's impressive form continued into his quarter-final with Sampras, which Sampras won on four tiebreaks in one of the highest-quality matches of recent years. Having beaten Rafter, Agassi and the defending champion, Marat Safin, in successive matches, Sampras seemed on course for a fifth US Open title, but he was undone in the final by the coming-of-age performance of Lleyton Hewitt, who had continued his quicker development to beat Federer to the Grand Slam roll of honour by twenty-two months. The feisty Australian was to beat Federer to the number-one ranking by twenty-six months.

From the high of his win over Sampras, Federer had been brought down to earth. After beating the great man at Wimbledon, he'd had good reason to hope for enough subsequent wins to enable him to qualify for the Tennis Masters Cup, the eight-man year-ending elite tournament that took place that year in Sydney. But his defeat to Henman and the groin injury had left him with just five matches in two months, and, when he lost to Nicolas Kiefer on a final-set tiebreak in the first round of the Moscow indoor event in the first week of October, his year was fizzling out.

But there was still Basel. As the beaten finalist in 2000, Federer was hoping to improve on his previous year's performance for the third successive year and, when he beat Andy Roddick 3–6, 6–3, 7–6 in the quarter-finals, his route to victory looked clear. A straight-sets win over Julien Boutter in the semi-finals then set him up for his first meeting with Tim Henman since Wimbledon three months earlier. With his groin strain now healed, with the Swiss public behind him, and without the kind of strength-sapping semi-final that had wrecked his chances the previous year, this was surely his moment.

Henman had other ideas. He'd won Basel three years

earlier, taking Agassi apart in the final, and once again he showed his comfort in the Swiss metropolis by turning Federer's dream into a nightmare. The Briton won 6–3, 6–4, 6–2 in a one-sided match that took the sting out of the Basel crowd and left Federer numb. 'I just wasn't there,' he said afterwards. 'I played a bad match. I think I just put too much pressure on myself.' More than that, he was building up a complex about Henman, who had now beaten him in all of their four encounters on the tour.

Although he went into the last Masters Series tournament of the year – the indoor event in the Paris district of Bercy in late October – with an outside chance of qualifying for the Sydney Tennis Masters Cup, a first-round defeat to Jiri Novak killed off that hope and suddenly Federer's tennis year was over. He finished 2001 ranked thirteenth and having won his first ATP tournament – a respectable achievement, and an improvement on his 2000 year-end ranking of twenty-ninth. But it could have been so much better.

Having witnessed Federer beating Pete Sampras at Wimbledon, the tennis world was expecting him to press on in 2002, and the Australian Open seemed the ideal venue. He arrived in Melbourne fresh from his second tour title in Sydney the previous week – the arena in which he'd been so frustrated at missing out on a medal at the 2000 Olympics proved a happier hunting ground sixteen months on. The draw fell kindly for him, but his experience seemed to add more weight to the growing bank of evidence that this was a great talent who just couldn't hack it at the highest level of the sport.

After straight-sets wins over Michael Chang, Attila Savolt

and Rainer Schüttler, the eleventh-seeded Federer came up against Tommy Haas in the round of the last sixteen. Although the German was enjoying the spectacular run of form that would take him to number two in the rankings by mid-May – the highest position of his career – Federer should still have beaten him that day. In fact, he had Haas beaten – only to let his fish off the hook. After losing the first set, the Swiss came back to win the second and third, but then lost the fourth 6–4. But he had the advantage of serving first in the fifth set, in which both men were increasingly battling fatigue. At 6–5, Federer had Haas at 30–40, but then made five consecutive errors to turn match point for him into a 6–7 deficit. Haas – at seventh the highest remaining seed left in the tournament after a first week of carnage among the big names – served out an 8–6 final-set victory. A golden opportunity for Federer had gone begging.

And a week later, he failed to defend his title in Milan. He went all the way to the final, but lost to Italy's Davide Sanguinetti, seriously folding in the final set to lose it 6–1. It was an emotional win for the twenty-nine-year-old Italian, who posted his first career title, and in his home country.

Then came a week that, in retrospect, proved to have massive emotional value to Federer. Switzerland hadn't played a Davis Cup tie since that turbulent weekend ten months earlier in which he said he just couldn't play under the Swiss captain Jakob Hlasek. With the threat of losing not just his best player but the one who single-handedly carried Swiss hopes in tennis's top team competition, Hlasek had no option but to step down in the interests of team unity.

Federer then made it clear he wanted his former coach Peter Carter to become the Swiss Davis Cup captain, but there was a problem: Carter wasn't a Swiss national, and according to Davis Cup rules the captain of each team has to be a citizen of the country he's captaining. In 2001, however, Carter had married his Swiss fiancée and was in the process of applying for Swiss citizenship, so a deal was struck by which he became the head of the Swiss team (under the term 'Teamchef', literally team boss) while Ivo Heuberger – the fifth member of the four-man playing staff – was nominated as captain, with the sole responsibility of sitting on the bench and chatting to the players at changes of ends. This model proved sufficiently successful that the Swiss still use it today, several changes of personnel down the line.

Switzerland were drawn away to Russia in the 2002 first round. For the trip to Moscow, Federer's personal coach Peter Lundgren was allowed to be part of the Swiss entourage. By some accounts, not everyone was happy with Federer's influence on team affairs. The Swiss journalist Roger Jaunin says Michel Kratochvil – Switzerland's number-two player by a long way – felt he was denied any such privilege, though it should perhaps be pointed out that Kratchovil was never the most popular member of the Swiss team and was less crucial to its success than Federer. Be that as it may, with Carter pulling the strings off the court and Marc Rosset still offering an option in the doubles, the Swiss had a more powerful team than they'd presented for some time.

In Moscow's indoor Olympic Stadium, the Swiss were up against a Russian team desperate to win the Davis Cup. Well, Yevgeny Kafelnikov was desperate to win it, in what looked like being his last year on the tour, and in Marat Safin he had a partner who – if he was on his game and sufficiently motivated – could beat anyone on any surface, other than grass. The Russians chose to play on clay and, when Russia plays at home on clay, the clay is frequently very damp and heavy. So it proved for this tie, but Federer played superbly on the first day to beat Safin 7–5, 6–1, 6–2 to win in one hour and thirty-six minutes.

When Kratochvil took a two-sets-to-one lead against Kafelnikov in the second singles and then served for the match at 6–5 in the fourth set, the Russian plan to play on clay looked to have backfired miserably. But beautiful ball-striker that he was, Kratochvil often had difficulty in finishing off big matches, and so it proved on this occasion. 'I didn't play defensively or afraid,' he said after the match. 'I went for my shots, but I just lost them.' Kafelnikov won the fourth set on a tiebreak and took the fifth 6–2.

A crowd of 8,000 surged into the stadium for the doubles, and they were rewarded with one of the best displays of teamwork Kafelnikov and Safin ever put together. Federer and Rosset didn't play their best on that occasion, indeed Rosset had a particularly bad day and felt he was to blame for the Russians' 6–2, 7–6, 6–7, 6–2 victory, which was also Federer's first-ever defeat in a Davis Cup doubles rubber. They almost got back into the match after saving four match points in the third set, but then lost it in four. It was no disgrace, but it meant Switzerland's fate was now out of Federer's hands.

All he could do was win his second singles and hope for an unlikely Swiss victory in the deciding rubber. The next day, he played his part, putting in his second outstanding display of the weekend to crush Kafelnikov 7–6, 6–1, 6–1, which threw the initiative back to Kratochvil. Although Kratochvil lost the first set to Safin in just twenty-two minutes, he led

4–1 in the second and had a point for a double-break. But once Safin had won the second set on an 8–6 tiebreak, the mountain proved too high for the Swiss to climb, despite leading 4–2 in the third, and Safin took Russia into the quarter-finals with a 6–1, 7–6, 6–4 win.

After the final match, Federer observed, 'For myself and my singles matches, there was some great tennis from me this weekend. I couldn't have expected much more. I would have loved to win the doubles, but they played very well. In the end it was just tough that we lost the tie.' One can, of course, read too much into casual comments made in post-match press conferences, where emotions often run high, but the impression these words leave behind is that Federer fully expected that, in order for Switzerland to win, he had to win all his three matches. As the British journalist Neil Harman had written in the Davis Cup yearbook about Switzerland's win over the USA the previous year, 'The result might just as well have read, "Federer 3, USA 2."' It seemed that, at least in terms of the Davis Cup, Switzerland *was* Federer – even if Kratochvil would have a solitary moment of glory the following year.

It took until the end of March for Federer to play a consistent tournament from start to finish, and, in the weeks between the Davis Cup tie in Moscow and his run to the final in Miami, there were signs that the man was still being formed from the remnants of the boy. One salutary lesson came in Dubai, where Federer lost 6–3, 6–1 to the German Rainer Schüttler in the second round. It was not that he lost, rather the manner in which he lost, that caused concern. To those watching the match, he hardly seemed to care in the second set. Most tournaments below Masters Series level tend to pay either appearance fees or minimum prize money guarantees to their bigger names – it's a practice no tournament likes to talk about, but it's recognised as part of what oils the wheels of the global tennis machine. Federer had been offered an appearance fee for Dubai, but such was his slapdash showing against Schüttler that the tournament threatened not to pay it. After lots of to-ing and fro-ing with Federer and his agents, the tournament agreed to hold the agreed fee, to be paid if he turned up the following year and made the appropriate effort. Federer did turn up the following year and did make the effort, winning the first of three back-to-back Dubai Open titles. He had clearly profited from Dubai's lesson.

At the end of March 2002, he finally played a consistent tournament from start to finish: the Nasdaq-100 Open in Key Biscayne, Florida. As well as being one of the nine Masters Series tournaments (ie the level of men's event immediately below the four Grand Slams), it's also arguably the most prestigious. Back in the 1980s, its organisers even hoped it would take over from the Australian Open as the fourth Grand Slam. Although that plan was foiled and the event is now probably sixth in prestige behind the four majors and the year-ending ATP World Tour Finals, it is still an event all the major players turn out for.

That year, Federer had to face two of his bogeymen, Tim Henman and Lleyton Hewitt. Henman was dispatched in the third round (albeit on a retirement), while Hewitt was beaten majestically in the semi-finals. This second victory was something of a prized scalp for Federer. Not only was Hewitt the world number one at the time – and Federer had never beaten a number one before – but he was also on a winning streak of twenty-three matches on American hard courts. Yet the contrast between his game and Federer's proved the Australian's undoing. Hewitt's principal weapon, the ability to run down every shot and wear opponents out, cost him much more energy than Federer's bigger hitting. And with Hewitt stretched to his limit in his first four matches, he went into his semi-final having played more than eight hours, while the more economical Federer had spent less than four. With Hewitt looking tired, a break early in each set sufficed for a 6–3, 6–4 Swiss victory and, with it, passage into Federer's first Masters Series final.

After the match, Hewitt offered his own thoughts on Federer's form. 'I think this could be a breakthrough year for him,' he predicted, 'but whether he's going to get up to the top four or five, that's another question.'

Hewitt, whose gruff on-court manner often hides a highly perceptive tennis brain, knew Federer's strengths and weaknesses, and the remark proved highly accurate: Federer did improve, but he finished the year just short of the top five.

With the jinx players Hewitt and Henman vanquished, Federer found himself up against Andre Agassi in the final. They had played just twice before – in Basel in 1998 and at the 2001 US Open – and Agassi had won both. This time it should have been a five-setter: Agassi took the first two sets, and then Federer came back to take the third and served at 4–3 in the fourth. Until the final, he hadn't dropped serve all tournament and, after being broken three times in the first two sets, he seemed to have steadied the ship. But then Agassi – by then just four weeks short of his thirty-second birthday –

showed why he was one of the sport's greatest-ever returners. He broke Federer's serve twice in succession to take his fifth Key Biscayne title in his 700th full tour win.

It was a lesson to Federer that he still needed to raise his game to another level if he was to pick up one of the nine Masters Series glass shields the male players compete for every year. But his first shield was not long in coming – only another seven weeks, in fact.

When Federer speaks today of the matches that served as turning points in his career, he often mentions one that few might consider: his win over Marat Safin in Hamburg in May 2002. Perhaps it signified coming full circle after his ill-disciplined outburst in the German city the previous year. 'It was my first Masters Series win,' he says, 'and probably my second-biggest breakthrough after the Sampras match.'

It had always been something of an oddity that a player who'd learned his tennis on clay was thought to be so vulnerable on the red stuff. A little relativity is called for here. For a start, Federer was not alone in this: both Boris Becker and Stefan Edberg had honed their skills on clay (though also on fast indoor courts during the winter months) and it always proved their least favourite and least effective surface. More importantly, by going on to reach four successive French Open finals and lifting the trophy, nobody could possibly claim that Federer has a weakness on clay. Had it not been for the presence of Rafael Nadal, who is certainly one of the greatest clay-court players ever – if not the greatest – it is highly likely that Federer would have won the French Open several times, and it is only his superb achievements on grass and hard courts that make his clay achievements pale in comparison.

However, from the vantage point of mid-2002, Federer did

seem vulnerable on the principal European tennis surface. He had lost his first dozen or so tour matches on clay, and by May 2002 he needed a tournament at which he could show that he did have the game for the underfoot conditions that demand so much patience and fitness. The Hamburg Masters was to be that tournament.

His first four wins – the first three in straight sets – were against players of proven clay-court pedigree: Nicolas Lapentti, Bohdan Ulihrach, Adrian Voinea and Gustavo Kuerten. He then saw off the big-serving Max Mirnyi in the semi-finals to set up a final against Marat Safin, the man who had just gone to the top of the 2002 'Race'. (The 'Race' is similar to the rankings but is based solely on results since 1 January of each year, so it gives a fairly reliable indication of recent form in the first few months of the year.) Two years earlier, Safin had lost a fifth-set tiebreak to Kuerten in the Hamburg final, and the mercurial Russian seemed well set to avenge his defeat to Federer in the Davis Cup three months earlier. But it was to be Federer's day, and one of the best of his year.

'It was definitely the best match of my career,' Federer enthused after his 6–1, 6–3, 6–4 win in barely two hours. 'I thought it would be much tougher, but I played unbelievable tennis. I could risk a lot and the balls went in. It was just incredible. I always had the feeling I could break him.' Even Safin said, 'I thought he played the best match of his life.'

Winning the Hamburg Masters revolutionised Federer's clay-court status. He was suddenly installed as one of the favourites for the French Open. But he had yet to learn to deal with the pressure of expectation, and in Paris he froze in the first round against the highly gifted but frustratingly erratic Moroccan Hicham Arazi. Twice a quarter-finalist at Roland Garros, Arazi went into every match knowing he was probably ahead of his opponent on natural ability, even if he let himself down on discipline. Against Federer he was arguably only equal on natural ability and inferior on discipline, but he still ran out a 6–3, 6–2, 6–4 winner. 'I was hoping for so much from this tournament,' Federer said sadly after his defeat, 'but I put too much pressure on myself.'

At least there were still the grass-court tournaments to come. Federer put in his usual appearance in Halle, and looked best placed to win the title, but he came up short over the finals weekend, this time to Nicolas Kiefer, 6–4 in the third set of their semi-final. He then managed to get three more batches of match practice on grass before losing in the quarter-finals of 's-Hertogenbosch to Sjeng Schalken.

Next stop was Wimbledon, to which Federer returned in 2002 with the confidence of the previous year's win over Sampras still ringing in his ears. When he was put on Centre Court for his first-round match against the Grand Slam debutant Mario Ancic, he looked set for a comfortable win, but the big-serving eighteen-year-old from Croatia showed phenomenal composure to deliver a stunning 6–3, 7–6, 6–3 defeat that sent Federer home before he'd barely finished unpacking. Ancic later revealed that his tactics had come from the reigning champion Goran Ivanisevic – they had been merely to avoid the big Federer forehand and attack the second serve. So simple.

'It was a shocker,' said Federer pithily, scarcely concealing his anger. Had he known it would be his last defeat at Wimbledon for six years it would no doubt have been easier to take, but such things seem scarcely plausible in the immediate aftermath of such a frustrating defeat. Instead of Federer, it was his Davis Cup colleague George Bastl who made the Swiss tennis headlines at that Wimbledon, stunning Pete Sampras in the second round in five sets to draw a somewhat patchy close to the American's glorious Wimbledon years.

Back on the clay in Gstaad, Federer showed how easy it should have been in Paris by dispatching Hicham Arazi 6–4, 6–3 in the first round, but the following day he was again inconsistent against another gifted but erratic player, Radek Stepanek. It was time for a holiday and some fitness work before the American summer hard-court swing. But that season began badly, and swiftly got worse.

On 1 August 2002, Switzerland's national day, Federer lost 7–6, 7–5 in the first round of the Toronto Masters to the muscular Argentinian Guillermo Cañas, who went on to win the tournament. But the disappointment of defeat was as nothing compared to the news that greeted him when he arrived back in the locker room after the match: Peter Carter had been killed in a car crash while on his honeymoon in South Africa.

7

PETER CARTER HAD met his wife, Sylvia von Arx, in Basel. She was a receptionist at the *Paradies* indoor tennis facility owned by the Basel sports and entertainment impresario Roger Brennwald. Shortly after they'd got to know each other, she had been diagnosed with a brain tumour. For a long time the prognosis didn't look good, but in 2001 her condition began to improve. That year they got married, but decided to delay their honeymoon until she was fully fit and they could have the holiday of a lifetime.

In late 2001, Sylvia was finally given a clean bill of health, and the pair arranged a trip to South Africa the following summer, as a combined honeymoon and celebration of her recovery. They were touring in the Kruger National Park in separate four-wheel-drive cars, when the driver of the one Carter was in swerved to avoid an on-coming minibus and then had to veer back onto the road to avoid hitting a bridge near the township of Gravelotte. The soft-topped car overturned, landed on its roof, which caved in, crushing Carter and the driver.

When Federer came off court in Toronto, his coach Peter Lundgren – the man he had opted for ahead of Carter when he had to choose between them in early 2000 – rang him to break the news. For a while, Federer couldn't believe it. 'I'm very shocked and very sad,' he said in his first public statement. 'He was a very close friend. This is the first time a close friend of mine has died. He wasn't my first coach, but he was my real coach. He knew me and my game, and he was always thinking of what was good for me.'

Eventually, he and Lundgren decided Federer should play the following week's Masters Series event in Cincinnati, and then fly back to Switzerland for the funeral. Needless to say, he was in no fit state of mind for Cincinnati, and crashed out against Ivan Ljubicic in the first round. 'When something like that happens,' he said after the match, 'you see how unimportant tennis is.' Unlike in Toronto the week before, where he had played doubles the day after Carter's death, Federer withdrew from the Cincinnati doubles and headed for home.

In his book, *The Tennis Genius*, René Stauffer gives a very sensitive account of Carter's moving funeral in St Leonhard's Church in Basel. Around 200 people turned up, among them Andre Agassi's coach Darren Cahill, who had been Carter's stablemate at Peter Smith's set-up in Adelaide. The priest conducting the funeral had married Carter and Silvia just a year earlier. Silvia made a short and moving speech, as did three others. As well as Roger, Lynette and Robbie Federer were also inconsolable – as Stauffer points out, they had lost the man who had been such a vital channel of communication for them as Roger had gradually asserted his independence during his teenage years. A week after the funeral, Federer said, 'Compared with a moment like that, losing a tennis match is nothing. I normally try to avoid sad events, and it was my first funeral. I can't say it did me good, but I was very close to Peter in my thoughts and feel I've said goodbye in a dignified setting. Now I feel a bit better, especially in terms of tennis. The motivation that I felt I'd lost after the event is back.'

After the funeral, he honoured his commitment to play in Long Island, a small tournament just outside New York City which always acted as a curtain-raiser for the US Open, but again he lost in the first round, this time to Nicolas Massu. At least he salvaged something at the US Open, winning three rounds, but his mind still wasn't fully on the job, and Max Mirnyi beat him in straight sets in the fourth.

Speaking several years later, Federer says of Carter, 'He was a very important man in my tennis career, if not the most important. I had been with him from ten to fourteen years old, and then again from sixteen till twenty, so I knew him very well. He gave me a lot in terms of his personality, in terms of technique and on the court. It was a hard loss. In those weeks after he died, everything went very quickly. I decided that I would compete in the US Open because I guessed that that was what Peter would have liked to see me do, not just to sit around. I don't know if it was for good or for bad... It was also a very influential moment in my career. It certainly marked me, and there was a reaction in terms of how I look at life now. It was a hard moment, and I think of him very often still.'

In the months that followed, Federer frequently had to suppress tears. But the grief made him stronger. In an interview with the Melbourne newspaper *The Age* in January 2004, he said the period pulling himself together after the shock of Carter's death was one of the most crucial in his tennis maturity. 'I guess it made me strong mentally, and I started thinking,' he said. 'I suddenly had time to ask myself, "What do I need to do to get to the next level?"'

Federer's first commitment after the US Open had a poignancy about it that could have brought his grief-blighted tennis right back. But the opposite happened – he played three of his best matches of the year.

After losing to Russia in the first round of the Davis Cup earlier that year, Switzerland were drawn away to Morocco in a tie they had to win in order to maintain their membership of the sixteen-nation elite Davis Cup world group. At the time of his death, Swiss Tennis had been confident Carter would be granted his Swiss citizenship in time for the trip to Casablanca; that would have enabled him to assume the role of Swiss captain and thus sit on the bench coaching his players at changes of ends. But, with Peter Lundgren acting as temporary team supremo and Marc Rosset now promoted to captain, the tie became something of a homage to Carter. The Swiss team was united as never before, any unrest put aside for the tough assignment on clay in the heat of North Africa. At the official ceremony, all the Swiss players had their names on the backs of their shirts, but Federer and Rosset had Carter's name as well as their own. As the Swiss national anthem was played before play on the Saturday, Federer's eyes were moist with emotion. It was that kind of occasion.

When Younes el Aynaoui beat Michel Kratochvil in straight sets in the first rubber, the spotlight was on Federer, who faced Hicham Arazi, the man who had bundled him out of the French Open. On his least effective surface, it could have proved too much for the still just twenty-one-year-old Swiss. But if he froze under the pressure of expectation in Paris, he flourished under the opportunity to make a statement for his deceased friend in Casablanca. He crushed Arazi for the loss of just six games, playing as if in a trance and admitting afterwards that he felt the key was for him to be in 'a very good mental state'.

The trance continued into the doubles, in which Federer and George Bastl conceded just nine games in beating Younes el Aynaoui and Karim Alami, and in the first reverse singles el Aynaoui achieved no more against Federer than the six games his teammate had posted two days earlier. It was awesome stuff and, as the Swiss journalist Roger Jaunin reported, el Aynaoui recognised it as such. One of the game's most humane characters, the Moroccan gatecrashed the Swiss celebration party on the Sunday night to say to Federer, 'What you have done this weekend no one else but you could have done.'

Federer dedicated his first victory and his first tournament title after Carter's death to his former coach and mentor. The first victory was a four-sets passage to the second round of the US Open against Jiri Vanek, while the first title came in early October in Vienna. The weekend in Casablanca had restored the on-court confidence that now went with the off-court lessons in life Federer had learned since 1 August. He reached the quarter-finals in Moscow, and then won his fourth career title, the CA Trophy in Vienna.

The rest of the year continued in a similar vein, putting Federer in a position where, despite his barren fourteen-week spell from Hamburg to the US Open, during which he won just seven out of fourteen matches, he qualified for the first time for the elite eight-man Tennis Masters Cup, that year staged in Shanghai. His consistency at the start and end of 2002 allowed him to finish the year ranked sixth – another major improvement. But the two titles that had really mattered to him – the Swiss Indoors and the Tennis Masters Cup – were both won that autumn by players who continued to exercise something of a hold over him.

In his fifth assault on his home tournament, Federer managed to reach the semi-finals of the Swiss Indoors, again beating Andy Roddick in the quarter-finals. Everything seemed set for a final featuring the local boy and the French Open runner-up Juan Carlos Ferrero, but neither made it to the final; Federer was taken out in the semis by David Nalbandian, who had beaten him in the US Open boys' final in 1998 and who had yet to lose to Federer since their junior days, while Ferrero lost to another alumnus of the 1998 junior year, Fernando Gonzalez. Nalbandian's win over Gonzalez in the final cut very little ice with the aficionados in the St Jakobshalle!

And then, having battled through the round-robin stage of the Tennis Masters Cup, with wins over Ferrero, Jiri Novak and Thomas Johansson, Federer lost a high-quality semi-final to Lleyton Hewitt, the Australian winning 7–5 in the third set as he became only the fourth man since computer rankings began in 1973 to go a full calendar year in the number-one slot.

Federer himself finished the year ranked fifth, another

advance on the previous year, but still in the 'flattering to deceive' category. When he again stumbled against Nalbandian in the fourth round of the Australian Open in another mid-tournament five-setter, he had played the first Grand Slam of the year four times and got stuck at the half-way stage all four times (twice in the third round, twice in the fourth). After his five-sets defeat to Tommy Haas the previous year, Nalbandian took the fifth set 6-3, to make his record against Federer three wins in three tour-level matches. Federer was an acknowledged colossus on the tour, but still unproven in the tournaments that really mattered.

Roger Federer's Davis Cup career can be broken down into two phases. The first covered his first six years from 1999 to 2004, when he played every tie Switzerland contested. The second phase covers the years since 2005, when he has declined to play the first round weekend, but was always available for Switzerland's September tie. Because of his absence, the Swiss have never gone beyond the first round, so that September tie has since 2005 always been a promotion/relegation affair to stay in or return to the sixteen-nation World Group of the team competition. Inspired by the team effort that brought him his Olympic doubles gold medal in 2008, he declared his willingness to play in Switzerland's first round tie against the USA in March 2009. He ended up pulling out, citing back problems though concerns over Mirka's pregnancy were also a factor. He also declined to turn up for Switzerland's first round tie against Spain in 2010, which suggests that he might not value the Davis Cup, despite it being the one historic prize in tennis he has yet to win.

Of the six years that made up the first phase, the most successful was 2003, when Switzerland reached the semi-finals, its most successful run since the two-man team of Marc Rosset and Jakob Hlasek took the Alpine nation to its first, and so far only, Davis Cup final in 1992. Maybe having come so close in the semi-final in 2003, a little of the romance of the Davis Cup went missing for Federer. He has never said that, or blamed it for his early-year absences in recent years, but Switzerland's defeat to Australia in September 2003 took a lot out of him emotionally. He has also taken to criticising the Davis Cup calendar, which is a somewhat unfair pastime. There is much that could be improved in the Davis Cup's slots in the tennis calendar but, in 2007, the International Tennis Federation agreed to a calendar for tennis's premier team competition that it felt was far from ideal, but accepted because the players wanted specific dates. So for the players to say that the federation has not listened to them, as Federer has done, is a bit rich.

To play Australia, Switzerland had to win two ties, and the first of them suggested that the Swiss team of 2003 might be more than a one-man band.

The Swiss were drawn away to the Netherlands, and the Royal Dutch Lawn Tennis Association opted to play the tie in a corner of the Gelredome football stadium used by the top Dutch football club Vitesse Arnhem. The stadium not only had a retractable roof, but its grass pitch was on wheels, so it could be rolled out of the stadium for non-football events, or for a bit of fresh air during the week. When the grass was in the stadium, the venue had an extra car park.

To history scholars, the city of Arnhem is best known for

being the site of one of the bloodiest battles of the Second World War, when British troops looking to set up a bridgehead on the Rhine were shot down in their thousands in 1944. And the Davis Cup tie played there in February 2003 was one of the bloodiest in the 103-year history of tennis's premier team competition.

Before Federer had taken to the court, there was uproar in the stadium, and Rosset – who had been confirmed as Switzerland's captain after the emotions of Peter Carter's death had died down – had kicked a refrigerator in frustration. The Swiss number two, Michel Kratochvil, had battled impressively to come back from two sets down against the solid Dutch number one, Sjeng Schalken, but in the final set a small band of Dutch supporters unused to Davis Cup etiquette became increasingly loud and unruly. When Schalken had match point at 5–4, some of them threw celebration balls on to the court, only to find their hero hadn't yet won. Kratochvil saved a second match point, but on the third one of the troublesome supporters screamed during Kratochvil's second-serve ball toss, causing the Swiss to double-fault the match away. The visitors were furious. Rosset and Kratochvil railed at the umpire, Javier Moreno, and the referee, Brian Earley. As Rosset vented his spleen by delivering a massive kick to the courtside drinks fridge, the atmosphere became decidedly tense.

Into it stepped the man who as a boy had been unable to control his temper. But not any more. Federer kept his head down between points, and kept the points to a minimum in a 6–2, 6–1, 6–3 win over the dangerous though inconsistent Raemon Sluiter. It was his sixth successive Davis Cup singles win and his third consecutive victory for the loss of just six games.

There was some talk in the Swiss camp of Rosset leaving the bench to partner Federer in the doubles, but, having seen Federer team so well with George Bastl against Morocco, Rosset stuck to his role as captain and left the work to his pairing from Casablanca. It was not to work a second time. Against the veteran Paul Haarhuis and the Davis Cup debutant Martin Verkerk, the Swiss took the first set but then faded in the second, third and fourth, Federer playing one of his least distinguished doubles matches. He almost gave the impression of being depressed on court; when asked about it after the match he snapped, 'Bad question! I wasn't at all.'

Once again, the Swiss squad were in a position where their fate no longer hung entirely in Federer's hands. He certainly wasn't expected to lose to Sjeng Schalken in his next match and, while the match was no formality, his 7–6, 6–4, 7–5 victory was a fair reflection of the two players. 'I played better and better,' said Schalken after the match, 'but Roger does that to me – he brings out the best in me. But then he proved himself even more.'

Federer had done his bit, but now he had to watch as Kratochvil again held Switzerland's fate in the decisive rubber. This was his sixth live Davis Cup match, and he had yet to win one. After Verkerk's impressive showing in the doubles, the Dutch captain, Tjerk Bogtstra, opted for him over Sluiter for the final match. It looked a good choice when Verkerk had set points at 5–0 after less than twenty minutes of play, and Kratochvil looked a fish out of water. But the Bernese son of Czech immigrants, who had grown up at a tennis centre run by his dad called TC Flamingo, put both feet on the ground to score the biggest single win of his career in one of the most raucous environments ever seen for a tennis match.

During the second set, Kratochvil just about held his own and went on to sneak it on a 7–5 tiebreak, winning four points on the run to make good a 3–5 deficit. He then held his nerve in a third-set tiebreak that involved five contentious line calls, two overrules and a set point played with a noise level more commonly associated with basketball than tennis.

Verkerk had two set points at 6–4, but Kratochvil saved both. With the Swiss serving at 7–6, the home crowd were still protesting about a call. Kratochvil waited for quiet. It never came. So, following a nod from the umpire Roland Herfel, who clearly hoped that starting the point would quieten the spectators, he served.

The Dutch thought the serve was out, but Verkerk played it, and a rally ensued.

The noise continued.

Then Verkerk made an error, Kratochvil took the set, the Dutch went wild with anger, and Bogtstra began climbing the umpire's chair in rage. But the point stood, and Kratochvil led by two sets to one, despite having been outplayed for most of the match. From then on, Verkerk was a broken man, and Kratochvil raced through the fourth set for a 1–6, 7–6, 7–6, 6–1 win that saw Switzerland into the quarter-finals.

What Federer thought of it as he sat by the court watching is anyone's guess. He made all the right noises afterwards, two months later he was to say Rosset had fostered 'a wonderful team spirit', and he was obviously pleased to have another chance of glory, one he was to seize in spectacular fashion in the quarter-finals. But it's never easy for someone used to being the undisputed hero to sit back and let a lesser teammate take the applause, even someone as balanced and OK with himself as Roger Federer. Whatever his inherent good manners and sense of team unity had taught him to say that night, there must have been a tiny bit of discomfort in the realisation that this was someone else's moment.

There was no question that Federer was the undisputed hero of Switzerland's quarter-final win away to France. Some veteran tennis watchers even described it as the most remarkable individual performance in the Davis Cup – high praise indeed from those who had seen Björn Borg and Boris Becker take Sweden and West Germany to team triumphs largely single-handedly. In the aptly named Zenith Stadium in Toulouse, Federer reached one of the peaks of his career, beating Nicolas Escudé and Fabrice Santoro in the singles, and teaming up with Rosset to scoop victory in the doubles.

In retrospect, the opposition Federer faced that year in Toulouse might not have been of the highest order, but playing France in the Davis Cup is always a tricky proposition. The French have a joker in the pack, an extra card to play, in the form of their captain, Guy Forget. The mild-mannered left-hander has somehow managed to get his teams to be greater than the sum of their parts and has captained a team to three finals without ever having a player regularly in the top ten. Before the quarter-final began, Forget observed, 'Roger Federer is a very good player, and he can cause us some concern, but he's not unbeatable'. The simple art of piling the pressure on the opposition while at the same time letting your own players know they can win.

Federer was more than up for the task. Again he had to steady the Swiss ship after a defeat in the opening singles, but this time it wasn't Kratochvil flying the Swiss flag but George Bastl. Instead of propelling him into a confidence-laden surge up the rankings, Kratochvil's win in Arnhem was followed by a serious knee injury that required surgery, and he missed several months of 2003. Bastl replaced him, but was no match for France's Sébastien Grosjean in the first singles. Yet Escudé, who had beaten Federer two years earlier in Federer's worst-ever day in the Davis Cup, was no match for the man now in the world's top five, Federer notching up a 6–4, 7–5, 6–2 win, despite a slow start.

The agonising in the Swiss camp that Friday night concerned who would partner Federer in the doubles. The choice was between his old friend from childhood days, Yves Allegro, who had yet to play a Davis Cup rubber, and the thirty-two-year-old Rosset. The decision was made easier by an appointment made at the start of the year. The experienced French coach Georges Déniau has many connections with Switzerland, dating back to his days coaching Jakob Hlasek. After being appointed captain, Rosset brought in Déniau as one of his backroom team, and that night in Toulouse Déniau was instrumental in persuading Rosset to take to the court with Federer.

The gamble worked. Rosset played what he described as 'my best match since... an eternity!', he and Federer posting a 6–4, 3–6, 6–3, 7–6 win against Escudé and Santoro, the pair who had won the doubles in the Davis Cup final against Russia four months earlier. After the match, Rosset confessed, 'I didn't sleep or eat last night because I was so nervous to get on to the court. But Roger is a great doubles player; he helped me tough it out psychologically, and this is a wonderful win for the Swiss team.'

In beating Bastl on the Friday, France's top player Grosjean had pulled a thigh muscle, and couldn't play. Forget threw in Santoro, knowing his unorthodox game might cause problems for Federer. It had on several occasions – only six months earlier Santoro had beaten Federer in similar conditions in Madrid, and Santoro had won their first meeting in 1999 which happened to be in Toulouse. But the Santoro wizardry was not going to work this time; Federer was relentless, and the Frenchman won just three games as Switzerland moved through to the semi-finals with their fifth consecutive away win.

In the aftermath of Peter Carter's death, the Swiss and Australian tennis associations had taken up a suggestion made by Australia's captain John Fitzgerald that, when the two nations met each other in the Davis Cup, they would play for the Peter Carter Trophy. Fitzgerald had a personal interest, having known Carter from their time together as boys at Peter Smith's set-up in Adelaide. The first opportunity to play for the new trophy came in September 2003, when Australia hosted Switzerland in the semi-finals. Tennis Australia chose to stage the tie in the Rod Laver Arena in Melbourne and, with the previous two Wimbledon champions spearheading their teams, the stage was set for a cracker of a tie.

At that time, however, there were large question marks hanging over both teams. Federer came to Melbourne having made no obvious progress since Wimbledon. Switzerland welcomed back Michel Kratochvil as its second player, but he was woefully short of match practice. The same could also be said of Australia's number two, Mark Philippoussis, and even their number one, Lleyton Hewitt, hardly came into the tie with the best of records; he'd lost his Wimbledon title on the first day to Ivo Karlovic, he'd lost in the quarter-finals of the US Open to Juan Carlos Ferrero, he'd lost his number-one ranking, he'd lost his coach, Jason Stoltenberg (and people weren't at that stage sure whether his replacement, Roger

Rasheed, was a mate standing in or a genuine coach – he proved to be the latter by working with Hewitt for well over three years), and there was speculation about whether he was spending too much time with his girlfriend, Kim Clijsters, rather than concentrating on his tennis. It meant that all five rubbers of the semi-final seemed up for grabs.

With rain causing the roof to be closed for all the opening day, Hewitt crushed a disappointing Kratochvil 6–4, 6–4, 6–1. Then, in the second singles match, Federer and Philippoussis faced each other for the first time since their Wimbledon final eleven weeks earlier. The Australian claimed to have learned a lesson from the Wimbledon final, but what it was nobody could quite work out as Federer won 6–3, 6–4, 7–6. Philippoussis had led 5–3 in the third set, but that had been his only period of hope.

With the opening singles matches split, the doubles assumed massive importance, and it turned into what the Australian journalist Craig Gabriel described as 'a fiesta of enthralling tennis'. Since the retirement of Mark Woodforde in 2000, Australia had struggled to find a doubles pairing that did justice to the country's tradition of producing great doubles teams; the best option seemed to be Todd Woodbridge and Wayne Arthurs, but they had never looked totally convincing. So, when they faced Federer and Marc Rosset, it seemed a genuinely fifty-fifty match, and indeed it went the full distance. Unfortunately for the Swiss, that was the day Woodbridge and Arthurs played their best match together for Australia, sneaking a 4–6, 7–6, 5–7, 6–4, 6–4 win in a magnificent spectacle.

The pressure was then on Federer in the first reverse singles against Hewitt. When he won the first set 7–5, Federer equalled John McEnroe's record of thirty successive sets won in Davis Cup singles rubbers. When he won the second 6–2, he beat it. When he led Hewitt by two sets and 5–3 in the third, it seemed the formbook was holding firm and a live fifth rubber was imminent. But two things remained in Hewitt's favour: he had a good record against Federer (he'd won six of their eight matches as professionals) and he becomes even more passionate than normal when playing for his country. This is the man who, when his clothing company (the same as Federer's at that time) refused him permission to put the name of his country on the back of his shirts and wouldn't give him any in Australia's colours, got up early one morning to dye some white shirts yellow and some white shorts green. He is a patriotic Australian to the core, and that day he showed it.

The British tennis journalist Neil Harman described the match as 'the indomitable will against the extravagant talent'. On the point of victory for the talent, the will took over. Federer was within two points of levelling the tie, but Hewitt was determined not to be beaten in front of his own people and, when Federer gave him a couple of cheap points, the tide turned. After Hewitt had taken the third-set tiebreak 7–4, Federer took a breather; it's called a 'bathroom break', and no doubt there was a genuine call of nature, but he was clearly hoping to take the opportunity to regroup. He did for a while, but it didn't last. At 5–6 in the fourth set, he served a double fault to give Hewitt a set point. Hewitt then lunged at a volley to claim the set, and with it effectively break Federer's spirit. The final score read 5–7, 2–6, 7–6, 7–5, 6–1, and Hewitt enjoyed one of the biggest adrenaline rushes of his life. 'You can take your

Wimbledons and your US Opens,' he said in an on-court interview. 'This means more to me than anything.'

Even if Federer had won, Switzerland would still have had to rely on Kratochvil to beat Philippoussis. Kratochvil would have been the underdog in a match few would have felt confident about. In theory, Philippoussis, the man who had reached two Grand Slam finals and beaten a world number one (Pete Sampras in 1996) should have had the edge against a player with a fragile match temperament and on the rebound from knee surgery. But having won a live fifth rubber in his previous Davis Cup tie, Kratochvil might well have risen to the occasion against the flaky 'Flip'. We will never know.

At the end of the tie, Federer was in tears as the Peter Carter Trophy was presented to Australia's captain, John Fitzgerald. He knew his great run in Davis Cup singles would one day come to an end, but for it to do so in the crucial rubber of the tie for the trophy named after his mentor was hard. He restated his wish to have another go in 2004, and he duly turned out for Switzerland's first and second ties. But maybe something of the Davis Cup magic died in Federer that September night in Melbourne. It certainly slipped down his priority list after April 2004, and only resurfaced when he won the Olympic doubles gold medal with another Swiss player in the top ten, Stanislas Wawrinka. While he always said he enjoyed carrying the entire Swiss cause on his shoulders, it could be that the pressure of doing so was losing its allure, and only when he had someone with whom to share the load did some of his enthusiasm for the team variant of tennis return.

The dignified Fitzgerald was no doubt trying to be consoling, though in no way untruthful, when he said after the Hewitt-Federer match, 'They're going to have some battles over the years and, goodness, what a talent Roger is! What he can do with the ball – it's like a magic wand in his hand.' 'Fitzy' was right about Federer's talent, but proved totally wrong about the future battles. Though no-one could know it at the time, Hewitt was a largely spent force, and was soon to lose his status as a serious challenger to Federer.

In sport and other disciplines such as music and dance, there is a phenomenon whereby some highly gifted players find it tough to reach the very top – footballers who are giants in the club game but can't get comfortable in the national team, or runners who beat the best in Grand Prix meetings but who freeze at the Olympics and world championships, and golfers who on the tour hit round after round below par but who miss the crucial chips and putts in the majors. Similarly, numerous musicians and dancers offer scintillating performances in unpressured situations but can then lose something of their lustre on the biggest stages. All join the ranks of the nearly-men and nearly-women who look like getting to the top but never quite make it.

That was the prospect facing Roger Federer after the first few months of 2003. His form on the tour had gone up to another level, landing him titles in Marseille, Dubai and Munich – none of them massively prestigious events on their own, but thanks to those wins, together with reaching the semi-finals in Rotterdam and the fourth round in Miami, he'd climbed into the world's top five. Among those who ply their trade writing and broadcasting about tennis, the general view was that he was probably heading for the top but he was taking a devil of a long time getting there.

A little irritation – understandably – seeped out at a press conference when he was once again asked about getting to number one. 'I believe I will get there one day,' he said politely yet through somewhat gritted teeth, 'and, when I do, I'm a bit concerned that I won't get the credit for it, because people will have said for so long that I'm going to get there.'

As it happened, he needn't have worried; such was the elegance of his play and the dominance he showed when he finally made it to the top of the rankings that people couldn't help but give him the credit. And the fact that he had appeared to stumble so much en route to the pinnacle probably added to the public's appreciation of his success.

There was another unofficial school of thought at that time, which can best be summed up as 'he'd be better if he wasn't so good'. Behind the obvious illogicality of the statement lay a belief among some that he was so gifted and had so many options on the tennis court that he couldn't work out the right options at the right time. Federer himself said in early 2010, 'I always knew I had it in my hand – the question was: do I have it in my mind and my legs? That's something I had to work extremely hard at.' That is not only a fair assessment, but seasoned tennis watchers know that gifted and all-court players take longer to mature, often because it takes them longer to assemble the experience of putting more components together, unlike baseliners, who have fewer options and so are surer of what they should be doing. But then many gifted all-court players never quite put it all together, and this was the quiet fear behind where Federer stood approaching the mid-point of 2003.

A fourth title of 2003, and a second clay-court Masters Series shield, seemed on the cards when Federer reached the final in Rome in May, beating some quality clay-courters en route. In that final he came up against the revitalised Felix Mantilla, a twenty-nine-year-old former French Open semi-finalist whose best days were behind him, and who later fought a successful battle against skin cancer (one of the few touring professionals to be afflicted by a disease they are all very vulnerable to). It seemed a formality that Federer would win. But the old demons returned.

Mixing the pace of his groundstrokes, Federer made all the early running but then failed to convert his seven break points and lost the first set. In the third he had three set points but ended up losing the tiebreak 12–10 and, with it, the two-hour-and-forty-one-minute final. It left the unseeded Mantilla somewhat astonished and tearful, having won 7–5, 6–2, 7–6. Federer had created seventeen break points but had converted just three of them.

A defeat in a tournament final offers no immediate escape – no rushing off court, no quick exit to dodge the cameras and seek sanctuary in the locker room. While the winner cavorts around the stadium in his or her moment of triumph, the loser has to sit there, waiting for the presentation ceremony, working out what nice things to say through the disappointment of a match that has just got away.

When Federer finally got back on to the court, he found himself at the end of a long line of dignitaries, the last of whom was Francesco Ricci Bitti, the International Tennis Federation's president and one of Federer's greatest fans. 'I found myself standing next to Roger,' recalls Ricci Bitti, 'so I took the liberty of saying a few words to him. I said, "Roger, I don't think you should be losing this kind of match. You have to start winning this kind of match, or this is going to become sad for you and sad for tennis." It was totally the wrong moment to say something to him, but I am such a fan of his that I couldn't control myself saying something. Some players would have thought it very bad, but Roger was polite enough to accept it, and that restrained reaction impressed me greatly. He's a very sensitive guy but very controlled.'

Mantilla made a comment after the match that to some seemed to sum up where Federer might be failing. 'I believe I won today because I had the hunger,' he said. 'I played with heart and courage and everything I had.' Was that what Federer wasn't doing? In truth, no. Federer was working very hard away from the public gaze, and was to a certain extent suffering from the curse of the gifted performer: it always looks so easy that the hard work put in behind the scenes doesn't show.

The following week was the Hamburg leg of the Masters Series, and Federer proved somewhat touchy when asked if he thought he was playing too much tennis and thereby jeopardising his chances at the French Open. Even after losing in the third round to Mark Philippoussis, he declined to take any comfort in the fact that his defeat effectively gave him ten days rather than seven in which to prepare for Paris. Hamburg, it seemed, was becoming a place of contrasting emotions for him, with his smashed racket in 2001, his victory in 2002, and now a slightly edgy run-up to Roland Garros 2003.

In most people's eyes, after his first round defeat in 2002 to Hicham Arazi, he was due a reasonable run at the French. And the draw was kind to him, or so it seemed. Seeded fifth, in the first round he came up against the sixty-seventh-ranked Luis Horna, a player who attracts that unkind and dishonest epithet of the 'tennis journeyman'. The match was scheduled for the main Philippe Chatrier Arena at the start of the first day. A couple of hours beforehand, Federer had been given the customary chance to hit on the greatest clay-court arena in the world, but instead of grooving his strokes he flicked the ball casually around and never looked fully focused. Not that this seemed to matter when he led by a break early in the first set. But Horna broke back, Federer's angst set in as the first set wore on and, once he had lost it on a tiebreak, his self-belief ebbed away. Though a hardened clay-courter from Peru, Horna was making his Roland Garros debut, and playing his first match since becoming a father a couple of weeks earlier. Surely Federer would come back. But the second set rattled past and, while Federer made a better fist of it in the third set, he lost another tiebreak, allowing Horna to walk away victorious after just 131 minutes of play by almost exactly the same score by which Mantilla had beaten Federer in Rome.

'I played a poor match and he played well,' was Federer's assessment through the disappointment. 'And, when those two combine, it doesn't help my cause.'

For the second year running, Federer had fallen at the first hurdle in Paris. Was he the real deal, or was the great Swiss talent flattering to deceive?

GRAND SLAM CHAMPION

3

8

FEDERER'S GRAND SLAM period began at the time when people were seriously beginning to question whether he might ever get there. With the benefit of hindsight, it's hard to imagine that he was still very much an unproven quantity as he arrived at Wimbledon in 2003. His victory over Pete Sampras was two years back, he had lost to Mario Ancic in the first round the year before, and for the second year running he was coming to south-west London fresh from a first-round defeat at the French Open. Since beating Sampras in 2001, he hadn't got past the fourth round of any of the four Grand Slam events.

At least he'd notched up his first grass-court tournament. That came in Halle, but even there he'd come very close to losing his semi-final against Mikhail Youzhny, and in the ten previous stagings of the Gerry Weber Open, the best the Halle champion had done at Wimbledon was the fourth round. According to Gerhard Weber, the women's clothing magnate who launched the Halle tournament in 1993, the idea was that 'Wimbledon starts in Halle', and his press officer Frank Hofen had even cajoled a couple of local radio journalists into using the term 'Kleinwimbledon' (Little Wimbledon) to describe the German grass-court event. Yet the failure of those who had done well in Halle to go on and do well at Wimbledon was beginning to undermine the reliability of the Halle event to offer valid pre-Wimbledon preparation. By 2003, Weber was becoming desperate for the champion of his tournament to go on to win Wimbledon – and in his 2003 champion, he finally seemed to have someone with the potential to win the world's biggest grass-court tournament. With Sampras announcing his retirement a few weeks before Wimbledon and the reigning Wimbledon champion, Lleyton Hewitt, struggling for form, the way seemed open for a new name on the Wimbledon roll of honour. The British thought they knew what that name would be – and it wasn't Roger Federer.

Andy Roddick began working with Andre Agassi's former coach Brad Gilbert after suffering a frustrating first-round defeat to Sargis Sargsian at the 2003 French Open. Like Federer, he had been the-next-big-thing-waiting-to-happen since becoming the Swiss's next-but-one successor as the world junior champion in 2000. He needed something to take him to the next level, and in Gilbert he found it.

The effect of Roddick bringing Gilbert on board was instantaneous. In their first event together, Roddick stormed through the pre-Wimbledon tournament, the Stella Artois Championships at London's Queen's Club, beating Andre Agassi in a glorious semi-final (saving a match point in doing so) and humbling Sébastien Grosjean in less than an hour to claim the title.

The British press went mad about him, nominating him as the favourite for Wimbledon, even though he was seeded fifth behind Hewitt, Agassi, Juan Carlos Ferrero and Federer. Of course, the locals still harboured hopes that Tim Henman might finally win their event, but the serious money was on Roddick. And the dramatic events of the first day hardly slowed the Roddick bandwagon.

The Centre Court programme at Wimbledon is always opened on the first day by the defending champion, and the match is normally something of a formality. Not so in 2003. For the first time since the 1966 champion Manolo Santana lost in the first round in 1967, the champion was struck down at the first hurdle, Hewitt losing in four sets to the big-serving, stammering giant from Croatia, Ivo Karlovic.

More fuel was added to the Roddick fire in the second round, when the American kept his cool while Greg Rusedski lost his. Roddick played a much more assured match than the indignant Brits were willing to acknowledge in beating Rusedski in straight sets. Rusedski led 5–2 in the third set, but then at 5–3 he let a ball go when he heard the call of 'out'. The call proved to have come from the crowd rather than the line umpire and, with his serve under threat, Rusedski went wild. With several million people watching at teatime on British terrestrial television, Rusedski let fly a tirade of expletives towards the match umpire, Lars Graff, who had been one hundred per cent correct in his application of the rules. Rusedski lost the match shortly after the outburst, and he was the talk of Wimbledon until the following day.

Meanwhile, Federer cruised comfortably through his first

couple of matches, beating Hyung Taik-Lee and Stefan Koubek each in straight sets, and then in his third match he beat Mardy Fish in four. Although no one could have guessed at the time, the thirtieth-ranked Fish was to be the only person to win a set against Federer in the whole tournament. But, after three rounds, nothing had been proved – yet. After all, Federer had never been beyond the quarter-finals, and his next opponent was Feliciano López, a Spaniard with a passion for fast courts who had reached the fourth round the previous year and whose big left-handed serve was particularly effective on grass. Yet, with Hewitt gone and Agassi, Henman, Nalbandian and Ferrero all in the bottom half of the draw, anticipation about the projected Federer–Roddick semi-final was growing.

A personal recollection perhaps illustrates this sense of anticipation. Over the middle weekend of that year's tournament, London's oldest Sunday newspaper, *The Observer*, asked me to write a preview of the likely semi-final between Roddick and Federer. The brief I was given was 'to look at the two players' strengths and weaknesses, explain why it should be a great match, and why Roddick should win'. 'But I don't think he *will* win,' I replied. I was allowed to make my case for Federer, although this was very much against the tide of opinion in the British media.

Fifteen minutes into Federer's match against López, the prospect of a Roddick–Federer semi-final was receding rapidly. On a cold, overcast June Monday, the two players walked out on to what was then Court 2, the showcourt nicknamed 'the graveyard of the seeds'. After the first game, Federer called for the trainer, and after three he took an injury timeout. His back had seized up. 'I felt a twinge in my upper back,' he said later. 'I told the trainer what I was feeling and he massaged it but couldn't tell me what it was, so I just went on playing.'

To this day, Federer doesn't know what went wrong with his back that day. The fact that he had no further problems with it, either during that Wimbledon week or at any time in the subsequent years (the back problem he suffered from in late 2008 and early 2009 was not the same injury), suggests it was the nerves getting to him. Was the perennial prodigy about to flop again and fuel the growing suspicion that he was a little flaky in the big tournaments?

No, he wasn't. In fact, the injury may have been the best thing that happened to him. Fearing he might have to retire, he relaxed, and while he trailed for most of the set, a run of López errors helped Federer to break back to level at 5–5. Once he had taken the first set on a 7–5 tiebreak, he was never in trouble again.

That day, Roddick dropped his first set of the tournament, beating Paradorn Srichaphan in four and adding to the aura of the seemingly phenomenal effect Gilbert was having on his game. Nine matches the two had had together: nine wins, just three sets dropped.

Another man on a run of nine successive victories was Sjeng Schalken. The Dutchman had won the pre-Wimbledon grass-court tournament in 's-Hertogenbosch, and must have hoped Federer's back problem would help redress the balance from when the pair had played in Arnhem earlier that year, a match Federer had won in straight sets. But a break in each set sufficed for Federer to sail through. With Roddick beating the Swede Jonas Björkman, also in straight sets, the match all the neutrals wanted to see had been secured. Having a Roddick–Federer semi-final was also some minor comfort for the home fans, who that day had to endure another Tim Henman defeat, this time in the quarter-finals to Sébastien Grosjean.

If the hype surrounding the Roddick–Federer match had turned the semi-final into a spectacle that threatened to eclipse the final, it wasn't a sentiment shared by Federer. 'I expected to win it,' he says today. 'It was just the media that was hyping up everything, that he was the big favourite to win the tournament. I – how shall I say this? – I wasn't of the same opinion. Because he won Queen's and I won Halle, and because Queen's is in England, everybody was talking about him more, for about a month. But I knew that if I played my game correctly I should beat him.'

The word 'correctly' doesn't seem sufficient to describe one of the most emphatic performances of Federer's career. Even if his passage to his first Grand Slam final wasn't as big a breakthrough for him as certain other matches had been, it was the one at which he effectively announced to the tennis world that, if he was on his game, it was virtually impossible for anyone else to beat him. Roddick's comment 'I got my butt kicked' was short and to the point, but doesn't give sufficient credit to the sublime display his opponent offered on what was America's national day. Writing in a British newspaper, Boris Becker said of Federer's display, 'A video cassette of this should be sent to every tennis coach in the world.'

One point in particular stays in the memory: the point with which Federer reached set point in the second set. Rallying from the baseline, he came in to the net on a late decision and found himself having to play a low volley. To experienced tennis watchers, he appeared to have made a tactical error that left him stranded in no-man's land. But playing the kind of shot he would normally attempt only in the last few minutes of a practice session when the fun and artistry takes over from the hard work, he flicked the low ball cross-court, driving it ferociously into the forehand corner of Roddick's baseline. Federer himself couldn't suppress a wry smile. Even he knew it was sheer brilliance.

'I know I played a fantastic match with fantastic points,' he says today of the 7–6, 6–3, 6–3 win that took him into his first Grand Slam final, 'but that made it all the more necessary for me to settle down in the final. I got praised like crazy for beating Andy, because people had seen him playing so well, but I'd already beaten him before. It was the final I had to get up for, and that was the real breakthrough.'

Facing Federer in the final was Mark Philippoussis, the big-serving but injury-prone Australian whose five-sets victory over Andre Agassi in the tournament's fourth round seemed to have relaunched his career. Philippoussis had two advantages over Federer: he had the bigger serve and he'd been in one previous Grand Slam final, the 1998 US Open decider, which he'd lost in four sets to his compatriot Patrick Rafter. For those reasons, he had a chance – theoretically, at least.

Federer, however, had the momentum. After beating Roddick so convincingly, he could probably have lost the final and still claimed to have exorcised his demons. But, with the wind in his sails, he wasn't going to let himself be blown off course.

In the final, he out-aced Philippoussis by 21 to 14 in notching up a 7–6, 6–2, 7–6 win that was effectively decided in the first set tiebreak. At 6–2 in the third-set tiebreak, Federer had four championship points. On the first, Philippoussis delivered a big serve: 6–3. On the second, the Australian netted a return, and Federer fell to his knees.

It was what happened in the moments after Federer became Wimbledon champion that really sold him to the British public. Tears in the moment of winning a major sporting event are nothing new, even in a country like England where men crying openly is still not something many are comfortable with. By the time Federer faced a live on-court interview that was broadcast around the world, it was assumed he had 'regained his composure', as the British like to call it. He had already answered a couple of questions from the former French Open champion Sue Barker, when he described how he was finally living one of his childhood dreams. As he uttered the words 'And now I'm here!' his voice cracked with emotion, the tears of joy flowed, and he captured the hearts of a lot more than the 13,800 people in the venerable arena that day.

'There's no rule about how you should conduct yourself in the moment when you win or when you lose,' he said the following morning. 'The only thing you mustn't do is throw your racket into the crowd and injure someone. There are people who don't smile when they win, and there are people who smile for weeks afterwards. I'm the kind of guy who lets the tears flow, and I think that goes down pretty well, especially when people see this is the realisation of my biggest dream and that it's just amazing for me. I got a lot of feedback that people in the crowd also cried and enjoyed it, and it's nice to share this with a lot of people.'

One of the photographs taken immediately after the final

that frequently gets reprinted shows a fan in a Swiss shirt with tears streaming down his face. That man was Michael Purek, a member at Old Boys Basel, who had been a sparring partner of Federer's in his teenage days.

While Purek was lucky enough to watch his old mate's performance courtside, most of the rest of the Old Boys fraternity were glued to the television set in the Old Boys' cramped clubhouse. 'That was a great day at the club,' said Seppli Kacovski, the man who'd taught the Wimbledon champion to play tennis. 'I was OK at the beginning, but I got so nervous that I could hardly watch in the tiebreak, and then I got so nervous I uncorked the champagne too early. It was his first match point, and suddenly there was champagne everywhere, and then Philippoussis saved it. Everyone was laughing at me, but only for one point, because Roger then won it. We drank and cried. We sang. We toasted Roger. We were so proud.'

Lots of people were proud of Federer that night, among them Peter Carter's parents, Diana and Bob, who watched the match in the South Australian town of Nuriootpa and shed their own tears at Roger's victory. It was still less than a year after Peter's death, but Bob admitted in a television interview around this time that Federer's success had helped ease the pain of their loss. 'I feel really good about it,' he said of Federer's title. 'It's a wonderful feeling, really, because Peter had such an influence on his career, and to watch Roger play you can sort of see a little of Peter there.'

Although keen not to praise any single person's contribution to his success when he faced the media after the final, Federer was happy to acknowledge Carter's role in his moment of triumph. 'Peter was one of the most important people in my career. We would have had a big party together if he was still here. I'm sure he was watching it from somewhere.'

That night, Federer was invited for the second time to the Wimbledon champions' dinner at London's Savoy hotel, and this time he accepted. The dinner always takes place very late because all champions and finalists are invited, including those from the junior events, and some don't finish playing their finals until well into the evening. The tradition of the men's and women's singles champions having the first dance with each other has long since gone (in fact, there's no dancing at the Wimbledon champions' dinner), but both singles champions are asked to make a small speech, and the moment normally falls sometime after midnight. In his, Federer said, 'This is the first time I've attended this event. Five years ago, when I won the junior title, I declined your invitation because the following day I was playing in Gstaad. I now realise I made a mistake. I'm really proud to be here and to have earned my membership of the All England Club. I look forward to dropping by to hit a few balls at Wimbledon just for fun. If anyone wants to hit with me, give me a ring.'

Sitting close to Federer at the dinner was Francesco Ricci Bitti, the president of the International Tennis Federation. Referring back to their on-court conversation at the Rome prize-giving ceremony eight weeks earlier, when Ricci Bitti had chided Federer for the way he had lost to Felix Mantilla, Federer looked into the Italian's eyes and said, 'You see, Mr President, I *can* win these kinds of matches. Aren't you proud of me?'

Luckily for both the media and himself, Roger Federer is a good communicator. For any tennis player who does not enjoy chatting with journalists and television crews, winning a Grand Slam singles title is a serious health hazard.

As well as the obligatory post-match press conference and interview with the host television broadcaster, there are usually at least half a dozen one-on-one interview requests, often a dozen, with everyone considering it their moral right to have at least three minutes with the new champion. And that's just for the English-speakers; for someone who has their own language, you can double the time. And for someone from Switzerland, where trilingualism is nothing special, the process can take even longer. As a result, Federer has become accustomed to allowing at least an hour and sometimes much more for his media obligations after Grand Slam quarter- and semi-finals, while, for finals, it's normally about two hours, plus time for photo-shoots with whichever trophy he's won.

After winning Wimbledon in 2003, Federer duly discharged his two hours of media responsibilities before heading back to the family house in Wimbledon he'd rented for the fortnight, where he showered, shaved and quickly changed into his dinner jacket and Swiss-red bow tie. Then he was off to the Savoy, before returning home in the small hours of the morning. After a few hours' sleep, there was another round of media appointments, starting with radio and television appearances, followed by breakfast with first the British press and then any journalist wanting to converse in French, High German and Swiss German. He could have said no and enjoyed a lie-in; indeed, many champions do just that. But this wasn't just Federer's first Grand Slam title where the novelty was something to be enjoyed, he is also someone who understood early the responsibilities of promoting his sport that come with being one of its high-profile figures.

That morning, the papers had glowing accounts of Federer's success, and he continued to charm them. There was no hint of irritation, or even the tired autopilot of answering the same questions over and over. He listened to every one, thought about his answers and allowed his simple humanity to shine through. 'Life will change in some ways,' he said when asked how his victory would affect him. 'I'm more famous now, a celebrity. Before, I was just a good tennis player. I don't know how that's going to be. My star sign is Leo, and Leos like to be the centre of attention, but I'll do the same work on court because, if you don't work, people will catch you.'

A bit of context is needed here. At the time that Federer won his first Wimbledon, the ATP was publicly fighting the four Grand Slam tournaments for a share of their profits. In addition, a list of tennis grandees was calling for the permissible dimensions of rackets to be reduced because, they said, tennis was getting 'tedious'. And the previous August, Lleyton Hewitt became embroiled in a dispute with the ATP that seemed to sum up tennis's problems.

At the time the undisputed world number one, Hewitt was asked to do an interview with an American television station. Both the station and the ATP had been chasing him on the matter for some time, and at the Cincinnati Masters the patience of both the ATP's communications managers and Hewitt himself snapped. Astonishing as it might seem, the matter escalated to such a degree that the Australian took out a $1.5 million lawsuit against the organising body of the men's professional tennis tour. Irrespective of the arguments on both sides, the case seemed a metaphor for an epidemic of ills at the top of world tennis.

Into this tense environment steps a striking twenty-one-year-old man, with a personality of open emotions, considerable decency and the ability to express himself with great eloquence in three languages. And he wins the most prestigious prize in tennis! Federer was the kind of ambassador tennis could only dream of; the PR folk couldn't have staged it better. No wonder the sport felt good at that Wimbledon champions' dinner.

The message Federer was giving out was summed up in one sentence from his post-match press conference: 'There was big pressure from all sides, also from myself. I've proved myself to everybody. It's a big relief.' Now the real part of his career could begin.

It began with a flight on a private jet from London to Saanen, a tiny airfield high in the Swiss Alps and a few kilometres from arguably the most picturesque venue on the tennis tour: the small town of Gstaad, set amid the stunning splendour of the Bernese Oberland. The small club that hosts the tournament builds plenty of temporary seating for its week in the spotlight, but breathtaking vistas of chocolate-box scenery are always in the players' and spectators' peripheral vision, as is the fairytale castle towering over the town that looks like a drawing from a children's storybook. Gstaad is home (or second home) to many big names of the stage and screen, as well as sport (including the twelve-times Grand Slam champion Roy Emerson) and other celebrity walks of life, and the tournament would have featured more prominently on the tennis map if it hadn't for many years had a graveyard slot the week after Wimbledon. The calendar was re-jigged in 2009 to put a couple of weeks between the end of Wimbledon and the start of Gstaad, but that was still not enough to fit into Federer's tournament schedule, nor to change the unfortunate but understandable fact that Gstaad attracts only the hardened clay-courters for whom Wimbledon is an interruption – albeit a lucrative one – from the European red-clay season.

But in 2003 and 2004, Gstaad had the Wimbledon champion, an almost unheard-of occurrence. And it has the legacy of a decision taken back in 1998 to thank for that.

All tournament directors like to look for promising youngsters, on the basis that promising youngsters are looking for tournament opportunities, so, if a tournament director offers a player a chance to play while the player is on the way up, that same player might look favourably on the tournament when he or she is at the top.

In 1998, the Gstaad tournament director Köbi Hermenjat had offered Switzerland's promising junior Roger Federer his first-ever match at ATP tour level and, although Federer had lost in straight sets in the first round to the Argentinian doubles specialist Lucas Arnold, he never forgot the gesture of assistance. So, instead of feeling an imaginary twinge of pain in his left calf which might have emerged during the second and third sets of the Wimbledon final and thus forced him to withdraw from a tournament which made no sense from a tennis or physical point of view, Federer honoured his commitment to Gstaad and showed up. He might also have been forgiven for tanking his first or second match, knowing that he would have turned out for the fans and could always say the tiredness from Wimbledon or his becoming reaccustomed to clay had been his undoing. But Federer isn't like that. The tennis verb 'to tank' is barely in his vocabulary, and it's certainly not in his mentality; if he's out on a tennis court, he plays to win. Besides, he had given his word to Hermenjat that he would be there, and anyway this was the chance to celebrate. He knew his countryfolk wanted to see him, and he was determined to oblige them.

There was always going to be some sort of token present in Gstaad for the returning hero, but what a present the tournament in Gstaad hit on! After Federer's opening-round win over Marc López in three sets, his gift was brought on to the centre court. Her name was Juliette, and she was a tan-and-white Bernese Oberländer milk cow weighing something close to 800kg. She was presented to Federer decked out in a garland of sunflowers and wearing a traditional Swiss cowbell.

For a while on court, Federer looked nonplussed, but then he entered into the spirit of the gesture. Asked later by the media where he would keep her, he questioned whether she would really be happy either touring with him around the world or watching the trams go by in the streets of Basel, so he agreed to leave her to graze on the slopes of the Oberland mountains. She clearly did more than grazing; when asked at Wimbledon the following year how she was, Federer replied, 'She's doing well, and she has a calf now.'

As for the tournament at Gstaad, it was almost a phenomenal victory to follow Federer's heroics at Wimbledon. He beat the quality clay-courter Gaston Gaudio in the semi-finals in straight sets, before losing a five-set final to Jiri Novak, a Czech whose best year was the one before and whose star was beginning to fade. There would have been yodelling in the streets of Gstaad that night if Federer had won, but he'd still performed heroically; after his efforts at Wimbledon, he had not only shown up but had played all matches asked of him and fought to the end. 'I really wanted to win this for you,' he told the crowd after the final, 'because the way you have received me here has touched me greatly.'

After giving his all at Wimbledon and Gstaad, Federer admitted to being 'dead on my feet'. It was almost time for a holiday, but there was one more obligation.

Six months earlier, back in January 2003, his old friend and flatmate Yves Allegro had asked Federer if he would come to his home town of Grône, near Sion, to put in an appearance as part of the Grône tennis club's twenty-fifth anniversary celebrations. Federer had agreed to appear, telling Allegro in March that the evening of Tuesday 15 July would be the best time to appear. 'Gstaad finishes on the Sunday, we're off on holiday on Wednesday, so we'll fit it in on Tuesday,' he had said.

When Federer won Wimbledon, the folks at Grône thought he'd now be too big to spare an evening to play a set at their club. And when he got to the final in Gstaad, they all but gave up hope. Only one person was sure Federer would show, and that was Allegro. 'I know Roger,' he says today, 'and I knew that, once he'd said he'd come, he would come unless there was really something unavoidable that would prevent it. Everyone at the club was convinced he would cancel, but I knew he wouldn't.'

Federer did indeed show up at Grône as promised and provided a memorable night for the townspeople, playing three sets against Allegro, signing autographs and posing for the camera – all without even the mention of a fee. He saw at first hand how much it means to people to have him around, and his appearance allowed the club to raise enough money to wipe out debts that were threatening to close it down.

The following morning, it was off to Sardinia for a hard-earned holiday, but off court the sweet smell of success took a different form.

In the months after she became his girlfriend, Mirka Vavrinec persuaded Federer to launch his own range of cosmetics. Ever open to new ideas, Federer agreed, and the resulting RF cosmetics line became Vavrinec's project. She developed the logo, which features Federer's autograph, and worked on the development of the range's four products: eau de toilette spray, aftershave balm, body wash and deodorant stick, plus special sets – all made in Switzerland and marketed under the slogan 'Feel the touch'. The advertising blurb describes the range as 'fulfilling the highest demands of modern sports-oriented men'.

'It's something we've done all ourselves,' said Federer proudly in an interview with the tennis-x.com website. 'It's the Roger Federer fragrance. I helped a lot with it, including the selection and refinement of the fragrances. It's something that means a lot to me. We'll see what happens.'

One can only hope Federer wasn't involved in drafting the RF advertising literature, which in places puts the most pseudo of art critics and wine writers in the shade. The eau de toilette spray, with its 'elegantly sporty fragrance', is described as having 'citrus chords and ozone elements... with a hint of green tea'. The blurb goes on: 'Transparent floral themes, noble woody notes and sensuous ambergris tones create a lingering background to round off an unmistakable, sophisticated fragrance image.' The unmistakable, sophisticated fragrance image is available only in

Switzerland, although the products can be bought internationally via the internet.

Another significant off-court development in the weeks after Wimbledon was Federer's declaration of independence from his former management, a decision that sat well with his sense of self-determination.

Most tennis players – indeed, most top athletes – are 'managed' by a player agency. Such agencies look after advertising deals, contracts with clothing and racket suppliers, media appearances and in a few cases some of the minutiae of everyday life. The majority of tennis players are with one of three companies: the International Management Group (IMG), set up by the pioneering Mark McCormack in the 1960s when he turned Arnold Palmer from a successful golfer into a highly lucrative brand; Octagon Worldwide (formerly Advantage International); and SFX (formerly Pro-Serv).

Since 1998, Federer had been with IMG, but by mid-2003 he had come to the conclusion that he wanted control of his affairs closer to home. There were murmurings that he was unhappy about the way IMG had handled the renegotiation of a contract and Federer would not have been the first player on the rise to feel his management company may not have appreciated what an asset he was. Whatever the reason, he ended his relationship with IMG and set up Roger Federer Management. Federer himself and the people close to him were in a better position than many on the tennis circuit to take matters into their own hands. And take them they did.

Roger Federer Management had a number of high-profile officers, notably Mirka Vavrinec as Roger's diary secretary and Lynette Federer, Roger's mother, as a secretary for bigger projects. The Basel lawyer Bernhard Christen had a prominent position, and even Federer's coach Peter Lundgren was part of the team, giving him an air of permanence that proved to be illusory. The company was based in the offices of the law firm that Christen worked at in Bottmingen (the same suburb of Basel to which Lynette and Robbie Federer had relocated, though 2003 was the year Roger first moved in with Mirka in the neighbouring suburb of Oberwil), while publicity was handled by a communications firm in Germany. Chairman and chief executive was Roger Federer – and anyone assuming this was nothing more than a figurehead position misunderstands him; he might be willing to listen to advice, but he makes his own decisions.

Many people criticised the arrangement, notably those from other player-management companies who saw it as setting a precedent that didn't augur well for their own credibility. Others suggested there was a risk that in-house management would take up too much of Federer's time and distract him from tennis. His results in 2004 safely scotched that fear, and if there was a risk of becoming distracted from his tennis, that probably came more from the generous way in which he gave his time to the media, sponsors, tennis politics and outside initiatives than from any internal management issues. But Federer's entrepreneurism was hardly a unilateral declaration of independence; other players – notably the Spanish contemporaries Albert Costa and Alex Corretja – had also split from recognised agencies and put their management trust in friends and family. The critics no doubt saw themselves vindicated when, two years later, Federer went back to IMG and Roger Federer Management dwindled to looking after little more than Federer's charitable activities (see page 220). But given the personnel involved, in particular Roger Federer himself, it was clearly an experiment worth trying, and it means that Federer today probably enjoys a vastly more lucrative deal with IMG than he might otherwise have done, given that IMG had to coax him back after he'd gone his own way.

The Wimbledon honeymoon lasted well into August. Federer came within a point of reaching the final of the Montreal Masters, losing his semi-final to Andy Roddick on a final-set tiebreak. Had Federer won that match, he would have gone to the top of the rankings, but somehow he didn't seem ready for it and the result didn't feel altogether wrong. After all, Roddick was on the best roll of his career, one that would see him take the US Open and finish the year ranked number one. Nonetheless, Federer still had a match point, and the match remained Roddick's only win against him until March 2008, when the American capitalised on Federer's sluggish form to post only his second victory.

Despite a second-round defeat to David Nalbandian in Cincinnati, Federer's Wimbledon honeymoon could be said to have lasted until the US Open, but it was there that it certainly ended. In fact, the next two months were to prove particularly troublesome for the young Swiss.

Although no one had done the Wimbledon and US Open double since Pete Sampras in 1995, Federer looked a reasonable bet to do so at a tournament without any obvious favourite. But, as the weather worsened, Nalbandian again showed up to spoil the party.

Federer cruised through his first three rounds without dropping a set, but then had to sit by as fine drizzle held up play for three days. Although only in its seventh year in the 'new' Arthur Ashe Stadium, the US Tennis Association had apparently not foreseen the problem of mild drizzle affecting the playing surface. The dark-green concrete court was fine, but at the slightest hint of moisture the white lines became as slippery as ice and play had to stop. The skies were grey for three solid days during that year's US Open and, while play seemed always on the point of starting, it never really did.

On the fourth day, the skies were still grey, but it was finally dry, and Federer took to the Arthur Ashe Stadium against Nalbandian for a place in the quarter-finals. He won the first set, but, once he'd lost the second on a tiebreak, his face took on the colour of the sky, and after that there was no way back. Asked after his 3–6, 7–6, 6–4, 6–3 defeat why he hadn't managed to beat the Argentinian in five previous meetings, Federer replied, 'I've never had a great day playing against him. I guess I'm struggling against him. I don't know how to comment on this. I'm trying to figure out how to beat him. He likes my game; that's all I can say about it.'

Nalbandian was no more illuminating, 'I like playing against him,' he said. 'What more can I say? I like his game. I don't know exactly why, but I think I know him.'

If Federer's defeat in New York against Nalbandian was demoralising, another was to follow against another nemesis in another Grand Slam arena that was more demoralising, more dramatic, and certainly more emotional.

From the disappointment under the ashen skies of New York, Federer went to the disappointment of his defeat to Hewitt under the bright lights of Melbourne Park (see page 127), and thereafter began to look tired. Many a breakthrough player plans his/her schedule on the basis of a given average of matches per tournament, and having won five titles in the first six months of the year, he had gone beyond whatever average he had anticipated at the start of 2003. As a result, he began to look like a teenager who hasn't had enough sleep. He won the title in Vienna and reached the semi-finals of the Madrid Masters, but he bombed out of Basel in the second round and was unimpressive at the Paris Masters. There he even talked about not wanting to go to the year-ending Tennis Masters Cup, which that year moved to Houston, and he certainly left observers in Paris with doubts about whether he would make the trip to Texas.

He probably always intended to go and, after the event, he was more than glad he did. For out of the tiredness of the year that had seen him inscribe his name on the Grand Slam roll of honour, he summoned a breakthrough that eventually enabled him to move from being a member of the elite with a Grand Slam title to the all-conquering undisputed world number one.

The round-robin format used at the year-ending tournament allows a player to lose a match and still win the title; Pete Sampras did it four times, and Gustavo Kuerten did it the year he went to number one in the rankings. Had Federer lost his opening match to Andre Agassi, he could still have qualified for the semi-finals, but he probably wouldn't have done. Coming through the Agassi match unlocked a door for him.

The 2003 and 2004 Tennis Masters Cups were staged more by an individual than a club or organisation. Jim McIngvale had made his fortune selling affordable home furniture, and had earned the nickname 'Mattress Mack'. A committed tennis fan, he'd become the benefactor of Houston's West Side Club and won a bid to stage the year-ending showdown there for two years. But McIngvale's tennis etiquette wasn't to everyone's taste – it seemed to the international community to be excessively pro-American, and of the eight qualifiers, there was a sense that the two Americans, Agassi and Andy Roddick, were getting privileged treatment. That seemed to irk the other six, and no doubt made Federer just that little more determined to beat Agassi on the opening day, even when he stared defeat in the face.

Agassi led Federer 6–4 in the final-set tiebreak. Federer saved the first match point with a service winner, but the second was a long rally in which both men missed chances. Eventually, a Federer forehand broke the deadlock. Federer had to save a third match point at 6–7, but, when he ran out a 9–7 winner, it was to release his potential like no other victory. He had beaten one of his bogeymen – three times he had played Agassi, three times he had lost. Having snatched victory from the jaws of defeat, he was never to lose to Agassi again.

Just what a sense of release Federer gained from the Agassi victory became clear the following day, when he came face to face with another of his bogeymen, David Nalbandian. Going into the match, the head-to-head record was a staggering 5–0 for Nalbandian; in fact, Federer's only win over his Argentinian nemesis had been in the Orange Bowl junior event back in December 1998. Yet the Swiss made mincemeat of the head-to-head, allowing Nalbandian just three games in a 6–3, 6–0 victory. And, in the final round-robin match, Juan Carlos Ferrero fared scarcely better than Nalbandian, picking up just four games as Federer raced to the semi-finals with a 6–3, 6–1 win.

By the time Federer and Roddick walked out for their

semi-final, Roddick had secured the year-end number-one ranking, but it looked like a miscarriage of justice when Federer won a convincing 7–6, 6–2 victory.

Then came the final, and once again Federer found himself up against Agassi. Just six days had elapsed since their meeting at the start of the tournament, but it might have been a light-year, such was the progress Federer had made. Agassi didn't play badly that day, but he failed to make any impression on Federer, the Swiss describing his 6–3, 6–0, 6–4 win as 'one of the best of my life'.

After the event, Federer talked about having found something within himself, but it was an observation by Agassi that stayed in the memory. In the on-court presentation ceremony, the American congratulated Federer on the way he'd played all that week and added, 'It's a pleasure to watch you play.'

Federer's Wimbledon triumph back in July had turned something that had until then been only a trickle into a deluge. The Federer family had been hatching the idea of establishing a charitable foundation and, when the handful of requests for money from good causes suddenly multiplied after Federer had become a Grand Slam champion, it provided the impetus the Federers needed to turn intent into action.

The result was the launch of the Roger Federer Foundation in December 2003, its trustees being Lynette, Robert and Roger Federer, the lawyer Bernhard Christen and Urs Wüthrich, a member of the Basel-Land cantonal council. The foundation's mission statement is to fund projects that benefit disadvantaged children and to promote sport for young people. There was also a wish to make the most of the family's connection with South Africa, so in June 2004 the foundation joined forces with a Swiss–South African initiative called Imbewu-Suisse, the name meaning 'seed' in the Xhosa language. Founded in 2001, Imbewu works to improve social conditions for children and young people in the New Brighton township on the edge of Port Elizabeth, one of the most impoverished areas in the country. Imbewu says its aim is 'not to awaken pity but to raise interest in people for another culture and for what is happening 10,000 kilometres down south'.

Imbewu's biggest project is a sponsorship scheme under which 100 Swiss families subsidise 100 children, while other projects include schemes aimed at improving the nutrition of over 200 children, promoting sport for young people, running voluntary work schemes and providing improved healthcare. The Roger Federer Foundation therefore agreed to fund improvements to Imbewu's infrastructure in New Brighton, including paying salaries to certain Imbewu staff, and providing funds for fifty children with which to pay for their schooling, school uniform, learning materials and two meals a day. In early 2005, the three schools attended by the children who benefit from the Foundation's money held a competition to find a motto to accompany the children through their school years. And the winner was: 'I'm tomorrow's future'.

In March 2005, Federer used his absence from the Swiss Davis Cup team to travel to New Brighton to visit the results of the funding that the foundation had provided, taking with him a consignment of T-shirts, emblazoned with 'I'M TOMORROW'S FUTURE', produced by his clothing supplier. As the Swiss journalist Freddy Widmer wrote, 'The children don't know that the young man visiting them is a world-famous sportsman. They only know that the Federer Foundation will allow them what it says on their T-shirts: a future.'

Cynics might wonder if the foundation is little more than a convenient financial arrangement. Doubtless Federer does reduce his tax liability when he contributes to the foundation, but those who know him are convinced that his primary motivation behind setting up the venture is a genuine concern to divert some of his riches to the benefit of those at the bottom of the financial ladder. At the launch of the initiative, he said, 'I chose a project in South Africa because my mother grew up there, which means that I have always had a close affinity to the country. But to me South Africa is also a shining example of a country that has overcome hatred and oppression, making it a potential source of inspiration for other crisis regions around the world. Another key factor, from my point of view, is that Imbewu will allow me to help people to help themselves by providing practical and tangible support in a highly deprived area. The vast majority of the aid will benefit children and young people directly.'

On 20 December 2003, when most people were thinking more of Christmas than tennis, Federer dropped a bombshell. The Swiss media were summoned to a hastily arranged press conference in the premises of Christen Rickli Partners, the official home of Roger Federer Management, to hear that Federer had parted company from his coach, Peter Lundgren. Federer sat there looking grim as Bernhard Christen made the official announcement. He said the Federer team had hoped to have a news conference with Lundgren present to show that it was a mutual and amicable decision, but a rumour had leaked out and had been printed in the *Neue Zürcher Zeitung* newspaper, so the announcement had to be made now.

The split would have taken no one by surprise had it happened in the first half of 2003. At that stage, Federer's game seemed to have got stuck, and tennis observers found themselves wondering – certainly before Wimbledon – whether he needed a new coach to take him to new levels. Although highly experienced as a player and coach, Lundgren's corpulent figure never quite fitted with the image of the highest sporting aspirations and, while his laidback approach might have suited Federer away from the court, was it really the right thing for him as a player? So went the whispers on the tour.

But the decision to part company after Federer's most successful year to date – when he was Wimbledon champion, had just finished the year as Tennis Masters Cup champion, and was within striking distance of the world number one Andy Roddick – took the tennis world by surprise. In Houston four weeks earlier, he'd said he had no intention of changing coaches, and indeed Lundgren had briefed the Swiss media on how he was intending to get Federer into shape for 2004, when he hoped his charge would take over the number-one ranking. But, as Federer and Vavrinec departed for a holiday in Mauritius, Federer phoned Lundgren to say their four-year professional relationship was over.

In the news conference, Federer said he'd made the decision himself. It was the result of a long process, he said, after he'd come to the conclusion that his working relationship with Lundgren had become 'everyday' and that he needed 'new impulses'. He said he was sure that he and Lundgren would remain friends.

On the day that the parting became public, Lundgren, at home in Gothenburg, declined to comment. Later, he said he felt it was a move that was always likely to happen at some stage. 'This is what happens with the kind of relationship we had,' he said in an interview shortly afterwards. 'We were so close; we did everything together. We ate together. We went out together. We even played PlayStation together. Now it's good for him to carry on with something else, and I'm happy to be doing something else.'

Several months later, when Lundgren had developed a fruitful working relationship with Marat Safin, he said Safin was easier to coach than Federer because he generally took Lundgren's advice, whereas his predecessor had listened politely but normally done his own thing anyway. While this remark might add an extra brushstroke to a picture of Federer's character, it should probably be viewed with a degree of caution, as any coach is likely to say the most positive things about the player they happen to be coaching at that moment, even if it's to the relative detriment of those they've coached in the past.

There are arguments that can justify almost any decision, but Federer had just contradicted the sporting proverb: 'Never change a winning team'. He had ended 2003 on the unexpected high of Houston that gave all his followers hope for 2004, but had suddenly parted with one of the cornerstones of his 2003 success. Moreover, he had not appointed a successor. Suddenly, Federer looked a shade vulnerable again as 2004 approached.

9

ANYONE WITH AN urge to create an obstacle course designed to test whether or not Roger Federer had dealt with his demons could hardly have done better than to present him with 2004's Australian Open. Over the previous two years, he'd been beaten in the tournament in winnable fourth-round five-set matches. And there he was in 2004, without a coach, facing a run-in that looked like producing three out of the quartet of Hewitt, Nalbandian, Roddick and Agassi in the last four rounds: three of his bogeymen plus the reigning world number one.

After the shockwaves of parting from Lundgren, the world wanted to know who was going to be in Federer's corner henceforth. Federer took full responsibility for the decision and said he was in no hurry to appoint a successor to Lundgren. 'Maybe it's good to be on my own for a bit,' he'd said before the 2004 Australian Open. 'I've been given good advice for most of my life, so maybe there's something good about looking after myself for a time.' Although no one could argue with that sentiment, nor the logic of not rushing into a new coaching arrangement, for the number-two player in the world to be without a coach was generally perceived as a weakness. At least it was at the start of the year – by the end, things looked a little different.

Federer took responsibility for something else at the start of that tournament: his relations with the Swiss media. Having opted not to play a tournament before the Australian Open, he took the opportunity to acclimatise himself to conditions in Melbourne by playing at an exhibition event held the week before the Australian Open at the Kooyong Club, the tournament's former home. There he spoke to a number of journalists, granting almost every interview request. Then, on the Saturday before the Open, he did a little more media work at Melbourne Park, before telling the media liaison people he wanted Sunday off. The following day, the majority of the Swiss press showed up and were most put out to discover that their crown jewel was doing no media that day. When it was put to Federer that the Swiss press were not happy, Federer told the International Tennis Federation's on-duty player–media liaison officer that he would deal with it himself.

And he did. At the first available opportunity, he explained to the Swiss journalists that he felt that he'd done more than his fair share of media work, told them that he really did want a day off and asked them to respect that. Barbara Travers, the ITF's head of communications, said, 'It's only the second time in the twenty-plus years I've worked with tennis players that a player has said, "Leave it to me." The other was Ivan Lendl. To me, it showed an unusual but refreshing sense of taking responsibility.'

The tournament began with Federer posting three straight-sets wins against modest opposition, but then the stakes were suddenly and theatrically raised. On 26 January, Australia's national day, he came up against Lleyton Hewitt for the first time – and on the same court – since he'd lost so dramatically to the Australian from being two sets and 5–3 up in the Davis Cup semi-final four months earlier. The two shouldn't really have met so early in a Grand Slam event, but Hewitt had deliberately stayed off the tour after the US Open until the end of the year, using the time to have a bunion removed and concentrating solely on the Davis Cup. His ranking had therefore slipped to fifteenth, and he landed in Federer's eighth of the draw. As the match started, Hewitt was quick off the blocks, winning the first set to suggest that he still had Federer's number. But then something changed.

A little luck is often needed at a crucial moment, and Federer got his luck in the sixth game when Hewitt was foot-faulted after serving an ace. It wasn't a major incident, but Hewitt is seldom called for foot-faults, and players who seldom infringe the foot-fault rule generally feel mightily aggrieved when it happens, especially when – as in this case – the serve in question would have been a winner. Had Hewitt been trailing in the match, it would probably have fuelled him with the necessary aggression to bounce back, but with everything going swimmingly for the Australian, the baseline umpire's call threw him momentarily off balance, Federer seized his opportunity to break, and the match turned. And, as it turned out, the destiny of the tournament too.

From then on, Federer was unstoppable. As he closed in on victory, the night skies were lit up with the traditional Australia Day fireworks display over the Melbourne skyline, adding a theatrical audio-visual backdrop to the on-court tension. But it didn't distract the champion-in-waiting. He later admitted to being a little nervous when he served for victory, the memories of the Davis Cup semi-final coming back to pose a psychological question, and when Hewitt saved two match points there was a frisson around the Rod Laver Arena, the electrified crowds daring to hope that maybe their streetfighter was to stage another comeback. But Federer was not to be denied, and converted his third match point.

After dispatching the somewhat match-rusty Hewitt to win 4–6, 6–3, 6–0, 6–4, Federer had brushed aside one jinx player – only to be greeted by another in the next round.

In the quarter-finals, Federer found himself up against Nalbandian. At least he had one win against the Argentinian from the round-robin match in Houston, but had that been for real or did Nalbandian still hold the key to Federer's game?

Among those players who did most damage to Federer in the early part of his career (mainly Nalbandian, Hewitt, Henman, Agassi and Nadal), the one thing they all have in common is their use of the full width of the court. Federer tends to dominate when he's able to stay mostly within the width of the 36ft (10.97m) doubles court, but like all players he becomes somewhat less effective when driven wide by angled and heavily kicking shots. It's therefore crucial for him to assert control from the outset against such players. And against Nalbandian in that quarter-final he did so almost to perfection, surviving a lapse at the end of the third set to win 7–5, 6–4, 5–7, 6–3.

Joining Nalbandian among the quarter-final casualties was the world number one, Andy Roddick, who was beaten in five sets by the mercurial Marat Safin. The Russian was playing his first tournament after a patchy 2003 which had been seriously disrupted by a wrist injury that took a good eight months to heal. His win meant Roddick would lose the top spot after the tournament, and either Federer or Juan Carlos Ferrero would take it from him.

By a twist of fate, Ferrero and Federer were up against each other in the semi-finals. It wasn't quite a straight title eliminator – had Ferrero won, he would have had to win the final to return to the top – but it felt like one. And there was no question who the better player was. If Federer had wobbled in sight of the number-one spot against Roddick in Toronto five months earlier, there was no wobble now. He was ready to rise to the pinnacle of his profession, and he did so with a crushing 6–4, 6–1, 6–4 victory (although in fairness to Ferrero, the Spaniard was carrying an injury that restricted his movement). Irrespective of the outcome of the final, Federer would become the twenty-third man to top the world rankings since the computerised system was introduced in 1973.

Not that there was any doubt that he wanted to ascend to the throne as a newly crowned Grand Slam champion, and few gave his final opponent, Safin, much of a chance. He'd reached the final after four successive five-set wins over Todd Martin, James Blake, Andy Roddick and the defending champion, Andre Agassi, spending nearly twenty hours on court, and, although he said his body would recover in time for the final, it was clear that he had to get off to a good start to have any chance.

He didn't. The first set went to the tiebreak, Federer took it 7–3, and, after that, the strength drained from Safin's limbs. Just over an hour later, Federer had claimed his second major title, taking the final 7–6, 6–4, 6–2.

'It's really nice,' he said later of his success, with his typical brand of understatement. 'It just gets me all emotional inside. To win the Australian Open and become number one in the world is a dream come true.' Then, when asked if he felt himself to be the best player on the planet, he replied, 'I feel I'm maybe the most natural ball-striker. I'm not going to start praising myself, but, for me, my game feels natural. I feel like I'm living the game when I'm out there. When a guy is going to hit the ball, I know exactly the angles and the spins. I just feel I've got that figured out.'

Being his first triumph in Melbourne, everyone wanted a piece of him. He did several hours of media interviews and photo shoots, and then got up early to do another round of breakfast shows on the Monday morning. By the time he reached Melbourne's Tullamarine airport, it was barely four days before he was due on court again in a match on the other side of the world. Looking at Federer's schedule in the first week of February 2004, it's hard not to have some sympathy with his decision to rein in his Davis Cup commitments.

That year, the Davis Cup first round was the week after the Australian Open. For some reason, the players seem to like playing Davis Cup ties the week after a Grand Slam, even though the team competition can require them to jet off in all sorts of directions at the flash of a boarding pass. Federer boarded his twenty-two-hour flight on the Monday, spent some of Tuesday being feted at a civic reception in Basel that included an appearance on the balcony of the 'Roothuus', Basel's striking sixteenth century Gothic city hall with its deep-red sandstone and gilded pagan figures, and then jetted off to Bucharest for Switzerland's first-round tie against Romania.

Sheer class overcame jetlag in the opening day's singles

when he crushed Victor Hanescu, but with the tie at 1-1 on Friday night, Federer's real heroics came in the doubles where, teaming with his friend Yves Allegro for the first time in the competition, the Swiss beat Andrei Pavel and Gabriel Trifu 10-8 in the fifth set. It was a thrilling match, lasting three hours and thirty-six minutes, and a thrilling personal climax for both men to play together for their country after sharing a flat in their formative years. And the effort was worth it, as Federer finished off Pavel in straight sets in the first of Sunday's singles matches to see Switzerland through to their third quarter-final in four years. But while he never said this out loud, he could have been forgiven for saying he was never going to fall into such a mad travel schedule again unless it was for a cause of great importance.

In the two months between the Romania tie and the quarter-final against France in early April, Federer broke another of his jinxes. When he lost to Tim Henman in the quarter-finals in Rotterdam in mid-February, he had just one win in six matches against the Briton. But the two met again three weeks later in the final of the Pacific Life Open at Indian Wells, a resort in the California Desert for the well-to-do where the balls fly slightly freakishly through the air, giving the venue a tendency for producing some unusual results. Federer won the final 6–3, 6–3 and, while the result bucked the trend of their head-to-head record, it was the end of Henman's hold over Federer, a hold he was never to regain.

The champion in Indian Wells has a record of doing well at the ensuing Masters-1000 event in Miami, but in 2004 Federer was bundled out early in only his second defeat of the year. He came on court for his third-round match nursing a cold, never easy at the best of times but especially so against a keen seventeen-year-old prodigy he had never played before. Cold or not, the seventeen-year-old challenger went about his business without fear and in a way that made everyone sit up and take note. And he won the match 6-3, 6-3. No-one knew it at the time, but this was the real deal. The youngster's name was Rafael Nadal.

Switzerland's 2004 home Davis Cup quarter-final against France was a chance for the Swiss to exact revenge after their defeat three years earlier in Neuchâtel, especially as the personnel were almost exactly the same as in 2001. There was no off-court unrest within the Swiss camp, but this time Switzerland's second-best singles player was the 134th-ranked Ivo Heuberger. Once again, the home nation's chances were highly dependent on Federer winning his two singles matches and the doubles.

The reception Federer received in Lausanne's Prilly Arena when he stepped out on court to open the tie against France's Nicolas Escudé gave even the neutrals and French supporters goosebumps. The predominantly Swiss crowd – all clad in scarlet T-shirts, creating an amazing visual tableau – were treating the match as their hero's festive homecoming following his ascent to the top of the rankings in Australia. An emotional character such as Federer could have been forgiven for taking a few games to get into his tennis after such a heartfelt welcome, but his start was anything but slow. He rode the tide of emotion to win the first four games, conceding just ten in total in a highly emphatic 6–2, 6–4, 6–4 victory.

Yet Switzerland's dependence on Federer was shown up in the second singles match. Ivo Heuberger made no impression on either his opponent, Arnaud Clément, or indeed his captain, Marc Rosset. After Heuberger's 6–3, 6–2, 6–2 defeat, Rosset made it as clear as he could without being insulting that he was singularly unimpressed with Heuberger's form and suggested that the man from eastern Switzerland would play no further part in the Swiss Davis Cup set-up as long as Rosset was in charge. Rosset didn't last much longer but Heuberger never played for Switzerland again. The suggestion also made it even clearer that Federer and Allegro needed to win the doubles if a home victory was a realistic possibility.

Hence the delight of the French pair, Escudé and Michaël Llodra, when they won the doubles. In fact, when Llodra made an interception at the net to win the third-set tiebreak 7–5, such was his demonstrative celebration that anyone watching could have been forgiven for thinking that France had won the Davis Cup. Llodra knew that France had broken the back of the match, and so it proved, the visitors winning 6–7, 7–3, 7–6, 6–3.

Once again, Switzerland's fate was no longer solely in Federer's hands, and once again Michel Kratochvil had to play a live fifth rubber after Federer's 6–2, 7–5, 6–4 drubbing of Clément. Persistent knee problems had reduced Kratochvil's ranking to 194th, and against the sixty-eighth-ranked Escudé he lacked both confidence and nerve. Although Escudé too had been off the tour for the last six months of 2003 with a hip injury, the Frenchman had too much nous for Kratochvil, and even came back from being 3–6 down in a third-set tiebreak to beat Kratochvil 7–6, 6–3, 7–6. Once again, Switzerland's reliance on Federer was just a bit too great.

At the Swiss team's post-tie press conference, Kratochvil got visibly irritated with one of Federer's off-the-cuff comments. Some of the things Federer said in interviews that day suggested the Davis Cup was losing its appeal. 'At least I now know where I stand in terms of tournament planning for the rest of the year,' he said with some relief. 'Last year I didn't know whether I'd be needed during the off season, but now I know I won't have to play Davis Cup for another ten months.'

As it transpired, he didn't play for Switzerland again for another seventeen months, and in the intervening period the Davis Cup weekends ceased to be one of the first entries in his schedule when he and his entourage began planning his itinerary.

As one of the top earners in the world of tennis, Roger Federer has a number of business interests. As many of these are conducted in his name by advisers, they don't add too much to the overall picture of him as a person and athlete. But one such venture from 2004 does stand out as an indication of how he clearly leans towards the country of his mother's birth.

That year, Federer – who has a South African passport – bought a plot of land on the Pezula private golf estate near Knysna, a resort in the Cape just north of South Africa's much-promoted Garden Route. And, when he travelled to South Africa in March 2005 to visit the Imbewu project that receives funds from the Roger Federer Foundation, he made arrangements to build a house on his plot, which could become an off-season base in years to come.

Pezula advertises itself as the place in which 'to rub shoulders with international tennis stars and local sports heroes'. Among others who have bought land there are the golfer Nick Price, the South African national cricket-team captain Graeme Smith and a handful of tennis players, including the Swedes Jonas Björkman and Thomas Johansson. The link with tennis comes largely from the fact that Gary Muller – a former doubles specialist and ATP council member – has not only bought property there but is also in charge of what a Pezula press release describes as a '50 million-rand "Field of Dreams" multi-faceted sports facility... in a central position on the estate... [with] three tennis courts (one in a stadium), squash courts, a golf driving range, an international-standard cricket oval, a gymnasium and a swimming pool – and it will be linked into an equestrian centre and Pezula's own sailing and beach clubs'.

There were suggestions that Federer might be building himself a base in South Africa at the Pezula estate, but his association with it faded, for reasons never fully revealed. Asked in March 2006 about plans for his plot, he said, 'It's on hold. We'll see. I had plans, but we're waiting at the moment.' A year later he was asked about it again, and all he would say was that he had no plans to have a base in South Africa as he was 'very happy having bases in Switzerland and Dubai'. And in January 2009 he described his plans for the Pezula plot as 'long since gone' and admitted he had been trying to sell it for a while.

Having notched up Grand Slam titles on grass and hard courts, Federer's next challenge was for one on clay and, after two successive first-round defeats at Roland Garros, 2004 had to be different.

Federer travelled to Paris having again won one of the clay-court Masters Series tournaments in the build-up. He won Hamburg for the second time in three years, but this time it didn't make him any more of a favourite for Paris than he would have been anyway, given that he was the undisputed world number one. And, just as Luis Horna had seemed a reasonable first-round draw the previous year, no one could assume that Federer's first opponent at the 2004 French Open, Kristof Vliegen, would be easy to beat. Perhaps for that reason, the poor Belgian became cannon-fodder for Federer's first win at Roland Garros in three years, winning just four games against the rampant top seed.

Following this trouncing, a second straight-sets win over Nicolas Kiefer set up an appetising third-round clash against Gustavo Kuerten. The Brazilian, known affectionately as 'Guga', had been Paris's darling since his first shock title in 1997 when he took the tennis world by storm by winning with a ranking of 66. In 2001, his relationship with the Paris public intensified when, after winning his third title there, he chalked into the clay a heart, in the centre of which he lay flat on his back. The Roland Garros crowd, so hard to please if a player once crosses them, just adored him, and he loved them back. By 2004, however, a troubled recovery from a complicated hip operation in 2002 had taken its toll on the likeable beach boy, and it was widely assumed that time and Federer would have caught up with him. By and large, that was the case, but, as with many greats who know their best is behind them, they can still summon themselves for the odd great match, even if they're no longer capable of winning a great tournament. That's what Kuerten did in the feature match of the first Saturday.

Playing some of the tennis that saw him top the rankings for forty weeks in 2000–01, Kuerten took Federer apart, winning 6–4, 6–4, 6–4. He took Federer's first two service games, broke early in the second and third sets and, apart from one dropped service game at the beginning, he was never broken. 'It's like a love affair between me and the crowd,' he said afterwards. 'If it wasn't for this tournament, I wouldn't be here. I'm just happy I can play here, given the way my physical condition has been. Any other tournament and I'd have pulled out.'

No doubt Federer wished he had. He clearly still had something to learn about dealing with true clay-court specialists. 'I tried but he didn't give me much of a chance,' he said afterwards. 'Usually I can control these kinds of matches, but today that wasn't the case. Guga deserved to win. Now I'm just looking forward to getting out on the grass.'

That third-round defeat has since acquired an element of Federer folklore, because it proved to be the last time he lost before the semi-finals of a Grand Slam. As this book went to press, Federer had made the semis or better in the subsequent twenty-three majors, failing to reach the final on only three of those occasions. Given that the next-best run of consecutive Grand Slam semi-final appearances is Ivan Lendl's ten, no-one could have suspected the streak that was about to begin following that Parisian Saturday afternoon in 2004.

Federer's second Wimbledon triumph will probably end up as one of his less memorable major wins, but it drove another stake through the confidence of his rivals.

He again warmed up by playing in Halle, defending his Gerry Weber Open title without dropping a set and cutting the entertainment in the final to less than an hour in a clinical demolition of Mardy Fish. The American had been the only player to take a set from Federer at Wimbledon the previous year, but in Halle in 2004 he won just three games in the fifty-nine-minute match.

Then at Wimbledon, he again dropped just one set en route to the final. That was against Lleyton Hewitt in the quarter-finals, but far from being a signal that he might be beatable, Federer was so stung to have lost a set that he won the following one to love, to run out a 6–1, 6–7, 6–0, 6–4 winner. Then a win over Sébastien Grosjean in the semi-finals set him up for another match against Roddick.

With a number of Wimbledon's spectators being very much occasional tennis fans (many Britons wonder what the players do during the forty-eight weeks of the year when the tennis circuit isn't in England), the final between Federer and Roddick was billed as a great rematch from the previous year's semi-final. It was in fact their seventh match, and Federer had won five of the previous six, but Roddick seemed focused and determined to make the most of his one advantage over the Swiss: his sheer power. While he'd lost his number-one ranking in Australia, Roddick was still the world number two and saw himself as the principal threat to the reigning champion. And with the fastest serve in tennis, Wimbledon was the place to make it pay.

On a showery day, Roddick came out fastest. He looked the better player before rain held up play after just five games. Rain breaks can turn matches, often because they allow players to consult their coaches in the locker room, but Federer had no coach. When the players came back on court, he looked subdued, and Roddick stormed to the first set.

Roddick couldn't hold his level, though, and Federer raced to a 4–0 lead in the second set without ever looking totally convincing. He'd created such a dominating reputation for himself that the set was as good as gone, but his curious display continued as Roddick got both breaks back and levelled at 4–4. Then, with Roddick serving at 5–6, Federer profited from a lucky net cord that gave him set point and, when he then hit a running forehand down Roddick's backhand wing to level the match, he screamed and punched the air with real emotion. The real Federer, it seemed, was back.

Or was he? In the third game of the third set, it was the passive Federer who dropped his serve, and at 2–4 he was in serious trouble. Then it rained again. Roddick walked off to talk to his coach, Brad Gilbert, while Federer went off to talk to... well, himself. During that period of introspection, he worked out that he had to be a little more pro-active to counter Roddick's aggression. And, when he came back out on court, it was a different match.

When Federer took the third-set tiebreak 7–3, Roddick could have folded, but the combination of his conviction that his power would win out and Federer's inconsistent display gave the American good reason to hope. Early in the fourth set he created six break points but converted none of them. That failure proved costly, for at 3–3 Federer broke, and the game was up for the American, Federer running out a 4–6, 7–5, 7–6, 6–4 winner.

The Reuters news agency tennis writer, Ossian Shine, used a nice analogy in his report of the match. 'Certainly,' he wrote, 'there was a moral in there somewhere, one of which Aesop would have been proud, regarding the Swiss's steady, deliberate progress overcoming Roddick's whizzbang fireworks and general uproar.'

'I got lucky, for sure,' was Federer's more modest verdict. 'I was down a break in the third set, and if Andy had served a few better games it would have been two sets.'

After the match, Sue Barker came on court to conduct brief interviews with the two players. Roddick must have felt sick about having let Federer get away, but he still managed to muster enough wit to charm the British public. 'I threw the kitchen sink at him,' he said, 'but he went to the bathroom and got the tub.'

Yet it was another bit of Roddick wit which told the truer story. Barker asked Roddick about the 'great rivalry' he had with Federer, to which Roddick replied, 'I'm going to have to start winning some of these matches if we're to call it a rivalry.' The crowd loved Roddick's humility, but his response had summed up what Federer's third Grand Slam title meant to the tennis world in general: while he had challengers, he certainly had no rivals based on equality of expectation, except perhaps on clay.

In the eyes of many tennis watchers, what Federer achieved over the four weeks after Wimbledon in 2004 enhances his claim to greatness. Not since Björn Borg in 1979 had a player won three successive tournaments on different surfaces, but Federer did just that.

Arriving in Gstaad the day after Wimbledon, Federer made the often difficult transition from grass to clay in a matter of hours and, six days later, Gstaad had its home-grown champion. Although the list of people Federer beat that week hardly reads like a who's who of clay-court tennis, it was still a momentous achievement when he beat Igor Andreev in a four-set final to finally win a title on Swiss soil. Although he didn't say so at the time, he'd come to the conclusion that Gstaad's position in the tennis calendar was too impractical for him, and in early 2005 he announced it would no longer have a place in his annual tournament schedule.

A short holiday followed, before he took to the court again on the concrete of Toronto. Again, Roddick awaited him in the final, and again Roddick's weapons weren't accurate enough to stop the Swiss clock. It was Federer's nineteenth tour title and his fourth Masters Series shield – and he wasn't even twenty-three.

As he left Toronto for the next Masters Series event in Cincinnati in early August, he had lost just four matches all year, and was unbeaten in his last twenty-three. But such success can work against players, especially if they plan their tournament schedule around an average of three or four matches per week. He was getting tired, and yet he was committed to play in Cincinnati the week after Toronto. Mercifully, he lost in the first round to Dominik Hrbaty, earning him vital recuperation time, and yet his defeat was no tank; he'd stormed through the first set to win it 6–1 before losing the match 1–6, 7–6, 6–4. It was the first time he'd been defeated in the first round since losing to Luis Horna at the 2003 French Open, but it was not a day for sadness. 'I had a great run,' he said later of his twenty-three-match winning streak. 'Maybe it was one tournament too many for me, but it's ended now. I'm not disappointed. No one should feel sorry for me. I'm going to take a few days off.'

During those days off, the Federer look began to change. At first, the changes were subtle, and the complete new look wasn't unveiled until the Tennis Masters Cup in November, but after Cincinnati he had a haircut that looked as if it hadn't quite worked, for when he turned up at the Olympics in Athens his hair was held in place not just by the usual bandanna and ponytail but by a set of hairpins, too. When he was on court, his hair didn't look that different, but when he appeared without the bandanna the layering effect was somewhat unusual.

The Athens Olympics gave him the chance of an honour he

was to appreciate to the full. Having put Switzerland not just on the tennis map but the general sporting map too, he was asked to carry the Swiss flag in the opening ceremony. But his bigger goal – in fact his main goal of 2004, he said – was to win an Olympic gold medal, either in singles or doubles.

His first match in Athens, a stuttering 6–3, 5–7, 6–1 win over Russia's Nikolay Davydenko, serves to emphasise that the volatile Federer hadn't disappeared; he'd merely hidden it from view, and occasionally a safety valve had to be released. Federer served for the match in the second set, but when he played a poor game and was broken he belted a loose ball on to the roof of the centre court and earned a code violation from the umpire. 'It's a long time since I got my last warning,' he said after the match. 'For me, it was a sign. I just needed to show a reaction because I was unhappy with the way I played in the second set. I got frustrated. But the important thing is that I won, not how I acted on court.' The hidden meaning behind that assessment can be found in his analysis of the outburst in Hamburg in 2001, when he felt that by learning to control his temper he risked becoming too passive. In other words: while he'd learned to keep his composure on court, even the cool, calm and collected Roger Federer needed to vent his spleen on occasions.

He also admitted he'd have to play a lot better in his next match, against a player he had never faced before, a tall eighteen-year-old Czech, Tomas Berdych. With his mop of tied-back ginger hair, Berdych had become known on the circuit as a promising prospect but was still ranked only seventy-fourth coming into the Olympics. On a windy day, on an outside court, he was to make his introductory statement to the tennis world. Why the world number one and gold medal favourite was on an outside court is perhaps another question (then again, why shouldn't the very best also play on the lesser courts as long as their safety isn't compromised?), but it clearly added to the effect of the swirling wind. And when, after the match, Andy Roddick walked into the locker room, having saved three match points in a thriller against Tommy Haas, saw Federer and threw him the casual question, 'How'd you get on?', he was astonished to hear Federer reply, 'I lost.'

Against Berdych, Federer looked sluggish, even in taking the first set, but a single break and adequate serving proved to be enough. Then, at 3–4 in the second set, Berdych broke Federer to love. Federer broke back but then lost his next-but-one service game with a run of errors and Berdych took the set. With the wind acting as a leveller and Berdych doing some tremendous retrieving, Federer began to lose confidence in his serve. It just about saw him through to 5–5, but he then had to save two match points at 4–5. Then, at 5–6, he hit a double fault and made three unforced errors to give Berdych the breakthrough win of his career, the final scoreline reading 4–6, 7–5, 7–5.

'It's hard to play these big players on centre court because they have more practice there,' said Berdych in the post-match press conference. 'It's easier on the outside courts, where they haven't been practising or playing.'

Federer didn't do his own press conference until much later. Immediately after his defeat, he sat motionless for several minutes in the locker room, not knowing how to take it in. And by the time he faced the media, he was even more demoralised, for by then he and Yves Allegro had lost 6–2, 7–6 in the doubles to the Indian pair of Mahesh Bhupathi and Leander Paes. 'It's a terrible day for me, losing singles and doubles,' he said. 'I've been playing non-stop, you know, and it's obvious it's going to catch up with me eventually. Unfortunately, it's during the Olympics.'

Hindsight is a wonderful thing, but, if Federer had known that day that it would be more than five months before his next defeat, he would probably have felt considerably better.

The US Open is more than just a tennis tournament. It reflects the city of New York, with all its brashness. As a tournament, it's a little less brash today than it was between 1978 and 1996, when the main stadium was a hurriedly rehashed version of an open-air concert venue used by the jazz musician Louis Armstrong during the World Trade Fair of 1964, but it still takes a certain mentality to get used to the environment, especially for non-Americans. In the late 1980s, when playing on the outside courts meant inhaling the aroma of barbecued spare ribs from the chaotic food court, the Swedish champion Stefan Edberg got so fazed by the atmosphere that he threatened never to return there, until his coach, Tony Pickard, suggested that he stay in a family house on Long Island to give him a little peace. (It did the trick; Edberg won the US Open twice and played his best match there in the 1991 final.) Even Jim Courier, an American who made it to number one in the rankings, suggested the site at Flushing Meadows should be 'nuked'.

Although he always professed to enjoy his trips to New York, Federer does not have the natural personality to thrive in New York conditions. And having failed to make any in-roads against Nalbandian in the 2004 US Open, there was a question mark hanging over his capacity to win the top American tournament, certainly at the age of just twenty-three. But it was in New York that he was to make one of the most emphatic statements of his career.

He didn't look totally comfortable in his second-round match against the smiling Cypriot Marcos Baghdatis, nor in his third-round outing against the wily Frenchman Fabrice Santoro, but he raised his game when he needed to and qualified for the second week. A walkover against the Romanian Andrei Pavel, who couldn't play because of a herniated disc, meant Federer could conserve a little energy for his quarter-final, in which he had to go to five sets to beat Andre Agassi in a match played in quite ridiculous wind. With much calmer conditions for his semi-final, he showed that he'd worked out how to play Tim Henman, beating the Brit for the loss of just eleven games. But those eleven games looked a massive achievement for Henman in the light of Federer's superb display in the final.

On 12 September 2004, Federer stepped out to face another old nemesis, Lleyton Hewitt. At that time, the Australian was the man of the moment, and in some people's eyes was the favourite for the Open title, having won it three years earlier. More pertinently, he'd won four titles on the 2004 North American summer hard-court swing and was clearly the form player coming into both the tournament and the final. Yet Hewitt was humbled by one of the most impressive displays of sporting prowess of modern times. Only once did Federer wobble, that was towards the end of the second set when Hewitt had a couple of chances, but, once the Swiss had taken the tiebreak 7–3, he was irresistible, storming to a 6–0, 7–6, 6–0 victory. The US Open – or US nationals, as it was called before 1968 – dates back to 1881, yet you had to go back to 1884 to find the last time there had been two 'bagels' (6–0 sets) in a final.

After taking out his hairpins prior to the trophy-presentation ceremony, Federer did an on-court interview with the veteran CBS sports commentator Dick Enberg, who had just commentated on the final. Enberg tried to do justice to Federer's performance by asking him, 'Roger, I don't know where to start. We're up in the television booth, raving about your forehand, then it's your backhand, and then all of a sudden you go to the net and you made all but four of thirty-two points at the net. What else do we have to look forward to in the future?'

To which Federer replied, 'That's all I've got!'

The world was on his racket strings. From America he next went to Asia, had a holiday, and then won the title in Bangkok, where he again beat Roddick in the final. And, when he flew back to Switzerland shortly afterwards, he must have been thinking that surely, this time, Basel would finally be his.

In the first round of the Swiss Indoors, Federer was scheduled to play Luis Horna, the last man to beat him before he'd become a Grand Slam champion. They were scheduled to play each other for the first time since that frustrating day in Paris, but on the Monday afternoon of the week of the tournament, he began to feel a twinge in his thigh. By the following day, it had become clear he'd torn a muscle and was forced to withdraw. In doing so, he had to wave goodbye not only to the Swiss Indoors tournament but also to the final Masters Series event in Paris as well.

Federer's absence from the last couple of weeks of the 2004 ATP circuit meant there was something of a question mark hanging over his participation at the Tennis Masters Cup. He duly flew to Houston, sporting the post-ponytail look for the first time, but as he took to the court of the West Side Club, a year after his breakthrough win there over Agassi, many felt that he might be vulnerable after his injury lay-off. Such feelings lasted about ten minutes into his first match against the shock French Open champion Gaston Gaudio. He took Gaudio apart in the first set and, while the Argentinian came back in the second, Federer still ran out a 6–1, 7–6 winner.

Although the cream of the tennis world was gathered in Houston, Federer no longer feared any of his rivals. 'I respect everybody but fear nobody,' was his stated philosophy.

His former bogeyman Lleyton Hewitt was dispatched 6–3, 6–3 in the next round-robin match, and even the Spaniard Carlos Moya – who was in good form and getting his playing level up for the Davis Cup final he was due to contest at home to the USA two weeks later – could do no more than take a set from the world number one.

But then in the semi-finals came one of those moments of theatre that make all the run-of-the-mill 6–1, 6–2 early-round scorelines worth tolerating. Federer's match against Marat Safin was always going to have a poignancy about it, because since May Safin had been working with Federer's former coach, Peter Lundgren. Here were the two players facing each other for the first time since Safin began working with Lundgren, and at the tournament that, a year earlier, had been the last in the Federer–Lundgren partnership.

There was just one break of serve in the whole match, and that allowed Federer to take the first set. But the key statistic was the tiebreak score with which he took the second set in his 6–3, 7–6 win: 20–18. The tiebreak lasted twenty-six minutes. Safin saved seven match points, Federer saved six set points – and the tennis was outstanding, pure drama. And when Federer converted his eighth match point to move through to the final, the two men had equalled the record for the longest ever tiebreak (measured in points) set by Goran Ivanisevic and Daniel Nestor at the US Open eleven years earlier.

After such a match, Federer might have been mentally exhausted, but he did an hour-and-a-half's media work, accepting every interview request handed in. Admirable though that was, such generosity of time and spirit created a rod for his own back and could never be sustained in the long run with the on-court success rate he was to have over the next three years. As he began to cut down on his media time, reporters and broadcasters felt unfairly rebuffed when he refused them an interview they had previously become accustomed to expect, but even they had to accept that his time is not limitless. Quite rightly, he sees his dealings with the media as part of his duty to the sport that has nourished his bank account so well, but, as he's subsequently learned, even the generous Roger Federer has to say no on occasions.

After such drama, the final couldn't hope to live up to the same standards – and it didn't. This was through no fault of Federer and Hewitt, who were facing each other for the sixth time that year and the third time in nine weeks. Heavy rain reduced the match to a best-of-three-sets contest (and ensured that the event will never be awarded to an outdoor venue again), and the rain meant it was played late at night, by which time many television stations had cancelled their coverage. Although Hewitt battled bravely, the match served only to show what the previous two had done: that, when Federer is on his game, Hewitt doesn't have a chance against him.

So ended a year in which Federer had become the first man since Mats Wilander sixteen years earlier to win three of the four major titles in the same year (although, in fairness, Pete Sampras held three of the four titles for much of 1994 but had won them across two calendar years). He'd won seventy-four of the eighty matches he'd contested, a ratio not seen since Ivan Lendl's most consistent year of 1986. He was clearly the tennis player of the year, but he was more than that. The World Sports Academy awarded him its Laureus Award as the 2004 world sportsman of the year, arguably the most prestigious honour in world sport, despite a rather notable bias towards tennis.

And all without a coach.

10

WHEN MATS WILANDER won three of the four major titles in 1988, the effort just about killed him. His victory over Ivan Lendl in the US Open final, in what was a direct eliminator for the world number one ranking, allowed him to achieve what he had struggled all his life for. He freely admits that, after his *annus mirabilis*, motivation became hard to find and his ensuing downward slide proved to be swift.

Although the same age at the end of 2004 (23), Federer was not at the same point in his career as Wilander had been when he ended 1988. The US Open title that saw Wilander to the top of the rankings was his eighth Grand Slam in a haul spanning six years, starting with his breakthrough French Open at just seventeen. No-one seriously expected Federer to have peaked after 2004 the way Wilander had done after 1988. And yet few could have expected him to have had as lustrous a year in 2005. It would have been no disgrace for Federer to have had a quieter year than 2004 – but if anything, he scaled even greater heights in 2005, certainly in terms of consistency.

He set out his stall before hitting his first ball of the new year by hiring the former Australian great Tony Roche as his part-time coach. Born in Wagga-Wagga, the wily but somewhat inscrutable Roche, a former French Open champion and thirteen-times Grand Slam doubles winner, made his name as a coach in the 1980s with Ivan Lendl. He'd taken on the task after Lendl had had a succession of coaches who'd failed to lead him to Grand Slam success, despite his immense potential. Had Federer signed up Roche in the first half of 2003, the circumstances would have been almost identical to those in which Roche began working with Lendl. In the 1990s, the Australian had worked as a casual coach to Patrick Rafter, escorting him to two US Open titles and a week at the top of the rankings. And he was also Australia's Davis Cup coach, under the captaincy of his former doubles partner John Newcombe, which allowed him to play a leading role in the development of the young Lleyton Hewitt.

Federer had first approached Roche in February 2004. The Australian – then fifty-eight and increasingly reluctant to travel both for personal reasons and because of a hip problem – turned him down, but did travel with Federer on two occasions. In mid-December 2004, Federer flew to Sydney, ostensibly to acclimatise for the Australian Open, but, as he was playing the Qatar Open in the first week of January, the trip had a different justification. He went to Roche's home to discuss the Australian becoming his coach. Roche again said he didn't want to do much travelling, so Federer worked out a part-time deal that would commit the Aussie to just ten weeks' travelling per year.

On 5 January, after beating David Ferrer in the first round in Doha, Qatar, Federer told the media of his new signing. 'It's good to know that there is help there, because I need someone to analyse and help improve my game.'

When the news was reported in Australia, the former doubles champion turned television pundit and politician John Alexander said, 'It's a great shame for Australian tennis.' Alexander's comment reflected not only the esteem in which Roche was held down under, but also the fact that one of Australia's top coaches was working not with Australia's top player Hewitt, but with Hewitt's principal rival. Roche did eventually work as Hewitt's personal coach but not until 2008, by which time Hewitt was a spent force, certainly at the very top of the game.

Federer went on to win in Doha, beating Ivan Ljubicic in the final, and then it was on to the Australian Open in Melbourne, where he teamed up with Roche for the first time since their new working relationship had been announced. There, playing what seemed effortless tennis, Federer breezed through to the quarter-finals for an eagerly awaited clash with Andre Agassi.

Although the American was fast approaching his thirty-fifth birthday, Agassi was still a factor in Australia, having won the title on four previous occasions, most recently in 2003, and had only lost in 2004 in a five-set semi-final to Marat Safin. If there was anywhere Agassi still had a chance against Federer, it seemed to be on the high-bouncing Rebound Ace courts of Melbourne. The theory might well have been valid, but on a balmy late summer's evening Federer won before the last of the daylight had disappeared, notching up a 6–3, 6–4, 6–4 victory over the popular

American in what proved to be Agassi's last-ever match on the Rod Laver Arena.

But he picked up an injury in the course of the win. He said nothing about it afterwards, but it was to hamper him in his eagerly awaited semi-final against Safin, their first match since the epic 20–18 tiebreak from Houston two months earlier.

The tournament had already been blessed with four matches of the kind of quality and drama that most tournaments would normally be glad to have one of – Hewitt–Nadal, Molik–Davenport, Hewitt–Nalbandian and Serena Williams–Sharapova – so drama was in the air when Federer and Safin entered the arena on the Russian's twenty-fifth birthday. The first of the men's semi-finals was a mouth-watering prospect, and the reality lived up to the promise.

When tennis watchers are asked for a list of their all-time most memorable matches, their responses are obviously many and varied. A truly great match normally has an off-court element alongside the actual tennis, like Jimmy Connors suing the ATP's president Arthur Ashe at the time the two met in the Wimbledon final of 1975, or Pete Sampras learning that his coach Tim Gullikson had an inoperable brain tumour just before his five-sets quarter-final against Jim Courier at the 1995 Australian Open (a match in which Sampras played – and won – the final set with tears streaming down his face). If an out-of-tennis element is a criterion for greatness, then the Federer–Safin semi-final of 2005 falls slightly short of the all-time great category, but it was nevertheless the most enthralling and entertaining match of the 2005 tennis year.

What had most people on the edge of their seats was the fact that Federer was clearly unsettled in the early stages of the match. Although hardly as volatile as he had been in his junior days, he was growling about the court as Safin matched him shot for shot. He won the first set, but then Safin came back to level. Federer won the third set 7–5 – the same score with which he'd won the first – and when the fourth set came to a tiebreak he looked set to edge through to what would have been the first leg of a dream final for the organisers. For waiting in the wings was Lleyton Hewitt, who was all set to become the first Aussie finalist at the Australian Open in seventeen years if he beat Andy Roddick in the semi-final the next day – which he did. In the centenary Australian Open, marketed under the banner '100 years in the making', the semi-final line-up offered the prospect of a home player contesting the final against the defending champion and world number one.

Back in the fourth-set tiebreak of the Federer–Safin match, neither player ever had a significant lead, but then Federer got to match point at 6–5. A baseline rally developed, then Federer went to the net, Safin tried to pass him on his backhand side and Federer stretched for an exquisite backhand volley that just cleared the net. Surely that was good enough to win the point? But no. Safin raced forward and got the ball back. Federer played a second volley at Safin. Safin played the only shot he could: a lob. Federer chased it back. He seemed to have the option of playing a high defensive lob or an audacious attempted pass – either would have made sense. Instead, the controlled, disciplined Federer – the man who'd supposedly put his junior tricks behind him – had a rush of blood and attempted a 'hot dog', the flamboyant but highly risky shot through the legs with the player's back to the net. It failed, and Safin levelled the tiebreak at 6–6. It was to prove Federer's only match point.

When asked after the match what he'd thought he was doing playing a shot like that, he seemed slightly nonplussed by the question. 'Well, the point was already lost, so I tried it,' he said. Maybe he believed it at the time, but more likely he felt very silly about choosing such an ambitious shot at such a crucial stage of the match and just wanted to keep the attention away from it. There are plenty of tennis watchers who would love to see Federer attempt a hot dog and a few other showy shots, but they would expect it in the early part of an early set, not at match point in the fourth-set tiebreak of a Grand Slam semi-final!

Being Federer, he might still have won the match, but from that point on the momentum changed. Safin won the next two points to take the match into a fifth set, at which point Federer called for the physiotherapist. The trapped nerve he'd sustained during his match against Agassi was sending pain right down his playing arm. The match, it seemed, was now Safin's.

It seemed even more Safin's when the Russian opened up a 5–2 lead in the fifth set. Federer was obviously in great pain but hanging in there. He saved a handful of match points, broke back in the ninth game and hauled the set level at 5–5. Then, at 6–6, with Safin serving, Federer led 0–30, but the Russian snuffed out the danger.

Because he was serving second, Federer was always under more pressure than his opponent, and at 7–8, it told. Safin worked his way to match point – his seventh in total. Federer couldn't gain an advantage with his serve, Safin hit a big backhand and Federer lunged for the ball, got it back but dropped his racket in the process. The court was then open for Safin, who might have been put off by Federer's loose racket, but he wasn't – his volley crashed into an unguarded court with Federer stranded. Thus, the Russian claimed the second-greatest victory of his career after his win over Pete Sampras in the 2000 US Open final.

The match had lasted four hours and twenty-eight minutes and was another triumph for the Australian Open in its centenary year. It was also a considerable triumph for Peter Lundgren, who had coached his charge to a win over the man he'd helped to make pretty much unbeatable in the first place. Little wonder the Swede was mildly tearful at the end.

When asked after the match about the injury that had proved to be his undoing, Federer was philosophical. 'It's always going to hurt, no matter how great the match was,' he admitted, 'but at least I can leave the place feeling good about myself, because I gave it all I had.'

Despite losing to Safin, the way in which he lost hardly made Federer appear vulnerable to the rest of the tennis world. His twenty-seven-match winning streak – dating back to the Berdych defeat at the Olympics – may have been broken, but Safin had played to his full potential and still needed a Federer aberration to stave off match point. Federer was still the man to beat, and he was to prove it decisively over the next two months.

Federer's next two tournaments provided finals against Ivan Ljubicic, the late-developing Croatian who finally came good in 2005, breaking into the world's top ten after reaching eight finals, winning two of them, and steering Croatia to its first Davis Cup title. Ljubicic might have won more than his two finals if three of the six that got away hadn't been against Federer. (Another was against 2005's second-best player, Rafael Nadal.) In Rotterdam's Ahoy Arena, Ljubicic took Federer to a final-set tiebreak that he led 4–2. But the tennis world knows Federer is never beaten until the final point has been won, and he showed it by bouncing back to take his second title of the year. It was to prove his last visit to Rotterdam; while he entered the tournament in 2006, he pulled out a few weeks beforehand – it had by then become too small an event to justify inclusion in his schedule at a time of year when he was trying to conserve strength for the intense three-month stretch from the French Open to the US Open.

Federer's third title of the year came in Dubai, again Ljubicic the beaten finalist, again in a third set but this time 6–3. He'd beaten Agassi in the semi-finals – in fact, he played Agassi twice that week, the first time in arguably the most spectacular setting ever for a tennis 'match'.

Dubai is home to the world's only seven-star hotel, the Burj al-Arab. Built on a man-made island in the Gulf of Arabia just off the main settlement of Dubai, the hotel was designed to resemble a graceful sailing boat from a distance. Near the top, at 211m (692ft) above sea level, it boasts its own helipad, a plate-like addition to the structure measuring 415sq/m (1361sq/ft) – almost big enough for a tennis court.

Almost? Why let a few missing metres stop the fun? On this plate, someone had the idea of laying a temporary tennis court and inviting Roger Federer and Andre Agassi to play on it.

And so, on 22 February 2005, Federer and Agassi played a gentle set on the makeshift court. It was a little shorter than a regular tennis court, but the length of the court wasn't of primary concern. It was billed by many in the media as the highest tennis court in the world, which isn't entirely true; Alpine resorts that host tournaments such as Gstaad and Kitzbühel are considerably higher above sea level than 211m, but, with no ground immediately beneath the helipad, it would have felt high enough.

'When I was asked to do this [play tennis on the helipad], I didn't know what to expect,' Federer said. 'The view is absolutely amazing. I've been in Dubai many times and have stayed at the Burj al-Arab before, but this was an absolute treat. To play tennis with Andre on top of such an amazing hotel and overlooking the whole of Dubai was absolutely spectacular.'

The two players were so taken by the experience that they wanted to continue playing, but the hotel had to chase them off because a guest was about to arrive via helicopter and the 'court' had to be cleared.

Before 2005 began, Federer had let it be known that, for the first time since making his debut in 1999, he wouldn't be available for a Davis Cup tie.

There were some raised eyebrows in the offices of the International Tennis Federation, the custodians of tennis's oldest and most prestigious team competition and the sport's overall governing body, which receives around half of its income from Davis Cup profits. To compound concerns, Carlos Moya and Tim Henman – two equally loyal servants of their nations' causes – also announced they would be missing the team variant that year. As it happened, both Henman and Moya went on to suffer an alarming slump in form, adding to the anecdotal evidence that players who skip the Davis Cup often do their tour form as much harm as good; the different sense of responsibility inherent in playing for one's country appears to give some players a dimension they don't get elsewhere.

The ITF's president, Francesco Ricci Bitti, was a voice of calm. He pointed out that Federer had always turned out, even when Davis Cup ties fell uncomfortably for his tour programme, and it was proper for the tennis community to grant him his break. After some rejigging of the tennis calendar, itself prompted by some rejigging in 2004 to accommodate the Olympic tennis event, the first-round week of the Davis Cup had slipped from the beginning of February to the beginning of March. In 2005, it fell the week before the Masters Series event in Indian Wells, a tournament Federer was prioritising in his bid to remain at the top of the rankings. Besides, he'd withdrawn from only one tie, giving the impression that he'd return for Switzerland's next Davis Cup match – either a quarter-final, if the Federer-less Swiss beat the Netherlands, or a play-off tie in the qualifying round for the 2006 world group if they lost.

More eyebrows were raised when Federer did not turn up in Indian Wells to acclimatise to conditions in the California Desert, as anticipated, but in South Africa, where he was visiting the Roger Federer Foundation-funded Imbewu project. Yet, when the photos of his visit to the project hit the world's newspapers, it was understandable that no one wanted to point out that he was supposed to have withdrawn from the Davis Cup in order to concentrate on the Indian Wells tournament.

Meanwhile, in the picturesque town of Fribourg, the rest of Switzerland's players were determined to prove they could win without their illustrious compatriot. And in the Netherlands, they had a beatable opponent. If Federer had played, the Swiss would almost certainly have won comfortably, but his absence proved a great leveller against another team struggling for survival.

The Dutch were without their former French Open finalist Martin Verkerk, who had undergone shoulder surgery; their top player, Sjeng Schalken, was on the comeback trail after contracting the strength-sapping condition mononucleosis; so their inspirational captain, Tjerk Bogtstra, had to motivate his other players to punch well above their weight. The result was a tie that proved so exciting that Switzerland's captain, Marc Rosset, said, 'In my fourteen years in the Davis Cup, I have experienced a lot, but this was one of the best weeks. Our comradeship was great, and we have shown that alongside Roger we have other players. We've waited a long time for that.' It was a lovely comment, although it proved to be one of his last as captain.

In a nice twist, Federer's place in the Swiss team was taken by Marco Chiudinelli. After expecting to play tennis just for fun and go to university, Federer's boyhood mate suddenly found himself with a spurt in form in his mid-teens, which prompted him to put his study plans on hold and try to make it as a tennis professional. After two or three meagre years, he finally put in the hard work and surged up the rankings in 2004, earning his Davis Cup call-up in March 2005. 'Roger phoned me a few days before the tie,' says the likeable and eloquent Chiudinelli, 'but we didn't speak much, only for about three minutes. I think he didn't want to say too much. We had coaches in the team, and Marc Rosset was the captain, so I think it was right that he didn't try to add much input. But he sent me a message from South Africa on the day of the tie.'

Chiudinelli had never played a best-of-five-sets match

before and fought gamely in his opening rubber against Schalken before succumbing in five sets. With Wawrinka losing in four to the Dutch debutant Peter Wessels, Switzerland were effectively beaten by Friday night, but their spirit had been good, and it improved further when Yves Allegro and George Bastl won the doubles, saving three match points in a contest lasting four-and-a-half hours. When Wawrinka had match points against Schalken in the first reverse singles, the Swiss were a point away from a deciding rubber, for which Wessels was reported to be injured; but Wawrinka just couldn't convert, and Schalken sealed the Dutch victory in dramatic circumstances. In the dead rubber, Wessels did indeed retire with back problems after one set, which told the Swiss just how close they had come to winning without their trump card.

Yet another narrow Davis Cup defeat could have been demoralising, but the Swiss came away from Fribourg with real hope for the future. The country was desperate for a quality second singles player, and in Wawrinka it seemed to have found one (even Chiudinelli seemed a possibility at the time but didn't play for Switzerland again till September 2006 because of a shoulder injury). And yet... There may have been 'comradeship', as Rosset put it, but the tie had done nothing to enhance the captain's standing with the members of his team.

Before doing anything drastic, however, they sought a chat with Federer. He had a sense of what was going on, having been in regular text-message contact with the Swiss team from South Africa during the weekend. The players knew Federer and Rosset went back a long way, so they sounded him out about his feelings with regard to a change of captain. 'We were all in favour,' recalls Chiudinelli. 'If Roger had been completely against it, Marc would still be captain.' With Federer happy to go along with a change of personnel – albeit keen not to be the instigator – Rosset was removed from the captaincy.

Using the model of the team supremo with a part-time captain, Swiss Tennis appointed Ivo Werner as 'Teamchef' (team boss), with Severin Lüthi as captain. Werner is a Czech-born German coach who coached Jakob Hlasek in the 1990s and took Petr Korda to the Australian Open title and number two in the world rankings in 1998. Lüthi had been a promising junior who never quite broke into the top 600, and then became a part-time coach and part-time businessman with a firm selling advertising merchandise at tennis events. He'd been brought into the Swiss set-up by Peter Lundgren for the Morocco tie in September 2002, and had proved himself a popular general aide to the players, who knew him from their junior days. His friendship with Federer also deepened to the point where, by 2008, he was travelling regularly to tour events as a trusted member of the inner sanctum of Team Federer, having evolved into the closest thing Federer has to a coach, albeit not in the mould of Peter Lundgren or Tony Roche. The result was a harmony in the Swiss camp for the following tie against Great Britain that had been absent since the Casablanca tie following Peter Carter's death three years earlier.

Despite the fact that Federer was no longer committing himself to the Davis Cup to the same degree that he had in earlier years, there seemed finally to be a sense of discipline and contentment in the Swiss Davis Cup set-up. The team could make great use of Federer, but they weren't totally dependent on him in order to remain a world-group nation.

Only if they harboured dreams of winning the competition was his presence still essential.

Federer's decision to concentrate on Indian Wells rather than the Davis Cup paid dividends. He won the first two Masters Series tournaments of the year, and by the time he reached Paris he had won three of the five played. His only defeat came in Monte Carlo and was one of the more bizarre matches of his career.

When Federer beat Fernando Gonzalez to reach the quarter-finals of the Monte Carlo Masters, he'd gone twenty-five matches unbeaten and had lost just once in his previous fifty-three. The Swiss radio journalist Marco Mordasini makes an observation about Federer: 'I'd go so far as to say that, if he loses a match, it isn't an opponent who has beaten him on tennis grounds but he's lost it for external non-tennis reasons, whatever they may be.' Whether that is true every time, there were certainly external, non-tennis factors at play the day that Federer's latest winning streak came to an end. Whether they accounted for his defeat can, of course, never be proved, but they created a very strange atmosphere for a high-level tennis match.

Nine days earlier, Prince Rainier III, the monarch and ruler of the principality of Monaco, had died. His funeral was scheduled for the day of the Monte Carlo Masters quarter-finals. With dozens of heads of state and government in town, security was tight and a curfew was imposed from breakfast time until mid-afternoon, which meant anyone wanting to go to the Monte Carlo Country Club – the site of the tournament (half of which is actually on French territory) – had to get there early. And, while the view across the Mediterranean from the clubhouse is one of the most spectacular in world tennis, there isn't a lot to do on site, so all the players were somewhat at a loose end. With the overall ambience in Monaco very subdued, it created an eerie atmosphere seldom witnessed at a top-level tennis tournament.

That atmosphere was heightened by a minute's silence before play began. And, although Federer's two-hour-eighteen-minute match against the French teenager Richard Gasquet was a cliffhanger, it was characterised more by nerves and errors than by the glorious aestheticism of both men's elegant strokes.

For Gasquet, that quarter-final provided the potential of a coming-out party. Three years earlier, he'd become the youngest player ever to win a main-draw match at a Masters Series tournament, when he'd come through the Monte Carlo qualifying tournament as a fifteen-year-old and then beaten the fifty-first-ranked Franco Squillari in a first-round three-setter. That success seemed to justify years of being hyped by the press after first appearing as a nine-year-old on the cover of France's principal tennis magazine, which had hailed him as the future of French tennis. Yet, after that breakthrough against Squillari, a series of injuries coupled with a belief that advancing up the rankings would be easier than it is in reality saw him slide out of public view. By now approaching his nineteenth birthday, he was finally working his way back, and in Monte Carlo he had the chance to measure his progress against the best in the world.

Federer broke early but Gasquet soon bounced back, and Federer was ultimately glad to take the first set into the tiebreak. Once there, he stormed to a 7–1 success, which looked to most observers to have broken Gasquet's resistance. But Gasquet broke the Federer serve early in the second set, which he went on to take 6–2, and, when he opened up a 2–0 lead in the final set and held the advantage up to 5–3, a shock result was on the cards. Gasquet then had a match point that he should have won but, having opened up the court for an easy volley, he fluffed it. When Federer then broke back for 4–5, Gasquet's chance looked to have gone. He had a second match point in that tenth game, but Federer saved it.

The tiebreak they played in that third set was full of drama and tension, with neither man able to finish the job. Federer had three match points; the first Gasquet saved with a service winner, but the second and third were squandered on Federer errors.

Gasquet then had his third match point at 9–8, Federer came to the net, and Gasquet ripped a backhand down the line to win the match 7–6, 6–2, 7–6. The shock result suggested to the world that Gasquet was likely to become a factor at the top of men's tennis. It also prevented Federer from becoming the first man to win three successive Masters Series tournaments.

But it had been a subdued Federer, and with his energy levels back to normal four weeks later, he showed the true balance of power between him and Gasquet by beating the Frenchman 6–3, 7–5, 7–6 in the Hamburg final, a tournament he won without dropping a set.

Before heading to the French Open, Federer had another appointment. He had been nominated for the top 'Laureus' award, that of world sportsman of the year for 2004. At the awards ceremony he beat off the competition of Lance Armstrong (cycling), Hicham el Guerrouj (athletics), Michael Phelps (swimming), Valentino Rossi (motor cycling) and Michael Schumacher (motor racing) to earn arguably the highest honour in overall world sport. (An interesting footnote is that the world sportsman of the year couldn't quite manage to win the Basel sportsman of the year award! A committee of sports journalists from his home city decided that naming Federer, the winner in 2003, would be boring, so they gave the award to Marcel Fischer, who had won a gold medal in fencing at the Athens Olympics.)

Federer therefore approached the high point of the clay-court season, the French Open in Paris, as the undisputed world number one and one of the front-line favourites for the title. But the tennis headlines in the weeks leading up to the 2005 French had been made less by him than by a phenomenal eighteen-year-old who was to play a defining role in Federer's career.

4

NADAL THE NEMESIS

11

IT WOULD BE EASY to see Rafael Nadal as bad news for Federer. After all, the Spaniard was a threat, and ultimately it was he who, in August 2008, finally ousted the Swiss from the top of the rankings after more than three years spent as world number two. But Nadal was actually very good news for Federer.

Much as people admire a master craftsman, what gets the pulses racing in sport is a rivalry. People never sickened of the Borg-McEnroe and Evert-Navratilova rivalries of the 1980s, and the ATP and the media tried their best to build up clashes between Pete Sampras and Andre Agassi into a rivalry in the 1990s (which it was for short periods). The exuberant and ebullient topspin-heavy Nadal – with his pirate-like appearance in sleeveless shirt, plus-four-length shorts and shoulder-length hair – provided a wonderful counterfoil to the calm, flat-hitting, neat Federer. The rivalry Nadal generated with Federer played a vital role, not just in lifting Federer's level of play, but in bolstering Federer's standing when the historians come to debate his place in tennis history long after his career is over.

Statistically, it is the greatest rivalry in the history of men's tennis. Nadal ascended to the number two ranking on 25 July 2005 and, with the exception of four weeks in August 2009 when Andy Murray briefly broke the duopoly as Nadal recovered from tendinitis in his knees, the pair occupied the top two positions for more than four-and-a half-years until 1 February 2010. Federer held the top spot for most of that time, Nadal taking over for just under a year from the 2008 Olympics to the 2009 Wimbledon. No other pair of players has ever dominated the rankings to such an extent, not even Chris Evert and Martina Navratilova who had the greatest rivalry in the women's game. The computer rankings have only existed since 1973, but it is hard to think of anyone who had such an enduring rivalry before then. One thinks of Rod Laver and Ken Rosewall, who played countless times on the professional circuit after Laver turned professional in 1963, and then in the early 1970s, culminating in a superb WCT final in Dallas in 1972 in which Rosewall won the fifth set tiebreak 7–5. Or of Bill Tilden, whose battles with Henri Cochet and René Lacoste in the late 1920s caught the imagination of the tennis world. But the tennis world was much smaller then, and Federer and Nadal have surely eclipsed them.

Rafael Nadal Parera (in Spain the mother's maiden name is often used as a second surname) was born into a sporting family based in Manacor, the second city in Spain's Balearic island of Mallorca. He is the elder of two children, but has a large extended family. His uncle, Miguel-Angel, had played football for both Barcelona and the Spanish national team, and the rest of the family had greater or lesser sporting involvement.

When young Rafa showed an aptitude for tennis, another uncle, Toni Nadal, became his coach. One of his first acts was to get the youngster to stop playing his forehand with two hands, and many expected the left hand to come off to leave a right-handed forehand – after all, he writes right-handed and kicks a football with his right foot. But the right hand came off, leaving a left-hander who has developed a fluency of stroke with immense power and, in latter years, a very effective serve and one-handed sliced backhand.

Federer first played Nadal in Miami in March 2004, when Nadal took advantage of a Federer head cold to win in straight sets. Their second match was again in Miami, in the 2005 final. Nadal had been long known as a great prospect, beating his fellow Mallorcan Carlos Moya in his Masters Series debut in Hamburg in 2003, and proving the find of the 2004 Davis Cup year. At eighteen, he beat Andy Roddick in the final to help Spain earn their second title. But, as Roddick correctly observed at the time, while the youngster had played some great individual matches, he had yet to string them together. Three months later, the string was about to begin.

In a superb best-of-five-sets final, Nadal won the first two sets, and then led 4–1 in the third. Federer pegged him back, but when Nadal led 5–3 in the third set tiebreak, he was just two points from a famous win. But then his lack of experience allowed Federer to win four points on the run, and the Swiss raced away with the fourth and fifth sets for a 2–6, 6–7, 7–6, 6–3, 6–1 victory. Nonetheless, the eighteen-year-old left-hander had served notice that he was ready for an assault on the top level of the sport and, by the time he and Federer next met two months later, he was ready to win on a bigger stage.

The defeat in the Miami final proved Nadal's last for a while. He arrived in Paris on a phenomenal run of twenty-nine wins in his last thirty clay-court matches, the previous seventeen having brought him the titles in Monte Carlo, Barcelona and Rome. Yet he had never played in the Roland Garros main draw, injuries having prevented him from competing there in 2003 and 2004.

So tennis fans were licking their lips at the prospect of a Federer–Nadal final, but the Spaniard still wasn't ranked high enough to be seeded second, the position that would have guaranteed he would be kept apart from Federer until the final. Instead, he was seeded fourth, and the draw wasn't in a mood to co-operate – he came out of the hat in the same half as Federer, which meant the two were projected to meet in the semi-finals. That seemed to play into Nadal's hands; Federer had after all won his previous nineteen finals, so most of his main challengers felt the best chance of beating him came in the semis or earlier.

Meanwhile, the draw was also unkind to Federer, who looked like he'd have to face Carlos Moya, David Nalbandian and Nadal before reaching the final. Moya he beat in straight sets in the fourth round, on the same day as the neat but unremarkable Romanian Victor Hanescu beat Nalbandian. Freed from having to face his Argentinian nemesis, Federer beat Hanescu comfortably to reach the semis without having dropped a set since losing to Richard Gasquet in Monte Carlo. As expected, Nadal awaited him.

On the night of his victory over Hanescu, Federer went to the ITF's champions' dinner, an annual black-tie bash staged on the second Tuesday of the French Open to honour the singles, doubles, junior and wheelchair world champions of the previous year. It was his second champions' dinner – he and Jelena Dokic had been the best juniors of 1998 and had received their award at Paris's Hôtel de Ville in June 1999.

It was a slightly off-colour Federer who showed up after beating Hanescu. Nothing of substance can be held against him – he turned up on time, carried out all his obligations, and, when all the speeches and ceremonies were over, he asked the ITF president Francesco Ricci Bitti if he was now free to go. That showed a sense of co-operation and responsibility not shared by some of his predecessors as world champion. And yet something didn't seem to be quite right. He showed up on his own, without his partner, Mirka Vavrinec, despite her having told an ITF official three hours earlier that she'd be there; he turned up unshaven; and, while his dinner jacket was immaculate and his black shoes brightly polished, he had omitted to wear a bow tie, and the top three buttons of his shirt were undone. It might have been just a fashion statement, but it contrasted with his two previous appearances at the Wimbledon champions' dinner at London's Savoy hotel, when he had shaved beforehand and had worn his bow tie.

Two days later, he walked out on to the Philippe Chatrier Arena at Roland Garros looking somewhat ashen faced to play his semi-final against Nadal. He was entitled to be a little frustrated, given that the most eagerly awaited match of the tournament had been delayed until 6.29pm due to rain and the fact that the first semi-final had gone to five sets. If the Federer–Nadal match had gone to five sets, it would not have been completed that evening. There was also an omen in Nadal's favour; the Spaniard was celebrating his nineteenth birthday that day, and four months earlier Federer had been defeated in the semi-finals of the Australian Open by another birthday boy, Marat Safin.

Both men were nervous in the early stages, and neither found serving an advantage. In fact, six of the nine games in the first sent went against the serve, with Federer losing a remarkable four out of five, as both men tried to sound each other out. Federer found his form in the second set and, at one set all, looked the stronger player. But Nadal's heavy topspin and use of angles – especially his looped left-handed forehand, which drove Federer well wide of his comfort zone on the backhand wing – was undermining Federer's confidence in his game, which in turn led to him serving poorly and committing an uncharacteristically large number of errors with his normally deadly forehand.

Serving at 2–3 in the third set, Federer was broken from 40–15 up, which proved enough for Nadal to take a two-sets-to-one lead. Federer came out with an early break in the fourth and led 3–1, but still he didn't seem comfortable. At 3–2 he was broken back, and when Nadal held serve to lead 4–3, with the clock striking nine, Federer had a word with the umpire about the light. Had he won the fourth set, they would have had to come back the next day, and maybe Federer would have been more on his game. But Nadal held firm, broke again and won the match 6–3, 4–6, 6–4, 6–3 on Federer's thirty-fifth forehand error of the match.

Later that night, Federer said, 'I had too many highs and lows. He was much more consistent. I started bad and finished bad. I was good in the middle, but it wasn't good enough.'

Federer is adamant he wasn't beaten by anything going on off court. Asked about it six months later, he said, 'There was no problem, and also during the match there were no problems whatsoever. I was even being pushed by the fans, which was exciting. I would have wished that things went better, but there was nothing upsetting me incredibly much, except that I thought they should have stopped the match because of darkness, but they didn't. But again, what can I say as a player? I could have addressed that later to the supervisor, but I didn't do that because the match is over and that's it. I don't want to make a scene here. No, there were no problems leading up to that match.'

Nadal had actually made his Wimbledon debut well before he played in Paris, and while Paris was to become his fortress, Wimbledon was always his biggest dream. Forever keen for a challenge, Nadal had worked out that a Spaniard winning Roland Garros would not get the same recognition as a Spaniard winning Wimbledon, so Wimbledon became the target. But in 2005, he was still too inexperienced on grass. He went to Halle to get some practice, but lost in the first round to the passionate but unsubtle Alexander Waske, and then succumbed in the second round at Wimbledon to Gilles Müller, the only player of note to have come from Luxembourg.

Given another year, Nadal and Federer might have met in the Halle final, for they were both in the starting line-up in the impressive but slightly incongruous northern German stadium. By the time another year had elapsed, they were so entrenched at the top that they had become rival attractions in the biggest grasscourt events leading up to Wimbledon – Federer in Halle, Nadal at London's Queen's Club. Though he was not to know it at the time, 2005 was Federer's last year on grass unencumbered by the challenge of his Spanish nemesis.

Federer won Halle, recovering from a tetchy first round and an uncharacteristic reluctance to oblige the media (he even refused to speak Swiss German, his mother tongue, in press conferences), to claim the title in a little gem of a final in which he beat Marat Safin in three sets. Many hoped the match would be a sign that Safin could play on grass, but the Russian's results on the surface continued to be patchy, peaking in a Wimbledon semi-final in 2008.

Halle had done its job for Federer. He had regained his confidence after the Nadal defeat in Paris, and went on to claim a third Wimbledon title – his fifth Grand Slam – for the loss of just one set. In the final he again came up against Andy Roddick, but a match that promised much ended with Federer winning 6–2, 7–6, 6–4. With refreshing frankness, Roddick said after the match, 'I'm a better player than I was two years ago and last year, but I have nothing to show for it. It's frustrating, but he's better too – head and shoulders better than the rest of us.'

The veteran American journalist Bud Collins, writing a Wimbledon Diary, used typically colourful phrasing to describe Federer's dominance: 'Federer was playing a game called run-sheep-run with Roddick as the scrambling lamb eventually getting shorn, just as Lleyton Hewitt had been in the semi-finals. Roger, constantly varying his farm tools, has so many ways to hit a tennis ball in so many directions, with so many shifting spins and speeds, that the best Roddick could hope for was to catch up with some of them. But far from enough.'

And still Federer continued to charm the tennis world in three languages. At the end of a long press conference at Wimbledon, when someone shouted to him across the departing journalists, 'Roger, are there any more languages you speak?' he replied, 'If I did I wouldn't tell you, or my press conferences would take even longer.'

With his Wimbledon victory in 2005, Federer had gone thirty-six matches unbeaten on grass, putting him within striking distance of Björn Borg's run of forty-one, posted between 1976 and 1981. Perhaps more significantly, he had reached the same stage Pete Sampras got to around 1998 – he had become so good that some of his major titles were becoming less memorable. In winning the Wimbledon final that year, he said he felt his display against Roddick was better than the way he'd played against Lleyton Hewitt in the 2004 US Open final, which was viewed by many as his greatest single match. He was beginning to transcend the excellence barrier and enter that realm where many people don't really appreciate the heights a player is scaling simply because he or she scales them so often. It was a problem he was to run into with his compatriots later in the year.

It was to be another nine months before Federer played Nadal again. Although Nadal rose to number two in the rankings three weeks after Wimbledon, he lost early at the US Open. In the autumn, after winning the Masters Series title in his home capital, Madrid, he suffered a foot problem, which robbed him of four months on the tour, including the Australian Open (until he was hit by severe patella tendinitis in both knees in

2009, his feet had been the most vulnerable area of his body, including having had a stress fracture in his foot at seventeen). They may have been the two top-ranked players in the world, but the rivalry hadn't really yet begun.

In those nine months, Federer was developing the statesmanlike image that was to define him both as a player and person, and to prove such a foil to the brash challenge of the rising Mallorcan.

From this period, three matches and one off-court decision stand out in the Federer legend. The off-court decision came shortly after Wimbledon, when he sought the help of the International Management Group (IMG), the company he had sent packing two years earlier when he declared independence in the matter of managing his commercial interests.

Federer used the absence of a commitment in Gstaad to accept an invitation to a civic reception in his home city of Basel. It allowed him to stand on the balcony of the 'Roothuus' city hall and greet 3000 adoring home fans. If one says it was 'good PR', that sounds like a backhanded compliment, and Federer has always seemed as comfortable with his home city as the folk of Basel seem with him. But the decision to return to IMG was a sign that his focus was shifting more to the international market and away from Basel, or even Switzerland.

To some, the return to IMG could be seen as an admission of failure for the independent Roger Federer Management model. That's not how it seemed at the time, though the conclusion is hard to disagree with several years later. Federer and his entourage had decided that, in order to exploit his full economic potential, he couldn't rely solely on a management model that was heavily dependent on the input of two retired people, namely his parents. It was initially put out to the public that IMG would look after the global commercial interests, while Roger Federer Management would continue the Swiss side of things. In reality, IMG handled the Swiss interests too and gradually Roger Federer Management dwindled to the point where it is today little more than a shell from which Lynette Federer runs the Roger Federer Foundation. It would be wrong to denigrate the role of Roger Federer Management, as it does a lot of work to keep the foundation bringing in money for good causes, including a very successful annual Roger Federer calendar that allows Federer's fans to contribute to the foundation and get something for their wall. But the original idea that Roger's own management company would take over his total global commercial management can be said not to have worked out.

A little context is necessary here. It was widely reported in Switzerland at the time that Federer's earnings were lagging behind other global sporting names, including behind the tennis stars Andre Agassi and Maria Sharapova. To some, that wouldn't matter; to others, it would represent underexploited potential – it all depends on how much value one attaches to judging someone by their monetary worth.

The fact is that, even in a league behind the likes of Agassi and Sharapova, Federer was still earning the kind of money well beyond what most people can imagine ever earning. As such, the decision to look to maximise his international value meant he was effectively entering a new table of comparison based solely on marketable value. To that extent, he was arguably no different from the bankers and senior corporate executives who insist on certain salaries, not because they need the money, but because their earning potential is the marker of their professional esteem. Should one condemn him for that? Probably not. The point is only worth making given that the widely held perception of Roger Federer is that he is a down-to-earth guy who understands the human values that money cannot buy; this may be an accurate perception, but it seems clear that the lure of mammon had attracted Federer at this stage of his career, even if he remained largely immune to the ostentatious displays of what money can buy.

But why IMG? There were the two other major player management companies at that time (Octagon and SFx), plus numerous smaller ones, and they certainly courted him. But he went back to the firm he had jettisoned in 2005 and entered a deal in which IMG would be responsible for marketing him internationally. On a personal level, he was assigned the IMG agent Tony Godsick, the husband of the former French Open finalist Mary-Joe Fernandez, whose other clients included another popular and eloquent world number one, Lindsay Davenport. There is no doubt his relationship with Godsick is a comfortable one – there were observers who felt Godsick was getting too close to Federer early on, but the American will have judged how much the Swiss will have wanted his own space – and subsequent developments showed IMG as being more resilient in the global economic downturn of 2008-09 than some of its rivals. But the suspicion abounds that Federer was tempted by a very lucrative offer, probably in person from IMG's then-new chairman, the financier Teddy Forstmann, whose company Forstmann-Little had bought IMG in 2004. Forstmann, a keen golfer with no lack of appreciation for his own ability to spot talent, conducted the personal negotiations with Federer that led to the player returning to IMG.

It would be wrong to read too much into the moanings of those who had massive access to the young Roger who then had to make do with crumbs from the master's table when Federer hit the heights. But it is interesting to hear the comments of Beat Caspar, the former sports editor of the *Basler Zeitung*, who observed, 'In 2002, Lynette made it clear that the BaZ had helped Roger in his rise to prominence, that Roger would never forget that, and whenever we wanted an interview we could have one. Not only did that assurance disappear after 2003, but it gradually became clear that his media time was to be spent on publications and television programmes that linked up with his marketing goals. He was still interested in Basel, but in commercial terms he wanted world exposure, and we couldn't give him that.'

Federer's gradual divorce – or at least amicable separation – from Basel was to culminate in him slipping away to live in a more tax-friendly Swiss canton in the spring of 2008.

When tennis fans discuss who the greatest ever player was, a pastime that will probably go on as long as tennis is played, Andre Agassi's comments after the US Open final of 2005 should always be among the evidence cited. It proved to be Agassi's final hurrah as a player, and his sheer persistence in getting to the final of a Grand Slam tournament at 35 years old (needing three successive five-set matches to do so) adds to Agassi's own legend. But on 11 September 2005 he added more to Federer's.

Although Agassi had missed Wimbledon with a back injury, he returned in great shape at the US Open to pick up the pieces of the shattered hopes of American tennis after Andy Roddick's shock first round exit to the unheralded Gilles

Müller. Roddick had been hyped in the weeks leading up to the Open, and his defeat silenced not only the American public but also the reams of advertising material in which Roddick had appeared in the run-up to the tournament. While Federer was nonchalantly disposing of Kiefer, Nalbandian and Hewitt to reach the final, Agassi had a run-in of three five-set matches, including a quarter-final against James Blake decided on a final set tiebreak and a semi-final against Robby Ginepri. Fortunately, none of them was particularly long, and the charismatic Las Vegan was sustained by steadily rising hype and anticipation of his final against the great Federer.

Though there were less than twenty-four hours between the end of the semi-finals and the first point of the final, the match was the talk of New York. When they finally began playing at 4.30pm on a sunny September Sunday, Federer struck first. He won the first set, but Agassi broke in the second game of the second set to signal his intention to make a fight of it. A second break allowed the American to level at a set all, and the crowd was right into the match. When Agassi broke to lead 4–2 in the third set, the crowd was going wild at the prospect of a sentimental victory for their thirty-five-year-old hero. An upset was a genuine possibility.

But that was Federer's cue to find some of his best form of the tournament. He broke straight back, almost broke in the eleventh game and then stormed through the tiebreak 7–1.

From then on, Agassi was a beaten man and, when, at 5–0 in the fourth set, Federer played a slack game, one could be forgiven for suspecting that a sense of charity had crept quietly into Federer's mind, so Agassi's last set of the tournament – and at the time it felt as if it might be his last set ever at the US Open – wouldn't end 6–0. It made the final score 6–3, 2–6, 7–6, 6–1 to Federer.

Agassi's parting words to the Flushing Meadows crowd were: 'Thank you, New York. It's been a great twenty years.' But it's what he said in his post-match press conference that carries most weight.

By winning his sixth Grand Slam title, Federer had equalled the number of majors won by Boris Becker and Stefan Edberg. 'That's fantastic,' he said, 'tying your idols. Isn't that great? It's every boy's dream, and I made it come true today in a memorable final.'

But Agassi was not talking about equality. 'There's only so long you can go on denying it: he's the best player I've ever played against,' he said. 'Pete [Sampras] was great, no question, but there was a place to get to with Pete. You knew what you had to do. If you did it, it could be on your terms. There's no such place like that with Roger. There's a sense of urgency on every point, on every shot. If you do what you're supposed to do, you feel like it gives you a *chance* to win the point. That's just too good. He plays the game in a very special way that I haven't seen before.'

Federer felt the American's praise was a little over the top. 'The best player of this generation, yes,' he accepted when Agassi's comments were put to him, 'but nowhere close to the best ever. Just look at the records that some guys have. I'm a little cookie.'

Modesty as a polite shield for immense self-belief is central to the Federer make-up. He knew, of course, that he was more than a little cookie; he was resorting to statistics, when what Agassi was saying was that statistics cannot do justice to what Federer brings to a tennis court. When people in later years argue in tennis bars over who's the greatest tennis player of all time, Agassi's words will carry immense weight in separating Federer from Sampras.

More was added to the Federer legend in the final tour match of the year, the Tennis Masters Cup final. But this time it was a defeat, or at least the nature of it, that stood out in the memory.

Pete Sampras found at the height of his career that defeats were so rare that if he lost a match narrowly he would often get immense credit for it. His dignified loss to Federer at Wimbledon in 2001 was one example; a better one was his defeat to the diminutive Peruvian Jaime Yzaga at the 1994 US Open, when he battled against dwindling energy and poor fitness following an injury lay-off to put up a magnificent fight, only to lose 7-5 in the fifth set.

Federer's defeat to David Nalbandian in the 2005 Tennis Masters Cup final falls into a similar category. The background to it began several weeks earlier when he returned to Basel after helping Switzerland crush Great Britain in the Davis Cup promotion/relegation round, winning the title in Bangkok, and then holidaying in Thailand.

A few days after returning from Asia, Federer was practising at the Paradies club owned by the Swiss Indoors' impresario Roger Brennwald. He was hitting with the rising Swiss player Michael Lammer, a contemporary of Federer's from junior days who had just had his breakthrough by qualifying for the US Open and reaching the second round. As the *Basler Zeitung* journalist Freddy Widmer reported in his short book *Moments '05*, on that occasion Federer had tried to book a court, only to find they'd all been taken. But then a genial octogenarian Ernst Schneider – the lifelong driving force behind the cigar and luxury-goods company Davidoff, which has sponsored the Swiss Indoors for many years – offered to give up the court he'd booked to allow Federer to practise. During that practice session, Federer felt a stinging pain in his right foot while running for a forehand, and landed on the ground in agony. A subsequent X-ray revealed he'd torn a tendon in his right foot and needed a plaster cast.

Three weeks later, Brennwald was faced with the same unpopular task he'd had a year earlier: he had to tell his loyal public that the man they really wanted to see in Basel wouldn't be competing for the second year running.

Following the X-ray, Federer's entourage began a race to get him ready for the Tennis Masters Cup, which in 2005 returned to Shanghai. Federer has always had a soft spot for Asia, and agreed to go to Shanghai after his triumph in Bangkok to take part in the official opening of the Qi Zhong Stadium, a purpose-built 15,000-seater state-of-the-art arena with a beautiful retractable roof made of eight interlocking petals. Now there was a serious danger that he wouldn't be able to compete in the event the stadium was built for.

Less than three weeks before the Tennis Masters Cup was due to begin, Federer was still on crutches, but some careful yet intensive rehabilitation work with Pierre Paganini got him healthy just in time to take part. It was the same as in 2004: he was fit, but was he match-fit?

The organisers desperately hoped he was. In the run-up to the elite event reserved for the best eight players of the year, there were three high-profile withdrawals: Lleyton Hewitt, Andy Roddick and Marat Safin. Rafael Nadal came to Shanghai with his foot injury, and concluded after practising that it would be pointless for him to take to the court, and Andre Agassi withdrew with an injury after losing his first match. After working so hard to get the tournament, and building a brand-new stadium for it, the Shanghai officials clearly felt they had lost face, and one of them made a stinging attack on Agassi that would have ensured the American never played in China again, had Agassi not retired anyway the following year. Losing face is a serious embarrassment in China; and in the absence of five of the six most illustrious names in tennis, Federer was effectively carrying the responsibility for the public credibility of the tournament.

He took to the court wearing a protective brace around his right ankle – a precaution, he said, more a comfort blanket than a real need – but came through his group matches, two of them going to three sets. That set up a semi-final against Gaston Gaudio, the Argentinian who had said the day before that he didn't really know how he could beat Federer – and promptly proved himself more than right by failing to win a game! Federer notched up the first 6–0, 6–0 victory of his career, the hapless Gaudio having lost heart early in the second set of what was only a fifty-minute match.

By reaching the final, Federer had done what the organisers in Shanghai had hoped: he had appeared in a maximum five matches, and had helped deflect attention from the five high-profile withdrawals. And he then ensured that the 2005 Tennis Masters Cup would forever be remembered for its best-of-five-sets final rather than for those who didn't show up.

When Federer led his opponent, David Nalbandian, by two sets to love, the match seemed to have been won, but it had taken him two hours and twenty minutes, the second-set tiebreak had been 13–11, and both players had done a lot of running. Instead of building on the momentum of winning the second-set tiebreak to plough home to victory, Federer suddenly began to feel very tired. The ankle wasn't a problem – or so he said – but the six weeks of practice and match time he'd missed while convalescing were beginning to take their toll. The turnaround was dramatic – Nalbandian took sixteen of the next nineteen games to open up a 4–0 lead in the final set. Federer looked beaten.

Federer has often said people didn't give him the credit for his talent until he showed that he could fight. 'It wasn't until I showed more grit when the going got tough that they started to respect me,' he said in a newspaper interview at the end of 2009. 'Then it was "Well, this guy is not just a wonderful shotmaker, he can also fight".' And faced with a 0–4 deficit in the Shanghai final, Federer fought. He fought his way back to 4–4, and when he broke to lead 6–5 he was serving for a third successive Masters Cup title. At 30–0 it seemed all over. Asked what he was thinking at that point, Nalbandian said, 'I can't go home like this!' And he wouldn't. He played four great points to break back and force a final-set tiebreak, and after a couple of points he was never behind, winning the tiebreak 7–3 to post the biggest win of his career.

That defeat meant that Federer was denied the opportunity to share a remarkable statistic with John McEnroe. In 1984, McEnroe so dominated world tennis that he lost just three matches out of the eighty-five he played that year. The final in Shanghai was Federer's eighty-fifth match of the year, and he went into it having won eighty-one and lost three; a victory would have meant tying McEnroe's phenomenal record. As it was, he finished on eighty-one wins and four losses, but with possible extraneous circumstances surrounding all four of his defeats in 2005. Nevertheless, it was a truly phenomenal year for Federer, in which he showed a consistency that outshines the fact that he 'only' won two Grand Slam titles, compared with the three he won in 2004, 2006 and 2007.

Yet such subtleties aren't always appreciated by the person in the street. And the Swiss can be a tough people to please.

After his heroics of 2004, those of 2005 probably seemed no better, or even slightly worse. When it came to the poll for the Swiss sportsperson of the year, Federer was beaten by Tom Lüthi, Switzerland's world motorcycling champion. Half of the poll is voted for by Switzerland's sports journalists in advance, while the other half is determined by the public via telephone voting during a televised awards gala.

Federer had won the award in 2003 and 2004, so in 2005 was going for his third in a row. In a three-way battle between himself, Lüthi and the ice-skating world champion Stéphane Lambiel, Federer led with forty-two per cent of the ballots after the journalists had made their choice. But the spectacle of Lüthi – who in 2004 was known more for his crashes, but who kept his bike upright in 2005 to claim the 125cc world championship at the age of nineteen – swayed many members of the public, and he edged out Federer. It was clearly no snub to Federer, who took it well.

If there was a minor consolation, it came not in his third successive nomination for the Laureus Award – although that in itself must have been immensely satisfying, and he went on to win the principal Laureus honour for the second year running – but in being named as one of 'the twenty sexiest men alive' by *People* magazine. When that particular accolade was announced during the Tennis Masters Cup,

Federer was more amused by it than anything else, but for a man who had won the highest honours the sporting world can bestow, having the attractiveness of his masculinity recognised was probably a more meaningful award than being Swiss sportsperson of the year would have been.

Federer's second Australian Open title in 2006, his seventh in the Grand Slams, will probably be remembered more for his emotional response to lifting the trophy than for much of his tennis. After receiving the Norman Brookes Trophy from Rod Laver, the only man to win all four majors in a calendar year with everyone eligible to play, Federer walked up to the microphone, said to the crowd 'I think you know how much this means to me,' and promptly burst into tears. Although he managed to finish his speech, in which he thanked the necessary dignitaries and sponsors, he did so with a quivering voice that clearly endeared him to the Melbourne faithful, just the way it had won over the Wimbledon crowd two and a half years earlier.

In some ways Federer was lucky at the first Grand Slam of 2006. The two players most likely to damage him were both absent – Rafael Nadal was still nursing his foot injury, while Marat Safin had wrist trouble. And in a fortnight when the temperature reached 44 degrees Celsius, Federer had the good fortune to play five of his seven matches – the last five – at night when some of the heat had gone out of the day. But neither factor should be allowed to detract from a victory which said much about his resilience under pressure.

In truth, he didn't play consistently well throughout the tournament. His backhand was unusually erratic, and his volleys were at best unreliable and at worst poor. But he did what all great champions do: he played well when he needed to most. He won his first three matches in straight sets, and when a 6–0 set gave him a two-sets lead against a highly impressive Tommy Haas in the fourth round, he looked invincible. But from that point he lost his way a little, and Haas was unlucky to lose that match in five sets. Federer admitted later that, after the second set against Haas, he never quite found a sustained level for the rest of the tournament.

He dropped further sets in the quarter- and semi-finals, and could have gone two sets down in the final against the twenty-one-year-old Cypriot, Marcos Baghdatis, for whom that Australian Open was a breakthrough event. Ultimately, Baghdatis didn't quite believe he could do it; Federer played his best tennis at the end of the second set, and then powered ahead to win eleven games on the run and put himself out of reach.

When Federer won 5–7, 7–5, 6–0, 6–2 to secure his second title in the Rod Laver Arena, there was Laver himself to present the trophy. That would have been enough reason to get emotional. Another reason would have been the presence of Diana and Bob Carter in Federer's own enclosure; Federer had invited the parents of his former coach, Peter, as his guests for the final. It also emerged later that he had been suffering more pain than he was admitting to in the right foot he injured in Basel three months earlier – that would have been another reason for a high degree of emotional satisfaction. But, when asked afterwards why the tears had flowed on the podium, Federer gave an answer that was almost banal: 'When I saw that [Baghdatis] was cramping on his calf muscle [early in the fourth set], and knowing I was in very good shape, so many things go through your head about the win already because you think, "Well, now nothing can go wrong." But, as we saw, it was still quite a long way to the finish line. I was getting emotionally ready for that, which I shouldn't, but I can't block it out. I'm also just human. And I guess, when I won, I was so relieved that I got it through. I wasn't emotional in the first minute, just relieved. It only came out later, when I was standing there with Marcos waiting for the ceremony. I was very relaxed. But once I got up on stage, it all changed.'

Who knows what brought on the tears? In Ancient Greece, the original Olympic athletes were extremely competitive, and it wasn't considered a sign of softness or effeminacy for men who had lost a race or a contest to cry or get very angry; in fact, it was considered quite normal. And for a man like Federer who has subverted most of his boyhood emotions in the quest to be the best in the world and who consequently gives little away during matches, no one should be really surprised if the emotions run free when the discipline is allowed to fall. The tears also allow people to respond to him as a human being. It just doesn't quite seem plausible that the intensity of emotion he expressed should all have been because of victory taking slightly longer to complete than he expected. But maybe he was just protecting himself by giving that answer.

As Federer left Melbourne to return to Switzerland, he and everyone else were well aware of his place in history. When asked after his victory at the Rod Laver Arena whether he'd one day like a stadium to be named after him, he replied, 'Yeah, it would be nice, but I don't think I'll get one at a Grand Slam. I don't expect anything like a court named after me. I'm not playing the game because of that, but obviously it would be nice.' Perhaps understandably, the gesture by the

Old Boys Basel tennis club to rename their main court the 'Platz Roger Federer' didn't quite register with him.

A golden opportunity for Federer to celebrate his Australian Open title on home soil presented itself eleven days later with Switzerland's home Davis Cup tie against Australia in Geneva. But again, Federer left his countryfolk on tenterhooks. As the official nominations were announced ten days before the opening day of the Davis Cup weekend, Federer's name was not among them. He issued a statement saying he wanted to play in Switzerland, but he also needed to rest his body. For three days he left the impression that he might play as a late replacement, only to decide finally that he needed to take a break. He announced his withdrawal not just from the Davis Cup tie but also from the following week's tournament in Rotterdam, an event that no longer forms part of his playing schedule.

A word should be said here about Federer's Davis Cup exploits – or lack of them early in the year. Since 2005, he has declined to play for Switzerland in the first round. Each year his country has hoped he would play, and his decision not to do so has seemed at odds with his stated aim of winning all the major titles in tennis, of which the Davis Cup is clearly one. In August 2008, flush from his Olympic doubles gold medal and with his partner Stanislas Wawrinka having broken into the world's top ten, Federer said he would play in the first round in 2009. The draw was kind to him, serving up a hard court tie in Birmingham, Alabama, the week before the Masters-1000 year began on the hard courts of Indian Wells, California. But Federer pulled out a couple of weeks beforehand citing back problems, though it later became clear there were concerns over Mirka's pregnancy at that time. Federer could have made good his promise a year later, but declined the chance to travel to the clay of northern Spain in March 2010.

Much speculation has been devoted to whether Federer really does want to win the Davis Cup. He says he does, but he appears to be running out of time, and it's not clear how long Switzerland will have the supporting cast of two top-sixty players in Wawrinka and Marco Chiudinelli, who could be crucial to winning four successive ties. But in fairness, context is needed again.

Federer has proved remarkably injury-free over his playing career. There may be several reasons for this, including a good physique, a playing style that puts less stress on his body than some of the modern tennis techniques, and a little luck. But he also works very hard with Pierre Paganini in the gym and plans his tournament schedule with great care. Paganini and Federer worked out that for Federer to survive the rigours of the French Open, Wimbledon and US Open swing that sees three Grand Slam tournaments held within fifteen weeks, it was important that he didn't overplay in the early part of the year. Federer had also set 'remaining number one' as his goal at the start of 2005 and 2006, and while one can criticise that goal – after all, one generally remembers players by the tournaments they win, not by the number of weeks they spent at the top of the rankings – that was what Federer was prioritising when he stopped playing the Davis Cup first round ties. Interestingly, he never took any criticism – at least not in public – from any of his team-mates whose prospects of success would have been much greater if he had played. And when an Italian journalist at the Beijing Olympics accused Federer of 'not playing Davis Cup',

Federer retorted defiantly, 'I have played Davis Cup every year since I was seventeen'. It's quite true, for while he didn't want to play in the early part of the year, he has always been willing to turn out after the US Open for what has, since 2005, been a promotion/relegation tie.

However questionable the aim of 'staying number one' was, it did mean that Federer had his concentration firmly on the tour when Nadal finally came back from his foot injury. By then, Federer's position as number one was pretty much impregnable ... but Nadal was to come back with a bang.

12

THE FEDERER-NADAL head-to-head record goes back to March 2004, when they first played in Miami. But the rivalry really took off in the four months between early March and early July 2006, when the two played each other five times. Nadal won the first four, leaving Federer in the strange position of having lost the same number of matches by early June that he had lost in the whole of 2005, and all to the same man. He was a runaway world number one who just couldn't beat the world number two.

With Nadal thought to be Federer's inferior on all surfaces other than clay, the Spaniard made a lot of people sit up and take notice when he came back from being a clear second-best in the final in Dubai to beat Federer 2–6, 6–4, 6–4. It was Federer's first defeat in Dubai since his ignominious capitulation to Rainer Schüttler in 2002.

It's often difficult to assess how much effort Federer puts into the Dubai event. As he has a spacious apartment there and does his December training in Dubai in readiness for the Australian Open, he always shows up for the tournament in late February (if fit) and is no doubt well remunerated for doing so. But it is very much in his quiet season, and while he has won the title three times, he has also lost early on at least as many occasions. While he is too well mannered ever to admit this, it is almost as if the tournament – which generally has a line-up of players to rival any Masters-1000 event – has the status for him of a practice match that a football team plays in the run-up to a major tournament.

But any suspicions that Nadal's win in Dubai was something of an aberration were brushed aside when Nadal beat Federer in two clay-court finals. The Spaniard won in four sets at the Monte Carlo Masters, and then inflicted probably the greatest psychological blow of the year on Federer by winning a quite superb final in the Rome Masters. It allowed him to equal Guillermo Vilas's record, set in the late 1970s, of 53 successive clay-court victories, a record he went on to break at the French Open. But that statistic was an incidental detail. What Nadal did at the Foro Italico was what Federer does to most of his opponents – makes them play their best yet find that it still isn't good enough.

Federer played near perfect tennis to take the first set on a 7–0 tiebreak, and seemed the dominant player in the second. But Nadal hung on, and took the set on a 7–5 tiebreak. That gave Nadal the momentum to take the third, but when he missed break points early in the fourth, Federer bounced back to take two breaks, and a third saw him lead 4–2 in the fifth. Federer's moment to beat Nadal on clay had surely arrived. Nadal levelled at 4–4, only for Federer to have two match points at 6–5. Remarkably, he missed both by making errors on his biggest weapon, the forehand. Still Federer should have won; he led the final set tiebreak 5–3 but mis-hit another forehand that would have given him a 6–3 lead. He didn't win another point, as Nadal wrapped up the glorious five-hour final on his first match point, the score reading 6–7, 7–6, 6–4, 2–6, 7–6.

A sign of the frustration Federer was feeling towards Nadal came with a slightly biting aside. At one stage in the match, Federer slipped out of his normally rock-solid focus and said to a person in the crowd 'All right, Toni?' Many thought he was talking to his IMG agent Tony Godsick, but it was an ironic quip directed towards Nadal's camp made to highlight what Federer perceived as unauthorised coaching Nadal was receiving from his Uncle Toni. There is a feeling on the circuit that Nadal gets away with more than he should, notably over the issues of mid-match coaching and taking too long between service points, and it can get under the skin of fair-minded players like Federer

Perhaps that match holds the secret of Federer's somewhat listless display in the French Open final. The scene was set for him to hold all four Grand Slam titles. When he beat David Nalbandian on a third-set retirement in their semi-final, he had made it to the final of all four majors. There were many respected pundits who were willing to say that if he won the final, he could be considered the greatest-ever tennis player. And when he won the first set 6–1 on the warmest day of the fortnight, he was just two sets away.

Nadal came back to win the second as Federer played a couple of sloppy games, but Federer looked to have regrouped early in the third. In the fourth game he had Nadal at 0–40, and seemed to have shrugged off the lull and regained control of the match. What happened next may never be fully explained.

Federer seemed to lose his intensity. He couldn't convert his break points, and in the following game Nadal broke. Federer's face suddenly took on the ashen look that had characterised his defeat to Nadal in the semi-finals the previous year. It was almost as if he didn't quite know what to do, as if Nadal's constant ability to make use of every conceivable angle, and thus make Federer use more of the court than he needs to against any other opponent, had finally ground the Swiss down. It was as if the Rome final had been the act of hypnosis, and the events of the fourth and fifth games of the third set had merely reintroduced the hypnotic effect.

Federer held his own during the fourth set, but never looked like seriously threatening the defending champion. And when Nadal won the final on a 7–4 tiebreak, it seemed a natural conclusion to what had gone on in the previous hour and a half.

Post-match press conferences are not always the best places to find the most telling analysis of how a match was won and lost – the players are often too close to the event and still emotionally involved. Yet there was something uncharacteristically incoherent about the way Federer was flailing about in trying to explain his collapse after the 6–1 first set. He first suggested it was because the conditions were slower than in Rome, then that he couldn't get to the net, he wondered if the heat might have been a factor, and ended up by saying he just didn't play the match he wanted to. 'I mean, I tried,' he said, 'I can't do more than try. Obviously it's a pity, but it goes on, right.'

There was no faulting Federer's attitude or sense of how a

single defeat in a final – his first French Open final – was hardly a tragedy. But the impression he gave after that final was that he still hadn't worked out how to play Nadal, at least not on clay.

There was no question of Nadal challenging Federer for the number one ranking. Federer left Paris nearly 3,000 ranking points (6,000 points by the ranking points system introduced in 2009) ahead of the Spaniard, the kind of deficit that could only have been erased during the remainder of 2006 if Federer had suffered a serious injury requiring a break of several months. But by the mid-point of the tennis year, Federer had lost four matches – as many as he had lost in the whole of 2005 – and all to the same man. The anomaly was clear to everyone in the game: the phenomenally dominant world number one had a head-to-head record against a young pretender (Nadal turned twenty during the French Open) of six defeats in their seven matches, and even the sole victory had been snatched from the jaws of defeat. Was the writing on the wall for the great man as he approached his twenty-fifth birthday?

Not yet. Roger Federer still reigned supreme at Wimbledon, and if anywhere was to be a Nadal-free zone for Roger Federer, Wimbledon seemed the most likely place. Even though Nadal had signalled at the age of seventeen his intention of breaking with the Spanish mantra that 'grass is for cows' (a casual remark attributed to the godfather of Spanish tennis, Manolo Santana, which came to characterise Spanish players' dislike of playing on grass courts), it was thought that, at twenty, he still lacked the necessary know-how, and that a realistic challenge to Federer's Wimbledon dominance was a long way off. But the Nadal challenge was for real, even on grass.

Federer came to Wimbledon on the verge of a piece of history he was trying very hard to play down. By winning the Gerry Weber Open in Halle for the fourth year running, he had equalled Björn Borg's record of forty-one successive wins on grass, set between 1976 and 1981, when the Swede won Wimbledon five times and reached a sixth final. Federer clearly wasn't that bothered by the record, choosing to view it partly as just another trick with numbers, and partly as being unfair on Borg, who had won all his forty-one matches at Wimbledon, while twenty of Federer's had come at the tour-level event in Halle which only attracted a sample of big names. Trick with numbers or not, it was further testimony to Federer's remarkable dominance of grass-court tennis. But then the streak very nearly snapped before Borg's record had been broken.

Many are the tournaments Federer has won without dropping a set. What was remarkable about Halle in 2006 was that only in his first round match against the 267th-ranked Indian, Rohan Bopanna, did he win in straight sets. The other four all involved a final set, and in the quarter-finals he had to save four match points. The man who very nearly beat him was his Wimbledon junior doubles partner, Olivier Rochus, the diminutive Belgian enjoying the best form of his career. Despite – or perhaps because of – his size, Rochus has learned not to fear anyone, and set about Federer as if he was just another opponent to be beaten. The Belgian had his four match points in the second set, three of them in a remarkable tiebreak that Federer eventually won 13–11. All three sets went to tiebreaks, and when Federer won the third of them 7–5, his winning streak stood at thirty-nine. After a three-sets win over Tomas Berdych in the final, he had equalled Borg's mark. 'It's very nice,' he said afterwards, continuing his underwhelmed attitude to the accomplishment, 'but just being able to defend this title after I really had to fight my heart out is great. Winning for a fourth consecutive time is something I've never done, so this is a great moment in my career.'

Barring some unforeseen catastrophe, the record was always going to fall on 26 June when Federer played his first match at Wimbledon, but bigger headlines that day were made by what he wore to walk on court.

Although Federer doesn't use the terms 'class' and 'classy' as much as Pete Sampras did in his playing days, he shares Sampras's appreciation for the classic traditions of the game. So it seemed entirely appropriate when he strode onto the hallowed turf of Wimbledon's Centre Court wearing a white blazer. On the left breast pocket was a crest made up of various symbols relevant to him, the whole lot in gold weave. The symbols included three rackets, one for each of his Wimbledon titles, and below the crest the name 'Federer' appeared in capital letters. There were a few suggestions that his clothing company, Nike, had come up with the idea in an attempt to steal the scene from its rival, Ralph Lauren, which was introducing its pioneering collection of clothing for Wimbledon's ball kids and line umpires that same day. But, by and large, Federer's jacket was universally acclaimed and helped add a modicum of fashion interest to the single-mindedness of the greatest tennis player on earth. It became his *leitmotif* for the 2006 Wimbledon championships: seven times he walked on court in it, seven times he walked off victorious in it, and he even wore it to the Wimbledon champions' dinner in place of a dinner jacket, complemented by a purple and green All England Club tie. By then the crest was out of date, Federer having won a fourth title, so the quick-thinking curator of the Wimbledon Museum asked him if he would donate it to the museum's collection. Federer agreed, and it is now on show fifty-two weeks a year to tennis tourists visiting the All England Lawn Tennis Club.

Federer swept into the final without dropping a set, despatching four players who had proved troublesome in the past. Richard Gasquet got just seven games as Federer broke Borg's record on the opening day, Tim Henman won a mere six, Tomas Berdych ten in the fourth round, and Mario Ancic twelve in the quarter-finals. Poor old Jonas Björkman managed only four as his reward for reaching the semis nine years after his first Grand Slam semi-final at the US Open. Federer was magnificent – in both tennis and sartorial terms.

But who should await him in the final? Yes, the man from Manacor: Rafael Nadal.

By his own admission, Nadal had a lot to learn about playing on grass when he arrived at Wimbledon in 2006. But good learners are often fast learners, and with a little luck, Nadal learned fast. He was two points from losing to the American Robert Kendrick in the second round; he showed up Andre Agassi's dwindling movement in the third in the match that ended Agassi's Wimbledon career; and his quarter-final opponent, Jarkko Nieminen, was coming off a long five-setter against Dmitry Tursunov and put up little opposition. By the time Nadal faced Marcos Baghdatis in the semis, he had worked out how to play on tennis's most idiosyncratic surface.

Now came Federer. It was a mouth-watering final, because of Nadal's hold over the world number one. The clay results could be dismissed as being merely a reflection of Nadal's best surface and Federer's worst. But the Nadal victory in Dubai, coupled with the two Key Biscayne results from 2004 and 2005, suggested Nadal could get under Federer's skin on any court. It wasn't quite in the 'make or break' league for Federer, but a defeat to Nadal on the surface on which he was supposedly impregnable would have been hard to take.

When Federer took the first set 6–0, he seemed to be making an emphatic statement. But there was a lot about that set which suggested Nadal was still adjusting to his first major final outside Paris. Once the Spaniard got going in the second set, it was suddenly a match. In retrospect, the second set tiebreak, which Federer won 7–5, decided the final, because while Nadal came back to take the third on a 7–2 tiebreak, the task was by then too much. Yet the fact that he had become the first man to take a set off Federer at that year's Wimbledon put down a marker, and with Nadal having recovered one of two breaks he conceded early in the fourth set, the feeling at the end was that the finish line had come just a little too soon for the twenty-year-old. Federer had won his fourth Wimbledon title, which seemed appropriate, but Nadal had made his point.

Tennis finally had the rivalry at the top that it craved. Nadal had proved himself on hard and grass courts, to go alongside his unofficial epithet of 'king of clay'. Federer and Nadal were so far ahead that they had reduced the title of world number three – which oscillated in 2006 between David Nalbandian, Ivan Ljubicic and Nikolay Davydenko – to denoting merely the best of the rest. Yet Nadal's challenge fell away in the second half of the year; he was to play Federer only once more, and it happened to come in the one tournament where the world's top two players can meet before the final. Despite Nadal's ability to trouble Federer, the gap between them was to widen before it narrowed.

One of the things that marks out the rivalry between Roger Federer and Rafael Nadal is the fact that, for all their contrasts, they are two incredibly decent human beings. There are a lot of good things that can be said about the great names of tennis history, but in many cases the good sides emerged as the competitive days waned. By contrast, for Federer and Nadal, it is almost as if the generous naïvité of youth was never crushed by the trappings of riches and fame, but has merely been modified to allow them to keep the worst excesses of mass adoration at arm's length.

As Nadal started to become Federer's equal in tennis terms, he managed to maintain his respect for Federer's achievements without being in awe of them. On beating Federer he was frequently asked whether he felt he should be number one, regardless what the rankings said. He always replied in the negative, saying Federer's achievements spoke for themselves and he wasn't going to let one match distort the big picture. Such respect, coupled with a modesty that was in no way false, allowed the two men to develop a friendship that, if not quite on the level of bosom buddies, stands out in marked contrast to several previous rivalries that included an element of personal dislike, whether real or manufactured.

John McEnroe has gone on record as saying that he is surprised at the friendship between Federer and Nadal, and Federer has some sympathy. In a candid 2009 interview with Paul Kimmage (a cyclist turned journalist for the British *Sunday Times* newspaper) he said, 'I'm surprised myself by the degree to which we actually get along, because we've had a very intense rivalry and you could say he has hurt my career and that I've hurt his career. But we've actually helped each other become the players we are today, and the rivalry has helped the game. It's nice that the two greatest players in tennis, or any sport, actually get along well, because normally there is all this hate and it's so negative – I don't like that. We've had enough controversy in recent years, so it's a welcome change. At the end of the day we are also role models for a lot of children, and sometimes that gets forgotten.'

But while Nadal was still finding his feet as a public figure, especially in the English-speaking world where he initially struggled with a tentative grasp of English, Federer enhanced his reputation as a statesman.

He was visibly affected by the Indian Ocean tidal wave, or tsunami, that wreaked havoc on many Asian countries right at the end of 2004. While many players donated rackets and other souvenirs for auctions to raise money for tsunami victims, and others said they would give the prize money they earned in a given week to the appeals, Federer dug straight into his pocket with a donation of $20,000. He was in Sydney when it happened, negotiating his coaching deal with Tony Roche, and went from there to Qatar, flying over many of the worst hit areas. He was apparently very affected by the carnage. The Swiss tennis journalist René Stauffer quotes a conversation he [Stauffer] had with Federer's partner, Mirka Vavrinec, at the time, in which she said, 'The whole thing has consumed him [Federer] like hardly anything else before.' Stauffer also points out that Federer's connection with Asia was particularly strong – he had played a number of Asian tournaments, he and Vavrinec had taken holidays on the badly affected Thai island of Phuket, and they had friends in other affected regions.

Federer had gone on to organise several initiatives to raise funds for the appeals coordinated by the United Nations children's fund, Unicef. The most high-profile was an exhibition tournament featuring a galaxy of top names, both men and women, which took place in California in March 2005. That event also saw the launch of a programme between the ATP and Unicef called 'Ace' ('Assisting children everywhere'), which was aimed at 'harnessing the power of tennis to help ensure the health, education and protection of the world's children'. One of Ace's fundraising stunts was a teddy bear called the 'Feder-Bear'. Launched at the 2006 US Open, they were loosely modelled on Federer himself, with a red tennis racket, white bandanna, and 'Federer' emblazoned on the back (it's doubtful Federer ever imagined having a lookalike teddy bear as a trapping of fame when, as a boy, he dreamed of winning Wimbledon!). They were sold at $8 per bear, with the profits – said to be $5 per bear – going to Ace funds.

Through working with Federer, Unicef soon realised they had a major asset on their hands, and moved swiftly to cement their relationship with the world's top tennis player. They invited him to become a United Nations 'goodwill ambassador' for Unicef, and on his way home from beating Ivan Ljubicic in the final of the 2006 Miami Masters, Federer stopped off in New York for his inauguration ceremony in the presence of the UN Secretary General, Kofi Annan. The official line was that the ambassadorship was a recognition of the interest in children Federer had shown through the Roger Federer Foundation and the tsunami efforts, but these reasons are probably of peripheral importance. By early 2006, Federer was established as a superstar with a conscience – that highly potent combination of name-recognition and admiration, coupled with a caring attitude to those less fortunate than himself, and a belief that he has been dealt a very fortuitous hand in life. That made him an ideal target for one of the highest-profile children's welfare organisations in the world.

'I've been lucky in life, and able to pursue my passion for tennis since I was six years old,' he said as he joined the ranks of goodwill ambassadors that have included David Beckham, Shakira, Youssou N'dour, Vanessa Redgrave, Roger Moore and the late Danny Kaye and Audrey Hepburn. 'It's important to me to help the many children throughout the world who do not have the basic resources they need.'

For his first field trip as an ambassador, Federer used the off-season in December 2006 to travel from Dubai, where he was preparing for the 2007 Australian Open, to Tamil Nadu, the south-eastern state in India which was the area of India worst hit by the tsunami. He met children whose school facilities were being rebuilt to a higher standard than existed before the tidal wave, chatted with orphans and psycho-logical support staff, and met teenagers being educated about HIV and Aids.

At the Australian Open that began three weeks after his visit to Tamil Nadu, he was asked jocularly by a journalist, 'What's the proper way to address you now – is it Mr Ambassador, or Your Honour, or what?' 'You decide,' said a slightly embarrassed Federer, 'you can also call me Roger, it's OK!'

There will be those tempted to cynically dismiss Federer's Unicef work as a good publicity stunt, but while those managing him will be aware of the benefits such visits give to his public image, Federer's own personality is a naturally caring one and he genuinely seems to want to make a difference. It's hard not to wonder whether his Unicef work might one day prove to be a small step on the road to some form of global statesmanship role Federer seems cut out for when he finally finishes playing tennis.

Another sign of Federer's 'diplomatic' work is his membership of the International Club. The IC is a club originally established to allow tennis players who have represented their country to remain competitive, but it has also taken on a more pastoral role alongside its central aims of promoting fair play and good sportsmanship.

Federer joined the Swiss branch of the IC in 2003, and later gave permission for his photo to be used on the cover of the IC brochure. He was recruited by Julian Tatum, who serves on the international council of ICs and, as a member of the All England Club championships committee, has become his personal invigilator for all his press conferences at Wimbledon. Federer's membership made it easier to recruit Nadal to the IC in mid-2008. Tatum says, 'Together they have brought great respect for the IC family of players. Since their behaviour is perfectly aligned with the IC ideals, it says a great deal to have them on the front of our official publicity. We have used this in all parts of the world to recruit international and ex-international players to the IC fold. It also encourages junior players to participate in IC events such as our Junior Challenge, an event held throughout the world on a continent-by-continent basis. Another aspect of the link is that, like Federer, the IC stages events and clinics for underprivileged kids. Our underprivileged events involve using IC players to give assistance with clinics that can start the thought process in the players' and volunteers' minds that (a) they are lucky to have all their faculties and (b) they are doing something for other people who are less lucky than themselves. Having Federer and Nadal as high-profile, fee-paying members allows them to follow the excellent examples they set.'

Federer has also become more politically involved in his own sport. Initially reluctant to express much of an opinion on tennis matters, he began to be less reticent in 2005 and 2006.

His views on electronic line-calling were well known by March 2006, when the Miami Masters tournament became the first tour-level event to use electronic review of line calls. The breakthrough had come in late 2005 when the British 'Hawk-Eye' system had its accuracy approved by the tennis authorities and was given the green light to be used in official competition. By the end of 2006, electronic review was an established feature of top-level tennis, and while it still has some detractors, it is now hard to imagine a Grand Slam, Masters Series stadium court or Davis Cup final without it.

Yet Federer was never a fan. Before it became accepted, he said it should not be used, and since it has been introduced he has left many with the strong impression that he doubts the accuracy of the system. It's possible that the system is accurate and Federer isn't entirely wrong – one of the central doubts about electronic review is that tennis is played to the human eye, and if a ball looks out but a tiny fraction of it did in fact catch the line, then electronic review will call a ball 'in' when no-one would have questioned a human call of 'out' if the facility to review it hadn't been there. But it is with us, and Federer knows he would be deluding himself if he felt he could somehow wish it out of existence.

Perhaps his attitude towards its legitimacy goes a long way to explaining his curious body language when it comes to calling for electronic reviews. When he challenges a call, he is highly dismissive – some would say arrogant – in the way he raises his arm like an ill-tempered guest in a restaurant who believes the waiters are beneath him. He barely looks at the umpire when he makes a challenge, almost as if he fears the eye-contact. And he has a grim record on challenges, frequently going a whole match without getting one right! His personality would be better suited to deciding in advance that he is not going to challenge at all, unless he's convinced the line call is so wrong there is no question of him getting the challenge wrong. The Williams sisters do that, and have done it very successfully.

Another issue on which he has spoken out is the tennis calendar in general and back-to-back Masters Series tournaments in particular. The level of men's tournament immediately below the four Grand Slams used to feature three instances of events in successive weeks. The revised calendar for 2009 reduced this to two – Indian Wells and Miami, and Montreal/Toronto and Cincinnati – and while the four days' gap between Indian Wells in the California desert and Miami on the Florida coast make the closeness palatable, the rush from Canada to Ohio has never been popular.

Federer's growing comfort with tennis-political issues culminated in him agreeing to run for the ATP Player Council, the advisory body made up of players and elected by players that feeds views and suggestions to the ATP's board of directors. He was elected to a two-year term in June 2008, and four months later voted in as president. The ATP Player

Council has four players from the top fifty, plus lower-ranked and doubles players. In the past it has at times struggled to get top-ranked players to stand, but not in 2008! For the first time ever, the intake included the world's top three players (Federer, Nadal and Djokovic) plus Fernando Gonzalez, with Federer and Nadal elected president and vice-president respectively. Not only were they the two players and personalities setting the tone in the player lounges, they actually held the leading administrative positions in the players' parliament.

One of the doubles players elected at the same time, the Australian Ashley Fisher, says of President Federer, 'Roger's leadership style in the meetings is very respectful and diplomatic. Although he is the president, he recognises that every member should have an equal say and makes a point of ensuring that everyone is satisfied with a decision.'

Such involvement in tennis-political issues has made Federer a harder person for the top ATP executives to deal with than he was earlier in this career. The South African Etienne de Villiers, who ran the ATP as chairman and chief executive from late 2005 to the end of 2008, began on good terms with the world's top player, but some see Federer's public statements as playing a quiet but key role in de Villiers' departure after just three years in charge.

De Villiers, a South African who came to tennis manage-ment after a career with some success at the Disney Corporation, was an instant hit with the players and with other tennis officials, and his South African background added a further sense of solidarity with Federer.

Despite the two men being on the same wavelength in the early days, Federer was opposed to de Villiers' plans to demote Monte Carlo and Hamburg from Masters Series status to general tour level once the majestic *Caja Magica* ('Magic Box') tennis complex opened in Madrid in early 2009. As world number one, Federer found himself as an impromptu shop steward, joining Nadal, the veteran Carlos Moya and the eloquent Ivan Ljubicic in a four-man delegation to see de Villiers. They were partially successful, winning the battle to keep Monte Carlo in the elite, but losing Hamburg.

A bona fide disagreement alone would not have turned Federer against the executive chairman, but the two men were, shall we say, of decidedly contrasting personalities, and de Villiers' relations with some in the tennis world seemed decidedly more strained at the end of his time than they were after his initial round of introductions.

And it was a single line from Federer that perhaps did most damage to de Villiers. De Villiers had pushed hard for an experiment in which the traditional knockout format was replaced in the early rounds by round robin matches in some lower-ranking ATP tournaments. Inevitably with an experiment, there was some learning as they went along, but the format hit crisis one Thursday night in Las Vegas in March 2007. A farcical situation developed in which one of the quarter-final places seemed to be in the gift of an ailing player (Juan Martin del Potro), who could have played his final round robin match to a conclusion to allow James Blake to go through, or could have retired injured to allow Evgeny Korolev to advance. No doubt unaware of his power, del Potro retired hurt. De Villiers got involved by telephone and ordered Blake to be put into the quarter-finals in place of Korolev, only to be reprimanded by his board for unjustifiably overruling an ATP supervisor who had followed the rules correctly. To a certain extent, de Villiers was the victim of unfortunate circumstances – he had been woken late at night and could justifiably claim to have acted in good faith. Federer was several thousand miles away in Dubai and could legitimately have declined to comment, but, never a fan of the round robin format, he said of de Villiers, 'He's got his fingers burned.' Federer's subsequent comment that 'He's doing his best' was largely overlooked or dismissed as faint praise, and the round robin experience was abandoned three weeks later.

The influence of the world number one is remarkably potent, both in terms of the mood in the locker room and players' lounge, and also in how the players feel about certain developments – it is as if they take their lead from the best player. With de Villiers clearly having a different view for the future of tennis from a number of key professionals including Federer, the South African's days were numbered, and one-by-one, his supporters were voted off the ATP Player Council during 2007 and 2008. De Villiers was gone by the end of the year.

The Roger-Rafa rivalry was interrupted in mid-2006 by a cameo comeback from Andy Roddick. By early 2006, the American had slipped out of the top five and showed no signs of breaking back. His one remaining citadel was Wimbledon, where he had been a semi-finalist once and a finalist twice in the previous three years, on all occasions losing to Federer. So when Roddick was beaten in the third round by Andy Murray, it was a wake-up call that he was losing ground against the true elite.

For several months, an unlikely rumour had been circulating that Roddick might be about to team up with the former world number one and street fighter par excellence Jimmy Connors, and after Wimbledon Roddick confirmed it. Despite having little experience of coaching at the highest level, the coaching input in his own career had been dominated by two matriarchal figures: his grandmother Bertha Thompson and his formidable mother Gloria Connors, who died a few months after Connors began working with Roddick. Connors was sufficiently well set in his post-playing-days life that he did not come cheap. But Roddick needed something a bit special, and Connors had become one of the greats in tennis by knowing how to get the best out of any situation, so Roddick took the plunge.

The first sign that some of the Connors magic was rubbing off onto Roddick came when Roddick captured his first Masters Series title for two-and-a-half years, winning Cincinnati in August 2006. Federer had been in the starting line-up, but had lost his first-round match to the rising Murray. The Scot's victories against Roddick and Federer within five weeks of each other served notice that he was set to become a serious challenger to Federer (and Nadal), but few read too much into this first win over Federer, and rightly so given that Federer had just won the Toronto title on four successive final sets, so his competitive hunger wasn't at its peak just two weeks before the US Open.

When Roddick followed up his Cincinnati title with a run to the US Open final, his meeting with Federer was the most eagerly anticipated match of the American hard court season. In many ways it was a repeat of the Federer-Agassi final of a year earlier. On that occasion, the excitement and anticipation meant people had rather turned a blind eye to the fact that Federer came into the final much fresher than Agassi, and the same happened again. The champion had dropped just one set and had played more than an hour less in his semi-final against Nikolay Davydenko than Roddick had done in beating Mikhail Youzhny in a four-setter that came close to three hours.

A year earlier, Federer had beaten Agassi 6–3, 2–6, 7–6, 6–1 to seal Grand Slam title number six. Grand Slam number nine was achieved by the remarkably similar scoreline of 6–2, 4–6, 7–5, 6–1, and the match followed a near-identical pattern. Just as Agassi – who ended his illustrious career at that US Open after losing in the third round to a solid but unremarkable German player with a loaded name, Benjamin Becker (no relation to Boris) – had led 4–2 in the third set, Roddick led 3–2 and had Federer at 0–40. Federer got back to deuce, saving all three break points with some sublime shot-making, but Roddick had a fourth, which he seemed destined to win, only to miss with a forehand. It was to prove his last chance. When Federer broke in the eleventh game and then served out to take the third set, he was unstoppable. 'At that stage of the match,' Federer said of the fourth set, 'I felt almost invincible.' As with Agassi a year earlier, Federer won the first five games, before Roddick picked up a lone consolation game to avoid the indignity of a 'bagel' in a US Open final.

History is likely to be kinder to Roddick than contemporary judges. A strange mix of class act and immature teenager, he has made absolutely the most of his talent, in particular a serve which is the fastest-ever measured in an official match. And if he was fortunate to catch the interregnum between the Sampras and Federer eras to reach the year-end number one spot in 2003, then credit to him for being there at all with a game that, by modern standards, is distinctly limited. He has been a colossus in the Davis Cup, where the pressure of expectation is often greater than anywhere else on the tennis circuit, and in some ways he has been unlucky to be around at the same time as Federer. For Federer has frequently played his best tennis with Roddick on the other side of the net, a circumstance that has made Roddick look unfairly ordinary.

Roddick came within a point of beating Federer at the 2006 Tennis Masters Cup in Shanghai, but even that seemed to emphasise Federer's unreachability for the big-serving American. As it was a round robin match, Federer could have afforded to lose and still win the tournament – a feat he achieved the following year – but Roddick was desperate to beat his long-time nemesis. When he failed to do so, the wind went out of his sails, and he didn't make it to the semi-final stage.

Roddick had another shot at Federer at the Australian Open two months later. It was at the semi-final stage, and in the build-up to the match he had expressed the view that he was 'getting closer' to the Swiss. It seemed an entirely reasonable statement at the time – Roddick had shown superb focus in beating Marat Safin in the third round, and had out-hit the big-hitting Croat Mario Ancic in the fourth. With Jimmy Connors now in Melbourne after the death of his mother, and Nadal out of the tournament, everything seemed set for Roddick to present a significant challenge to Federer.

How hollow those words 'getting closer' seemed after 83 minutes of play! Federer had won 6–4, 6–0, 6–2, taking eleven games on the run from 4–4 in the first set. It's easy for people to rush to superlatives when they have just witnessed a devastating display of sporting prowess, often forgetting that the passing of time offers a more realistic context, but there were many experienced tennis watchers not given to hyperbole who found themselves wondering whether they had ever seen a display of tennis quite so magnificent.

Roddick, who had been ticked off by Connors for overpraising Federer after the US Open final four months earlier, took the defeat well. A man for whom a five-second answer counts as long, he warmed up from a monosyllabic start to his press conference to offer the assessment, 'I've just got to keep doing what I do. I wake up every morning, I put in as much work as I can every day. You do your best not to get discouraged, you try to take it like a man. I caught an absolute beating tonight, there's no doubt about it. But you deal with it and you go back to the drawing board. You act like a professional, and you try to keep working hard.' Brave words, and realistic ones, but they hid the wreckage of hopes built up over several months that were destroyed in an evening.

During the Federer-Roddick match, a placard appeared in the stands bearing the words 'Quiet, genius at work'. It was not the first time it had appeared, but it seemed most appropriate that night. Asked whether he had seen it, Federer said, 'Yeah, of course', and was then asked what the word 'genius' meant to him. 'Look,' he began, showing he had picked up the Australian habit of starting every sentence with that particular word, 'I guess I'm the best tennis player in the world. You can call me a genius because I'm outplaying many of my opponents, kind of maybe playing a bit different, winning when I'm not playing my best. All of that maybe means a little bit of that.'

With Nadal once again failing to replicate the form he had shown in the first six months of the year in the latter five, Federer crossed swords with another rising rival. If Roddick was on the way down in terms of the challenge he presented to Federer, Novak Djokovic was most assuredly on the way up. And the normally mild-mannered Federer exercised the full weight of his office as world number one by branding the upstart 'a joke'.

When Switzerland were drawn at home against Serbia & Montenegro in the play-off round for the 2007 Davis Cup world group, it was to be a closer tie than many might have thought. The Serbian team (and it was all Serb – the 'Montenegro' was only a formality, and that for the last time) that travelled to Geneva had not only one of the world's top doubles players in Nenad Zimonjic, but one of the most promising teenagers in world tennis, Novak Djokovic.

Djokovic was very much grouped with Andy Murray. The Serb is just seven days younger than the Scot, and tennis watchers considered them prospects of equal promise. If Murray could beat Federer, the logic went, so could Djokovic. But Djokovic's first couple of years on the tour had been punctuated by a breathing problem that frequently caused him to call for the trainer mid-match, and there were those who wondered whether he had come to rely too much on his mid-match breaks. So when he called for the trainer to have his legs massaged, after going two-sets-to-one down on the opening day against Switzerland's second player, Stanislas Wawrinka, there were no doubt some who felt that there may have been a tactical element to the inquiry.

Djokovic denied there was, but Federer clearly felt otherwise. He became convinced that Djokovic's leg massages threw his team-mate off his game, and without the treatment, Switzerland would have ended the first day two-up. Wawrinka felt the same, but chose to view it as a failure on

ROGER FEDERER – THE GREATEST

his part to remain focused rather than blame it on anything approaching gamesmanship by his opponent. Whatever the interpretation, the first day score was 1–1, which meant the Federer-Djokovic match on the final day would be live. By the time the players took to the court, the Swiss were 2–1 ahead, and Federer was playing with a little venom in his veins. His 6–3, 6–2, 6–3 win was nothing unexpected, but his post-match comments took many by surprise.

When Federer said of Djokovic, 'I don't trust his injuries,' during his main post-match press conference, it drew a few nervous laughs from the audience. 'No, it's not funny,' he added admonishingly, 'I'm serious. I think he's a joke when it comes to his injuries. The rules are there to be used, but not abused. But it's what he's been doing many times, so I wasn't happy to see him doing it and then running around like a rabbit again. It was a good handshake for me, I was happy to beat him.' Later, Federer had an informal chat with the Swiss-German press, at which he added: 'I got irritated on Friday when he put on this show in his match against Wawrinka. Ninety-five per cent of players use these breaks fairly, but this isn't fair, and the rules need to be changed.'

Djokovic later admitted that the two men had chatted privately at the Madrid Masters three weeks later and cleared the air. The Serb claimed many of his withdrawals came from positions of strength, thus undermining the idea that his injuries and ailments had been psychosomatic responses to hopeless situations. A look through Djokovic's matches doesn't entirely bolster his argument, but to his credit, he does appear to have learned from it. His calls for the trainer and premature retirements became fewer and further between after that spat with Federer, and when the two men met in the fourth round of the Australian Open three months after their Madrid chat, there wasn't a hint of a time-out in another Federer straight sets win. Given that Djokovic was to get the better of Federer in the 2008 Australian Open semi-finals, maybe Federer's outburst has proved to be of some long-term benefit to the Serb.

When a player wins as many tournaments as Federer has, the currency gets devalued, and the smaller events get largely forgotten. Even some of the bigger ones can get forgotten too – not many among even the most ardent Federer fans could recite all his Grand Slam finals. So tour titles seem of peripheral importance, but there was one in the autumn of 2006 that counted for a lot more.

As Federer made his annual pilgrimage to the still barren venue of the St Jakobshalle in his home city of Basel, his battle was against the ill-fortune that had thwarted him in previous years as much as against any opponent in the 32-man field. Surely this year, nothing could stop him!

For any world number one, every match is a cup final for the opponent. Many falter in the presence of the illustrious standard bearer, but a few rise to the occasion and deliver the kind of performance that all giant-killers dream of. Paradorn Srichaphan, the likeable Thai, delivered a dream performance in the Basel semi-finals. Twice he led Federer by a minibreak in the final set tie break, but Federer just did enough to win. 'I obviously got a bit lucky in the end,' said the relieved local hero afterwards, knowing that his biggest obstacle to a first Swiss Indoors title was probably behind him. For in the following day's final would either be Fernando Gonzalez, the man he had beaten comprehensively in the Madrid final, or his Davis Cup teammate Stanislas Wawrinka.

It turned out to be Gonzalez, who was on the start of a rise up the rankings under the guidance of the experienced American coach Larry Stefanki. But by later October he was still a class below Federer. As with most of their previous matches, Gonzalez had one good set in him, in this case the third, but he lost it on the a 7–3 tiebreak as Federer sealed one of the least significant but most emotional titles of his career – completing the journey from Basel ball boy to Basel champion.

'It's one of the most beautiful moments of my career,' he said, 'and also one of the most important to me after Wimbledon. Although I always wanted to be a professional tennis player, I never dreamed that I would one day be the champion here. It's also my one thousandth day as world number one, so a very fitting day for this to happen, and one of those moments I'll never forget.'

Federer's sixth and final match against Nadal in 2006 seemed strangely out of character. In fact, the biggest thing one could say about it was that it was a match between the world's best two players that wasn't in a final, a situation that hardly ever happens. It only came about in Shanghai thanks to the one tour level round robin format that survived the battering to the round robin's reputation that was to come in Las Vegas three months later.

Nadal had lost in the round robin stages to James Blake, so only qualified for the semi-finals as second in his group. By contrast, Federer had gained revenge on Nalbandian for his defeat in the previous year's final (though it was hardly a real revenge – Nalbandian's mind was elsewhere as his godson had just been killed in an elevator accident and in tennis terms the imminent Davis Cup final between Russia and Argentina was a much bigger priority to him), survived a match point against Andy Roddick and beaten Ivan Ljubicic. As he won his group, it meant he came up against Nadal on the penultimate day of the tournament – if ever there was a reinforcement of Federer's aversion to the round robin format, this was it.

It was their least gripping match of the year, in fact one of the most anonymous matches they have played. Federer won 6–4, 7–5, and his dominance suggested to many that he had finally worked out how to play Nadal. Analysing Federer in the International Herald Tribune, the elegant tennis writer Christopher Clarey wrote: 'It was hardly the best Federer-Nadal duel, nor the most significant. But the match in Shanghai intrigues because of its relatively lop-sided nature, and because of what it said about Federer's drive and focus at the end of a globe-trotting, glad-handing year that would have drained many a top athlete of his energy and ambition. Instead, the Artful Roger (the best of Federer's several sobriquets) was in something like full flight in late November: swooping around the indoor, medium-speed court in Shanghai and giving a hint to his closest pursuer in the rankings, and frequent conqueror in head-to-head matches, that something fundamental had changed between them.'

It hadn't, actually. That result indicated that Nadal had still not learned how to deliver the blistering form he showed in the first half of the year in the second half, and while Federer was to beat Nadal in the following year's Tennis Masters Cup – again in straight sets, again in a semi-final – he had learned little of substance about how to beat Nadal on a regular basis.

Not that it seemed this way as Federer ended the year with his third title in the year-ending event. The ease with which he brushed aside the challenge of the likeable Blake in the final bordered on perfection. Afterwards, showing once again the fine line he manages to tread between the false modesty that would grate and the arrogance that would be equally a turn-off, Federer simply revelled in his achievement. 'I had to laugh at one stage about the way I was playing,' he said after his 6-0, 6-3, 6–4 victory. 'I always came up with a great answer, everything I wanted to do worked. To come to this point in my career where I feel so happy with my game, it's come such a long way that I am out of words really to describe this performance.'

As a display of craftsmanship, it amounted to excellence, yet the lack of a competitive culmination left the Shanghai organisers with a vastly less memorable tournament than the one a year earlier, in which they had torn their hair out in frustration at all the high-profile withdrawals but enjoyed an exhilarating five-sets final. Such is the unpredictability of sport, and the power of a great final to hide from the memory a somewhat dull event overall.

Thus ended a truly phenomenal year for Roger Federer. He surpassed his ultra-impressive years of 2004 and 2005 by a string of achievements: the first professional tennis player to earn $8 million in prize money in a single season (the first to earn $7 million as well) with a new record mark of $8,345,855; the most ranking points in a single year (8,370); the first man in the 'open' era of tennis to win ten or more titles in three consecutive seasons; the first for twenty years to win ninety matches in a season (he won ninety-two of the ninety-seven he contested); and for those who really revel in numbers, he took his winning percentage in finals to 77.2 (fifty-eight played, forty-five won) which elevated him above Pete Sampras on 72.7 per cent, John McEnroe on 71.3 and Björn Borg on 70.5.

But to most people, his single greatest achievement was in falling just one match – or two sets – short of doing a pure, calendar-year Grand Slam. Until Federer's ascent to the summit, it was generally believed that men's tennis was too competitive for anyone to win all four major titles in the same year. Yet here he was, the first man since Rod Laver did the only 'open' Grand Slam in 1969 to reach all four finals in the same year. But for his lame display in Paris against a man who may yet come to be seen as one of the all-time greats of clay-court tennis, he would probably have emulated Laver's achievement.

13

HE CAME EQUALLY CLOSE in 2007. Again three Grand Slams, again falling just two sets short of the fourth, and again Nadal standing in his way. And yet, many tennis watchers claim – with a justification that goes beyond mere twenty-twenty hindsight – that the writing of Federer's relative slump in form in 2008 was on the wall throughout 2007.

Not that there was any absence of quality in Federer's tenth Grand Slam title and third Australian Open. Where his emotional response to victory had been the defining feature of his title a year earlier, unbridled excellence was the leitmotif in 2007. The fact that he didn't have to face Nadal no doubt helped: the Spaniard emerged from an exhilarating five-sets victory over Andy Murray in the fourth round with an injury that made him dead meat against the big-hitting Fernando Gonzalez in the quarter-finals. But Federer did play two outstanding matches in Melbourne that year, and it's possible Murray and Gonzalez saved Nadal from a drubbing, such was the form Federer was in.

The bald statistics can record that he became the first man since Björn Borg at the 1980 French Open to win a Grand Slam singles title without dropping a set, and the first since Ken Rosewall in 1971 to win the Australian Open with the same distinction. But statistics don't do justice to the way he dismissed Novak Djokovic in the fourth round and Andy Roddick in the semis.

The match against Djokovic was their first meeting since the ill-tempered Davis Cup tie in Geneva four months earlier. Since then, Djokovic's stock had risen, and he came to Melbourne having won the tour event in Adelaide two weeks earlier. As the tennis world geared itself up for a classic, Federer simply raised his game, and beat Djokovic 6–2, 7–5, 6–3. The handshake at the net was unusually perfunctory by Federer's standards, despite Djokovic's smile and clear wish to impart a compliment or two. The sting from their spat appeared not to have been entirely eradicated by their *tête à tête* in Madrid.

The other outstanding display was against Andy Roddick, the American being made to pay for his seemingly legitimate comment that he was 'getting closer' to Federer (see page 258).

Despite his aversion to electronic line calling, Federer used one call to great effect in the final against Gonzalez, in which he delivered a performance not quite worthy of the 'genius at work' placard that again appeared in the stadium, but still more than good enough to snuff out the Chilean's challenge. Federer needed to save two set points on Gonzalez's serve at 4–5 in the first set, and a challenge to the electronic adjudication system that he got right gave him a decisive advantage at the start of the first set tiebreak. But the aura Federer had built up meant that Gonzalez was playing the reputation as well as the man. As the match wore on, the mental fatigue wore the challenger down as Federer ran out a 7–6, 6–4, 6–4 champion.

There is a school of thought that has the 2007 Australian Open – Federer's forty-sixth tour title and tenth Grand Slam – as the high point in terms of quality in his entire career. There are some, including Federer himself, who believe the tennis he played at the 2010 Australian Open was better, and in certain matches it probably was. But he had slip-ups in his matches against Igor Andreev and Nikolay Davydenko, dropping sets in both, whereas in Melbourne in 2007, he was consistently majestic from start to finish. It was as close to perfection as a tennis player can reasonably expect to get.

Yet where do you go after achieving perfection? What was to sustain Federer's motivation after a tenth major title? His oft-cited love of the game was in evidence, but was that enough to see him through the grind of the tour?

Signs that he might have been having difficulty motivating himself for events other than the Grand Slams were spotted when he lost twice in successive tournaments to Guillermo Cañas, a quality player on the comeback trail after a fifteen-month ban for taking a prohibited diuretic, but there was no doubt he was up for it when he resumed battle with Nadal on Nadal's favourite surface.

The rivals met in the finals of two of the three big lead-up tournaments to the French Open, Monte Carlo and Hamburg, yet there was something missing from both matches as a spectacle. Instead of celebrating the wonder of the best-of-five-sets format for the finals of its top tier of tournaments, the ATP used the superb drama of the epic Rome finals of 2005 and 2006 as an excuse to abolish the three-of-five-sets finals in all its Masters Series tournaments. It meant that when Nadal beat Federer in Monte Carlo and Federer then beat Nadal in Hamburg, it seemed to have less significance for the up-coming French Open than the Rome final of 2006, which seemed to have undermined Federer's confidence in his ability to win three sets on clay against his great rival. Many were happy to read into Federer's 2–6, 6–2, 6–0 victory in Hamburg proof that he had worked out how to play Nadal on clay, but in truth there were mitigating circumstances. Hamburg's clay is always somewhat lower-bouncing than that of Rome and Paris and Nadal was particularly tired after winning the titles in Indian Wells, Monte Carlo, Barcelona and Rome. In fact, had the two men not been in the vanguard of the players' attempts to show solidarity with Hamburg (the event threatened with the loss of its Masters Series status) it's possible neither might have played the tournament, and by the end Nadal was in serious need of some recuperation before the French Open.

Another interesting factor was that Federer's off-court set-up was in something of an upheaval. His coaching arrangement with Tony Roche, that had seen him win six Grand Slam titles, had slipped into a state of disrepair by the time the clay court season of 2007 came round, and when Federer committed 44 unforced errors to lose his second match in Rome 6-2, 6-4 to Filippo Volandri, a competent Italian who would never normally have threatened a player of Federer's class, even on clay, he promptly parted company with the respected Australian.

How much Federer needs a coach is a question that must always be asked before getting into a discussion of a specific coaching relationship. Having won three Grand Slam titles in 2004 without a coach, and three more in 2007 and 2008 with only informal support, it would be wrong to read too much into the demise of any individual coach of his. But what was interesting about Roche was that Federer was on record as saying he was looking for input as to how to win on clay, and Roche had encouraged him to slice more and go to the net to avoid the baseline wars of attrition that Nadal was always going to win. So for Federer to part company with a man he clearly respected just two weeks before the biggest clay court tournament in the world, and having seldom ventured to the net in his defeat to Volandri, suggested that the two were no longer on the same wavelength. Federer said in Hamburg it was 'a mental problem' and that a lack of communication was the cause – the two apparently didn't speak for nine weeks, despite Federer twice losing unexpectedly to Cañas. He is too discreet to have spoken intimately about it, and Roche's defensiveness with the media means he hasn't spoken at all, but those who saw the pair at close quarters during the Rome tournament were not surprised to see the parting of the ways.

The significance of the Hamburg final was to let the tennis world know that Roche's departure did not amount to Federer hitting the panic button. In fact some even saw it as a form of liberation, especially when he reached a second successive French Open final for the loss of just one set. But while Nadal had forced Federer to improve his clay court game, the reverse had also happened, and the match was to be decided by Nadal's ability to raise his game when danger threatened.

Federer arguably came closer in 2007 than he had in 2006. Although he was never ahead, he took the match to Nadal, attacking with his returns of serve, and created seventeen break points in the four-set final. Yet he converted just one of them, the other sixteen being largely saved by Nadal's burgeoning ability to play perfect tennis on the points that really mattered. By contrast, Nadal was brutal when he had break points on the Federer serve. The crucial break was the one in the second game of the third set, which wiped out all the momentum Federer had worked so hard to build up by taking the second set with a late break that momentarily ended Nadal's dominance. Federer had a break point in the second game of the fourth set, but once Nadal had saved it, he dropped just two more points on his serve in a 6–3, 4–6, 6–3, 6-4 victory.

Speculation about how much that victory had taken out of Federer, both mentally and physically, was fuelled by his decision to skip his hitherto traditional Wimbledon warm-up tournament in Halle. A man who is known for sticking to his word, his withdrawal was something of a shock and it earned him a fine because there was no question of his being injured. Federer returned to Basel to undergo medical tests (he was later to say of this period, 'I couldn't move for a week', so there was some sort of fatigue at play), but he was never going to dress these up as a reason for evading the fine that players incur when they miss without good reason a tournament they have committed to.

The Halle personnel, who were glued to the French Open final despite having the final round of their qualifying tournament to deal with, say they began to fear Federer might withdraw when they observed the change in his body language after he lost the first set. He had ten break points in three successive service games, but failed to convert any of them – 'once the set disappeared, we began to wonder,' said Frank Hofen of the Gerry Weber Open. 'It was during our qualifying tournament party late on Sunday night that Ralf Weber [the Halle tournament director] took a call on his mobile. It was from Roger, and he said he was just not able to play and he needed time to himself if he was to mount a realistic challenge for a fifth Wimbledon title. We got the impression that the fifth Wimbledon was the most important for him because it would put him on a level with Borg.'

A small detail to note is that Federer phoned Weber himself. Many players get their agent or someone else to pass on the message, but Federer carried his own responsibility. As a tournament director of fifteen years' standing, Weber will have known that the only response in such circumstances is to show complete understanding, as anything else will only worsen the chances of getting the player back the following year. But it's easier to show such understanding when the player has the decency to make his own call, and Weber's response was well rewarded, for not only did Federer sign a three-year deal to play at Halle from 2008 to 2010 (a commitment he honoured in 2008) but Weber, a competent club player, got to hit with Federer for half an hour on the Halle centre court during the 2008 event!

The break clearly did Federer good, because he returned to Wimbledon refreshed, and dropped just one set en route to his thirteenth meeting with Nadal. The Spaniard had dropped four in successive back-to-back matches against Robin Söderling and Mikhail Youzhny, and his subsequent performances on grass make it easy to forget that there were many who felt he was vulnerable in 2007, and that his run to the 2006 final had not delivered proof that he was the finished article on grass. The final he played against Federer put an end to any such thoughts.

With Björn Borg sitting in the front row of the Royal Box ready to witness Federer's equalling of his record of five successive Wimbledon titles, the two men played one of the great matches of recent times. It was in one way also unique, because the venerable stadium dating from 1922 was a completely open bowl, the previous roof having been removed but the new structure not yet in place – it gave the arena a most un-Wimbledon-like feel. Like the previous year, Nadal was slow to get going, but this time he got his act together early enough to make his mark, and Federer was taken to five sets for the first time at Wimbledon since he had beaten Pete Sampras in the 2001 fourth round. Many felt Nadal should have won.

Federer squandered a 3–0 lead in the first set, plus a 6–3 lead in the tiebreak before taking the shoot-out 9–7. Nadal should have broken at 3–3 in the second – Federer bounced back to save two break points, but Nadal did break in the tenth game to level the match. Federer had to save break points midway through the third set as Nadal upped his level. The Spaniard was making very few errors, but he played a poor tiebreak as Federer took it 7–3 to claim a two-sets-to-one led.

Nadal was ruthless at the start of the fourth set, reeling off four games as Federer looked lost. But then at 4–1, Nadal needed treatment for a niggle in his right knee. It didn't appear to hinder his movement, but the time it took to get the knee strapped allowed Federer to re-group, and the match was more competitive after that.

Nadal was far enough ahead in the fourth set for the match to go to a fifth, and when he had Federer at 15–40 at both 1–1 and 2–2 in the final set, the champion was wobbling. But Federer weathered the storm, played a superb sixth game to break Nadal, and from then on the Spaniard was broken. Another break made the final score 7–6, 4–6, 7–6, 2–6, 6–2.

A roving microphone caught snippets of Federer's conversation with Björn Borg as the two met in the lobby of the Wimbledon clubhouse after the trophy presentation ceremony. While it may have been a meeting of equals in terms of their Wimbledon achievements, it was decidedly unequal in terms of the conversation. Borg seemed limited in what he felt he should say – his normally easy-going demeanour with contemporaries such as John McEnroe, Mats Wilander and Yannick Noah was constrained in the company of his modern-day equivalent. By contrast, Federer was masterful in his ease of conversation, asking Borg plenty of questions and not getting deterred by the constricted answers he was getting. It was almost as if Borg was in awe of Federer.

Federer was also partly in awe of Nadal. In a formal interview after the match, he said, 'He's a fantastic player and he's going to be around so much longer so I'm happy with every one I get before he takes them all!' There was no doubt an element of politeness in that comment, but it proved remarkably prophetic over the subsequent eighteen months.

The final had been a great contest. It had ended a very wet Wimbledon on a real high, and it had put Nadal firmly on the map as a grass-courter of quality. Indeed there were many who wondered that Sunday night whether it was possibly the greatest Wimbledon final ever. Such musings lasted precisely one year.

As the world number one in a sport with as high a profile as tennis, Roger Federer has been asked to do his fair share of odd stunts. The set with Agassi on the helipad of Dubai's Burj al-Arab hotel was one such (see page 198), and when the ATP rebranded its tour at the start of 2009, he and Nadal were asked to hit some balls on a mini-court built on an Arabian dhow boat. But in May 2007 came probably the oddest of all stunts, staged to celebrate the rivalry between the king of grass and the king of clay.

With Nadal on his unbeaten clay streak and Federer unbeaten for four years on grass, the International Management Group got them to play a 'Battle of the Surfaces' – a match with one half of the court grass, the other half clay. The city tourism office of the Mallorcan capital Palma agreed to host and sponsor the event in the Palma Arena, and half a grass court was installed at an astonishing cost of $1.63 million. Even more astonishing, after nineteen days bedding down, it had to be ripped up again and re-laid (one report said the original grass had suffered an infestation of worms!).

As for the match, it went to the wire, Nadal winning it on a 12–10 third set tiebreak. With the players changing shoes at every change of ends, it was hard not to think of it as a gimmick, but both seemed to want to win the decider. Both men will have been handsomely paid for their efforts, so none of their comments about it can be taken to be a complete picture of what they really felt, but Federer is

Sky high – in February 2005, Federer and Andre Agassi were invited to play on the helipad at the Burj al-Arab hotel in Dubai, 211 metres above the sea.

Federer has been with Mirka Vavrinec, now Federer, since the Sydney
Olympics of 2000 – they got married in a private ceremony in April 2009.
They are pictured here at the Wimbledon Champions' dinner in 2004.

Keeping it in the family – Federer celebrates his 2005 Wimbledon title with his parents, Lynette and Robbie (*above*), while Lynette and Diana Federer watch Roger at the 2005 Tennis Masters Cup in Shanghai (*below*).

Above: Desert classic – Federer has always had a soft spot for the tournaments in Doha and Dubai, and no wonder when they arrange such adventurous outings!

Below: Trophies come in all shapes and sizes – Federer won the Dubai Duty Free Open four years out of five (2003-05 and 2007).

Above: Big weapon – Federer's forehand is the shot with which he wins more points than any other.

Below: Down but not out – even the best grass court soles can't always keep the best grass court player on his feet.

Above: The 'hot dog' – Federer playing the entertaining shot through his legs at the 2005 Australian Open; he tried it on match point in his semi-final against Marat Safin and went on to lose the match.

Below left: For Pete's sake! Federer emulating the 'slam dunk' shot made popular by Pete Sampras, pictured here at the 2004 Tennis Masters Cup in Houston.

Below right: Global statesman – on a visit to a shelter for people affected by the 2004 tsunami in the Indian province of Tamil Nadu, December 2006.

Above left: Birthday boy – on his 27th birthday, Roger carried the Swiss flag for the second time at an Olympics.

Above right: Golden games – Federer in action with his gold-medal-winning doubles partner Stanislas Wawrinka at Beijing in 2008.

Below: Back a winner – after a lapse in form, Federer beat Andy Murray to win the 2008 US Open, to the delight of his fans.

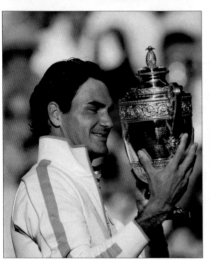

Above left: Young man comforts old – Federer's nemesis Rafael Nadal consoles the emotional former champion after winning the 2009 Australian Open.

Above right: Almost six years after winning his first Grand Slam tournament, Federer completes his set by winning the 2009 French Open. The trophy was presented to him by Andre Agassi.

Below left: Record breaker – his 2009 Wimbledon victory was Federer's 15th Grand Slam win, meaning he had broken Pete Sampras' record of 14.

Below right: Family man – Roger with his pregnant wife Mirka. The couple are now proud parents of twins Charlene Riva and Myla Rose.

always open to new ideas, especially those that are fun, while Nadal had the chance to play on his home island against his principal rival, so everyone got something.

Despite Nadal's achievement in the Wimbledon final, he again proved to have shot his bolt by mid-season. As he faded in the second half of the year, Novak Djokovic emerged as the leading challenger to Federer on hard courts.

The Serb had risen to third in the rankings on the back of semi-final showings at the French Open and Wimbledon, and a superb run in the Masters Series. That run continued when he beat Federer for the first time in the final of the Montreal Masters, and with a superior hard court record to Nadal, he seemed a bigger threat to Federer for the US Open than the Spaniard. Despite his aversion to back-to-back Masters Series tournaments, Federer nevertheless went to and won Cincinnati, which made him still very much the man to beat at Flushing Meadows.

After surviving a marathon second-round match against Radek Stepanek, Djokovic looked set to face Nadal in the semi-finals for the third successive major. But Nadal was beaten by Spain's number two player David Ferrer in the fourth round, leaving Djokovic with a clear run to his first Grand Slam final. With Federer looking slightly below his best, this was Djokovic's chance. But he wasn't able to take it.

Portents of Federer's drop in form in the first half of 2008 were very much in evidence in a final that was Djokovic's for the taking. In particular, the champion's big forehand was misfiring far too often, and he looked nervous in the early stages. The erratic forehand contributed to Djokovic leading

6–5 and 40–0 on his own serve, but Djokovic couldn't close out the set. Five set points went begging, before a double-fault allowed Federer to break back, and he won the set on a 7–4 tiebreak, Djokovic double-faulting on set point.

Djokovic should have won the second set 7–5, but he missed another two set points in the twelfth game, and then saw Federer play his best tennis of the match to take the tiebreak 7–2. Djokovic again had break points at 2–2 in the third, but he was looking increasingly tired and frustrated, and when Federer saved them, he was almost home and dry. A break in the tenth game of the set gave him a 7–6, 7–6, 6–4 victory that was as much attributable to his reputation as to the way he played on the day. It took him to twelve Grand Slam titles, and made him the first man ever to win the Wimbledon and US Open titles in the same year four times in a row.

The fact that Djokovic beat Federer in the Australian Open semi-final four months later suggests it was just inexperience that deprived the Serb of his maiden Grand Slam in September 2007. He joked afterwards that 'my next book will be called *Seven Set Points*', and it could well be that, in processing the defeat, the Serb worked out that he lost the match in his own head rather than on the court, and the only thing he needed to improve was his fear of the great man's reputation. Yet there is an equally compelling argument that Djokovic's success in Melbourne in 2008 was more down to Federer's ill-health than Djokovic being genuinely on the same level, and if one looks back through the head-to-head between the two men, that Australian defeat was the only one that Djokovic won that really mattered to Federer.

Two defeats to David Nalbandian meant Federer didn't add to his Masters Series haul, but he did defend his titles in Basel and the Tennis Masters Cup, the latter featuring another semi-final victory over Nadal. It was the pair's eleventh match, and Federer's easiest victory, though one that didn't mean a lot. The first set was close, but when Federer reeled off thirteen straight points at the start of the second, the contest was over. Federer's 6–4, 6–1 victory meant the head-to-head with Nadal read 8–6 for Nadal, as narrow a gap as Federer had enjoyed since early 2006, but one that was to expand again in 2008. The following day he beat the likeable and honest toiler David Ferrer comfortably in the final to win his fourth Tennis Masters Cup title.

As well as the usual rush of awards, the year ended with Federer playing three exhibition matches in Asia against Pete Sampras, the man he had played only once at tour level: Federer's fourth-round Wimbledon victory in 2001. They took place in Seoul, Kuala Lumpur and Macau. Federer won the first two and Sampras the third, a sequence that fuelled the thought that maybe Federer deliberately lost the third to keep interest alive for another – and bigger – match against Sampras scheduled for New York four months later. Although meaningless in historical terms, the matches seemed a harmless way of earning some extra pocket money, except that they came at the end of a long season which had seen Federer's dominance in the Grand Slams become less pronounced. And it more than likely contributed to Federer's hitherto reliable health suddenly rebelling at the start of 2008.

14

THERE COMES A PERIOD in any top athlete's career when their form dips. It happened to Tiger Woods in golf, it happened to Muhammad Ali in boxing (though with a more dramatic backdrop given his political activities), and it happened to Roger Federer in 2008. In some ways it's a totally natural phenomenon – a player will inevitably find that the constant drag of having to be at one's best the whole time eventually loses its attractiveness, especially after a great run of success. The hunger then goes, and the defeats – particularly those of a hitherto unexpected nature – follow.

There are then two ways to go: back up, or on down. The likes of Björn Borg and Mats Wilander hit that wall in their mid-twenties – both decided it wasn't worth the effort and gave up. They both made minor comebacks, but their best years were gone. By contrast, Jimmy Connors bounced back after seemingly losing his lustre as Borg and John McEnroe reached their respective peaks. The same can be said for

Andre Agassi, who was down to 141 in the rankings in November 1997 but returned to become French Open champion eighteen months later. In other sports, Muhummad Ali's regaining of the world heavyweight title against George Foreman in 1973 is one of boxing's defining moments; and Tiger Woods rebounded from a loss of form to add to his haul of major titles, until knee surgery and some high-profile sexual infidelity caused a second watershed in his career.

Roger Federer hit that watershed in the first half of 2008. There were extenuating circumstances, such as his health, but his air of invincibility disappeared. Viewed with the benefit of hindsight, it was hardly a disastrous period – in the first six months of the year, he reached two Grand Slam finals and one semi-final – and the fact that he went on to regain his number one ranking and beat Pete Sampras's record of Grand Slam singles titles in 2009 makes it seem like a blip. But in the fiercely competitive world of top-level sport, Federer went from being the untouchable at the top of the game to the wounded beast everyone was gunning for. And that spawned all sorts of theories about whether these were the early signs of a permanent decline, and whether there was some discontent in his private life.

The first indication that Federer might be a lesser force than he had been in 2006 and 2007 came in the third round of the Australian Open when it took him four hours to beat the steady but unremarkable Janko Tipsarevic. He eventually won the match 10–8 in the final set, which finally finished at 4.30 the following morning. When a listless display against another Serb, Novak Djokovic, in the semi-finals resulted in Federer's first defeat in Melbourne since the dramatic Safin semi-final of 2005, there were plenty ready to hail a decline in the great man's fortunes.

But there had been mitigating circumstances for these uncharacteristic performances. A week before the Australian Open, Federer had spent a night in a Sydney hospital with an upset stomach, which the doctors had initially thought was due to food poisoning. When his condition improved, the initial diagnosis appeared to have been confirmed. However, it seems few people knew then that Federer had come very close to missing his first Grand Slam tournament since the 1999 US Open, or that he was actually suffering from much more than just tummy trouble.

When Federer went on to lose to Andy Murray in the first round in Dubai and then failed to make much of an impression on either the American hard courts or the European clay-court circuit, there were many who were ready to believe that this was more than a mere blip in form and that perhaps Federer's career had, in fact, peaked. By the time he arrived at the French Open, he was something of a marked man. He had just one title to his name, the modest Estoril tournament in the Portuguese capital Lisbon, and he had lost to Nadal in the Hamburg final in another match which showed that not even the biggest lead Federer built up against his Spanish rival was impregnable. Yet, ironically, the French Open was the tournament he was supposed to be best prepared for.

At the end of 2007, Federer's fitness coach Pierre Paganini had made a few changes to the December practice schedule and to the regular regime in the early part of 2008, with the intention of having Federer in optimum shape by the time he arrived in Paris. However, those efforts were being undermined at the very time they were being undertaken. Unbeknown to all of Federer's entourage, the player was suffering from the strength-sapping mononucleosis, often known as glandular fever. He says he had it during the Australian Open, which, if that is the case, makes his victory over Tipsarevic and run to the semi-finals a remarkable achievement. He also says he had it very lightly, which explains why he missed very little time on the tour. But the nature of glandular fever is that, while the illness itself may be short-lived, the after-effect of fatigue can linger for several months, and doctors generally advise sufferers to give up sport for at least four weeks after 'mono' is diagnosed. He may well have had a very mild dose, but, looking back on Federer's 2008, the fact that he played on through it means it is medically quite plausible that it robbed him of strength for the first half of the year.

In retrospect, Federer's decision to play the three exhibition matches against Pete Sampras in Asia after the 2007 Tennis Masters Cup looks somewhat misguided. After a long and hard season, surely he should have rested, rather than played three interesting but ultimately meaningless matches against a man no longer in his prime. He was clearly handsomely rewarded for his efforts (some reports claimed he received $1 million per match, although fees for exhibition matches are seldom made public and are highly susceptible to exaggeration), and which of us would turn down such an offer, especially for an attractive assignment? By playing in Seoul, Kuala Lumpur and Macau, he could also claim to be doing his bit to spread the tennis gospel in places that are by-passed by the global tennis tours. But, even with the benefit of hindsight, he still chose to play three more exhibition matches in Asia at the end of 2008. Perhaps he figured the exhibitions would do nothing to undermine his general health. Interestingly, although his IMG agent Tony Godsick was on the record as saying Federer was cutting down on his exhibition matches, Federer began 2009 with two different exhibitions in the run-up to the Australian Open.

That having been said, it would be wrong to view his fourth exhibition with Sampras in March 2008 in the same light as the three in Asia three months earlier. The two met in a massively hyped occasion in Madison Square Garden, New York, in a match aimed at raising money for a programme to make vaccines available to people in poorer parts of the world. It was sponsored by the Net Jets company, which hires out private jets and which counts Federer as one of its best clients. It was also Federer's chance to play at the prestigious Madison Square Garden, a venue he was happy to describe as 'the greatest arena in the world'. Wearing an outfit all in black, to contrast with the angelic white of Sampras (very deliberately, as the two are clad by the same clothing company!), Federer won the match on a final-set tiebreak in front of 19,000 spectators. Taken as a sporting comparison of the two greats, it told the world little or nothing it didn't already know, but as a one-off competitive match, chance to experience playing in a historic venue and fundraising opportunity, it had some value.

Despite the spirited challenges of six players, Federer still made it to the Roland Garros final, to set up a third successive decider with Nadal. If Federer had done enough to get through the early stages without too much turbulence, Nadal had looked positively imperious in his run to the final, which involved no dropped sets and some crushing defeats for accomplished players, such as Nicolas Almagro and the Australian Open champion Novak Djokovic. To the sanguine observer, it appeared Nadal was in a class of his own and Federer was a step slower to the ball.

All that was overlooked on the morning of the final, as people got psyched up for what, for the third year running, was set to be Federer's moment of history. There were suggestions that he hadn't played well up to the final because he was saving everything for an assault on Nadal, and that a new Federer would turn up for the title decider. With the wily Spanish coach José Higueras in his corner, Federer clearly had a game plan based around attacking Nadal with his big forehand at the first opportunity.

The plan made sense, but the gun misfired. Federer was broken in the opening game as he made three forehand errors, and the writing was on the wall. He seemed to be making a match of it in the second set, but once he missed a chance to go 4–3 up, he didn't win another game, and Nadal handed out a humiliating 6–1, 6–3, 6–0 drubbing.

As Federer climbed on to the rostrum at the prize-giving ceremony to the sound of polite applause, he took the microphone and said, 'Oui, c'est moi' (yes, it's me) to the crowd. It was a neat encapsulation of how the man everyone had come to respect as arguably the greatest player of all time could look so unlike himself.

How much that defeat undermined his confidence and played a part in the outcome of the magnificent Wimbledon final they played four weeks later is difficult to gauge. A feature of the following four weeks was the amount of times he was to say that the severity of the loss wouldn't affect him if he met

Nadal at Wimbledon. To a certain extent, one must sympathise with players who get asked the same question over and over again, each journalist thinking he or she is the first to ask it. But there were times when Federer was volunteering the information unbidden, and it did tend to evoke a paraphrased line from Shakespeare: 'Methinks he doth protest too much.'

Whether Federer's sense of belief against Nadal had indeed been undermined by his crushing defeat in Paris, or whether Nadal was simply doing what he does best – moving his game relentlessly to a level few previously considered him capable of – what followed 28 days after the Paris massacre was a contest which surely has to make it into anyone's list of the ten greatest tennis matches of all time: the Wimbledon final of 2008.

In the run-up to the final, it seemed plenty of people were wondering whether the crushing defeat in Paris indicated that Federer was still suffering from the continuing after-effects of the glandular fever, although Federer denied that he was in any way below his peak of health. After winning his fifth Halle title with a level of play that rose steadily during his five matches, he said, 'People tell me when they saw my matches in Paris that I still have it in my system. I honestly don't feel it. I'm happy when people worry for me, but I don't wake up a single day any more feeling sick or tired or anything, so I'm not feeling the after-effects any more. The important thing was to be able to back up match after match, which I did since Indian Wells – I'm third in the number of matches played this year behind Rafa and Davydenko, so I'm really really pleased the way it's been going. This week wasn't a problem after the tough French Open, and things are looking good; it's where I want to be at this stage of the year.'

Federer also claimed – with some justification – that his defeat by Nadal in the Roland Garros final should not make people think he had had a poor French Open. And, when he stormed into the semi-finals at Wimbledon, it did seem to be a case of a few warm-up matches before his now customary meeting with Nadal in the final. The way he dismissed Lleyton Hewitt in the fourth round and the potentially more dangerous Mario Ancic in the quarter-finals was clinical. However, he faced a class act in the semis in the form of Marat Safin, the mercurial Muscovite who had dumped the third-seeded Novak Djokovic out of the tournament in the second round and gone further at Wimbledon than he had ever gone before.

Safin had taken a set off Federer in a superb Halle final in 2005. Now back in a Grand Slam semi-final for the first time since his Australian Open triumph in January 2005, all seemed set for a superb contest. Yet Federer snuffed it out with a three-set victory, which left some doubting how much Safin really believed he could win; it may also have eroded Safin's confidence for their meeting at the 2009 Australian Open, which Federer also won in straight sets despite Safin playing a very good match. More importantly, it established Federer as the champion who had finally rediscovered his best form. With Nadal demolishing Andy Murray and Rainer Schüttler to set up a third successive Federer–Nadal final, Wimbledon had the showdown it wanted, with both players seemingly in great form. Yet few could have expected the contest the two men delivered on a damp Sunday, 6 July.

As discussed elsewhere in this book (see page 194), what makes a match one of the all-time great contests is difficult to define. Obviously, a high level of tennis is an essential ingredient, as is the presence of at least one great player. But there are many great matches between great players, so many, in fact, that only a few stand out after the short-term memory has faded.

There is normally an extra component, a certain element that heightens the tension. It could be festering animosity between the players, or even extraneous circumstances that have nothing to do with tennis. Neither factor applies to Federer and Nadal; the two men are, in their different ways, so charming and inherently generous that their rivalry is based on a strict demarcation between intense competition on court and mutual respect bordering on friendship off it.

But there were two extra components in the 2008 Wimbledon final. The first was the historic nature of the moment, which would have been significant whatever the result. On one side of the net was Federer, looking to become the first man since William Renshaw in 1886 to win six Wimbledon titles in a row, and to go one better than Björn Borg, who in 1981 had fallen to a rising upstart of a left-hander in the match that would have given him six titles (a man he had beaten in five sets in the previous year's final). On the other side was Nadal, the undisputed king of clay who had set his heart on doing something that would really impress his countryfolk: winning Wimbledon. The second was the fact that the final finished in near darkness. There are many who say the most prestigious tournament on the global tennis calendar should never have been allowed to end in such gloom, and it's a powerful argument, but it unquestionably added to the drama.

The first set had tennis of an extrememly high quality. After his slow starts in the previous two finals, Nadal was quick off the mark, and broke Federer in the third game, a strike that sufficed for the first set. When Federer led 4–1 in the second, the match looked set for parity, but, with Nadal reeling off five straight games to take a 6–4, 6–4 lead, the champion was suddenly facing an uphill battle. Although he was to rally, those five games probably cost him the match.

When Federer trailed 0–40 on his own serve at 3–3 in the third set, Nadal looked like repeating his drubbing of Federer in Paris. But the champion found some of his best serves just when he needed them, and, with rain then forcing an eighty-minute interruption as the third set neared its conclusion, Federer had the chance to regroup. He came out looking more positive, and played by far the better tiebreak as the match went into a fourth set.

Nadal kept up his level, and, when he had Federer at 4–5, 0–30, the Spaniard was just two points from the title. Federer survived that storm but then found himself in deep trouble as Nadal led 5–2 in the tiebreak, again just two points from victory. The lead involved a double-minibreak, but Nadal – looking strangely unconfident for possibly the only time in his career – then played two of his worst service points to allow Federer back on-serve. Federer blew a set point at 6–5, and at 7–6 Nadal had championship point. Federer saved it with an unreturnable serve, but a stunning forehand passing shot gave Nadal a second championship point, this time on his own serve. Nadal followed his serve with a crosscourt forehand which seemed to push Federer hopelessly out of court, yet Federer calmly moved into position and stroked the most sublime backhand into the corner of Nadal's court.

'It was one of my first backhand passing shots all match,'

Federer said afterwards. 'With his forehand, I thought it was all over, so for me to come out with that one was a great feeling. I really thought, with winning last year in five and getting the momentum, that would be enough.'

With the tiebreak recalling the epic Borg–McEnroe tiebreak from the 1980 final – when McEnroe too saved one of six championship points with a stunning backhand winner – the tide ebbed and flowed. At 9–8, Federer had his second set point, this time on his own serve; Nadal's backhand went long, and the match was into a final set.

With the clock approaching eight in the evening, and the skies still leaden, the first fears that the final might not be completed that day began to surface. When rain interrupted play at 2–2 in the final set, those fears intensified. Wimbledon was desperately keen to get the match finished – going into a 'third Monday' is a logistical nightmare, and it rather wrecks the glitz of its official Champions Dinner on the Sunday night if one of the two singles champions hasn't been decided. The rain break proved short-lived, the players returned to the court at 8.20pm, with the meteorologists giving them 45–60 minutes of dry weather, and about the same in daylight.

If Federer had profited from the first rain break, the second break favoured Nadal. Although Federer served first and therefore had Nadal frequently just two points from defeat, Nadal never looked seriously threatened on his serve, while Federer seemed to have lost some of the bite from his fourth-set triumph. At 6–6 the players glanced up at the umpire, Pascal Maria, who himself glanced at the referee Andrew Jarrett. The signal was to play two more games. At 7–7, Federer looked for the signal to come off, but they were again told to play two more games. Nadal then broke Federer, and, despite losing the first point of the 16th game, held on to claim his first Wimbledon title as a Federer forehand went into the net.

The television footage of that match point, Nadal's fourth, is no guide to just how dark it was, as the cameras make it seem lighter than in reality. If Pete Sampras had beaten Pat Rafter in the gloaming in 2000, at least that was on an evening with relatively clear skies, and pretty much on the stroke of nine o'clock. This was an overcast day, with the final ball struck at 9.17pm. The brightness of the flashbulbs that illuminated Nadal's ecstatic fall to the turf, followed by his precarious walk up to his entourage and then over the fragile roof of NBC's commentary box to greet Crown Prince Felipe and Princess Letizia, and his holding of the trophy, testify to just how dark it had become.

Nadal admitted as much when, on the stroke of one o'clock in the morning, he strode, immaculately dressed and coiffed, into London's Intercontinental hotel to attend the Champions Dinner. His few words to the guests included the line: 'I couldn't see nothing at the end!'

In his post-match comments, Federer agreed, but he was in a more difficult position about saying so when he faced the media in his post-match press conference. He was well aware that, if he had said anything that could be remotely construed as complaining about the match conditions, there were members of the British media who would be only too happy to write 'Federer loses the final, and the ability to lose with dignity'. Therefore, he declined to comment in English about the light, saying merely, 'What can I say? It's over, so. What's the point in arguing about it? It's the way it is.' But in French and German, he was more forthcoming, saying, 'I could hardly see what I was playing at the end. The most important tournament in the world is decided in a light that isn't playable.'

Federer clearly felt that he and Nadal should have come back to finish the match the next day, but there are two important points to be made about this which are not readily appreciated. Firstly, the following day it drizzled at Wimbledon until mid-afternoon, which meant that, had they stopped at 6–6, 7–7 or 8–8, one of the great Wimbledon finals would have dragged on through a mist of cloud gazing and weather forecasting, before possibly being decided in a few anticlimactic minutes late on Monday afternoon. Such a final was surely worth more than that, and Andrew Jarrett showed good judgement in trying to get the match finished on the Sunday night. Secondly, over the whole match, Nadal had clearly been the better player. Federer looked slow in the first set, he seemed to have no answer to Nadal's surge in the second, he missed countless break points, and he was even slightly fortunate in the timing of the first rain break near the end of the third set. Even after his escapology in the fourth-set tiebreak, he never really looked like using that momentum to turn the screw on Nadal, and the Spaniard always seemed the more likely player to break serve as dusk set in. The triumph for Federer was that it was a rearguard action that very nearly succeeded in spite of his overall level – admirable though the champion's fighting qualities were, it was not a match he deserved to win more than Nadal did.

Apart from setting the record for the longest final in Wimbledon's history – at four hours forty-eight minutes it was more than half an hour longer than the McEnroe–Connors final of 1982 – Nadal had done what

Federer had until then always failed to do: win the French Open and Wimbledon in the same year. In fact, he became the first person to do it since Borg in 1980, another indication that Nadal was matching Borg's achievements as much as Federer was.

A feature of Federer's general disposition is the dignified way he is able to deal with defeat. However, after that final, his body language and tone of voice in his post-match press conference were most uncharacteristic. At the start, he was as dismissive as he has ever been and he only warmed up a little as the cathartic effect of talking about the match seemed to take hold. When asked what he was feeling, he replied, 'Nothing, it's over, I'm not feeling much, I'm disappointed. It's a disaster, I'm not joking. I'd prefer to lose the way I did in Paris than the way I did here.'

The media were keen to know whether he thought it was the greatest match ever, an understandable question, but one Federer was understandably keen not to get into. 'It's not up to us to judge whether it was the best ever,' he said, 'it's up to fans and media to debate. I'm happy Rafa and I put in a great effort, it was a fair battle which was tough with the rain delays. We both played tough till the very end, but in tennis there are no draws, there has to be a winner and a loser.'

Without resorting excessively to cliché or purple prose, there were actually two winners and one loser that day. Nadal won the match, Federer lost it, and the whole of tennis, if not the whole of sport, won through the sheer quality and drama of one of the best pieces of sporting theatre tennis has ever produced. Federer can be forgiven for not seeing that in the immediate aftermath of defeat, but he has since realised what a very special day it was.

In March 2008, a seemingly minor development took place in Federer's life that is worth noting. People may say it had nothing to do with his form – or loss of it – and it is an incidental detail in a sportsman's overall career. The development itself was no more than a house move, but there was a little more to it than merely quitting one building for another.

In the spring of 2008, it emerged that Federer no longer lived in Basel. And the news did 'emerge' – 'the Basel press heard about it after it had happened, almost as if he didn't want people to know about it,' says Beat Caspar of the *Basler Zeitung* newspaper. 'One can only assume he was embarrassed about it.'

It would be wrong to jump to adverse conclusions. Federer likes his home city, and clearly feels comfortable there. The words of the Basel tennis impresario Roger Brennwald about Björn Borg in the 1970s ring true for Federer today. 'Roger Federer can walk through the centre of Basel without bodyguards,' says Brennwald. 'I had Borg here in 1975 when he was the idol of the masses, and he said "I like coming to Basel, I can walk down the streets freely without being harrassed" and I've never forgotten that. You can walk down the street in Switzerland as a world star, which the stars appreciate.'

Federer and Mirka swapped their flat in the Oberwil suburb of Basel for a house on the banks of the Zurich Lake in Wollerau, in the canton of Schwyz. In scenery terms, it is an improvement on Basel – Schwyz is right at the heart of Switzerland, one of the four cantons that founded the Helvetic Confederation in 1291, the Swiss German name for Switzerland 'Schweiz' is derived from Schwyz, and it is so pure chocolate-box picturesque that you almost expect a purple cow to appear chewing the cud.

Perhaps more significant than the scenery, Canton Schwyz has a markedly lower level of taxation than the canton of Basel-Land in which Federer had lived all his life. Working on 2006 figures, its overall tax liability was 68.5% of the Swiss national average, while Basel-Land's was 96.2%. New financial regulations mean those figures are somewhat out of date, but if anything the discrepancy between Basel-Land and Schwyz is even greater now. A calculation based on an income of ten million Swiss francs a year (well below Federer's annual income) shows a resident of Wollerau would have a tax bill more than fifty percent lower than the same resident in Oberwil. Schwyz's tax level has also attracted other sports stars, notably Switzerland's top female tennis player Patty Schnyder, another exile from Basel who now lives near Wollerau in the village of Baech.

One thing the move to Wollerau allowed for was a bigger room to house his growing collection of trophy replicas. And that extra space prompted Federer to make use of an opportunity that Wimbledon offered him in 2008.

Up to and including the 2006 championships, Wimbledon awarded all its champions half-sized replicas of the trophies they had won. In 2007, it decided to make the replicas three-quarter-sized, so Federer's fifth replica was 50 per cent bigger than the other four. Because he is so proud of his Wimbledon record and because the place means so much to him, in 2008, Federer bought three-quarter-sized replicas for the first four years he won the title, in order to make up the full set. The All England Lawn Tennis and Croquet Club doesn't like talking about money, so it is not known how much Federer had to fork out, but, as the replicas are gold plated, they would not have come cheap.

The assumption after Federer's Wimbledon defeat was that he was now bound to lose his number-one ranking. But it wasn't a done deal. While Nadal was entering the least productive part of his year – at least on the basis of past form – Federer was returning to the hard courts where he was still a major contender; and he still had a lead of a couple of hundred points at the top of the rankings. But the damage inflicted by Nadal in Paris and Wimbledon was to have a continuing impact.

With the Olympics forcing the two hard-court Masters Series tournaments, Toronto and Cincinnati, to begin just two weeks after the end of Wimbledon, neither Federer nor Nadal had the time off that they needed. But, while Nadal bounced back to win Toronto and reach the semi-finals in Cincinnati, Federer lost his first match in Toronto and his second in Cincinnati. And his tone appeared to be that of a broken man.

After losing to Gilles Simon of France in Toronto from 3–1 up in the final set, Federer described the defeat as 'one of those matches I think I should never have lost' but, when asked about the four unforced errors he made in the final game, he replied, 'It's all a blur right now.'

When asked sympathetically, 'It seems you were mentally and physically drained since Wimbledon. Is that fair?' he replied, 'You wouldn't have asked me that if I'd have won, right?' and offered no more. And when a journalist asked, 'Do you agree with Justine Henin's decision to retire at the peak of her career?' (referring to Henin's sudden retirement two months earlier while well ahead at the top of the women's rankings), Federer retorted, 'Do I agree with that? Not today. Ask me another day, please. Don't kill me with questions like this.'

A week later, after he just scraped home in Cincinnati against Robby Ginepri, he talked about a 'one-match winning streak'. Ginepri had summed up the mood in the locker room by saying it was a good time to play Federer because 'he used to be a little more confident with his forehand and could win points more quickly, now he's a little more hesitant – I think guys have seen that he's human.'

Federer dismissed this, but two days later he lost again, this time to Ivo Karlovic on two tiebreaks.

With Nadal reaching the semi-finals at a time of Federer's abject form, the Spaniard had guaranteed himself the number-one ranking. Because of the intricacies of the generally logical 52-week rolling ranking system, the actual ascent to the top was to be delayed by two weeks, but the crown prince had acceded to the throne, and Federer's run at the top came to an end after a record 237 consecutive weeks.

He was gracious in his demotion. 'When I got to number one, I said I hoped I would keep it until someone else came along and took it from me,' he said. 'I didn't want to lose it because I was playing badly and it just slipped to someone else, so I'm pleased with what Rafa had to achieve to get it. If I'd lost first round in Paris and Wimbledon, I wouldn't be so nonchalant, but Rafa deserves it for sure.'

An interesting footnote to this period came in the offices of a Swiss newspaper. After Wimbledon, the sports editor told his long-standing tennis correspondent that he wasn't sending him to the US Open 'because Federer was finished'. No doubt financial considerations also played a part in the decision – the dollar was strengthening against the Swiss franc and the world economy was about to go into convulsions – but it seemed an easy decision to justify on sporting grounds.

The correspondent concerned asked not to be identified, nor his paper named, to save his boss from embarrassment. For, however much the boss in question saved financially, it was to prove a major sporting misjudgement.

Not that it seemed so for the first couple of weeks. Federer dismissed his defeat by Karlovic in Cincinnati by saying he was focusing more on the two big hard-court tournaments, the Olympics and the US Open, hoping that a good result in one of them could 'save' his year. There was no questioning his motivation for his third quest for an Olympic medal. But what of his form going into the Beijing Olympics?

What tennis has got from its return to the Olympic fold in the 1980s was always clear: the Olympic cachet that allowed all sorts of money to flow into the coffers of tennis-development projects that almost certainly would have gone to other sports if tennis had remained non-Olympic. What the Olympics got in return was never quite so clear. Until the first days of August 2008, that is.

When Federer and Nadal arrived at Beijing's new international airport, they attracted all the attention. Nadal arrived at the same time as Michael Phelps, the American swimmer who was a sensation even before the eight gold medals he won in China, but it was Nadal who garnered most of the publicity. In fact, most of the tennis players were captured on camera by the official television feed during the spectacular opening ceremony. Tennis's big names were enhancing the Olympics' credibility as the greatest spectacle involving the world's biggest sports stars.

Federer had long since decided that, for his third Olympics, he would not live in the Olympic village because he had been pestered so much in Athens by other athletes wanting their photo taken with him that he had had no privacy. In fact, his hotel room in Beijing had been booked as early as 2005. While some criticised Federer's decision to avoid the village, two separate incidents emphatically justified his reason for it.

On his 27th birthday, Federer did what few athletes have ever achieved – he carried his country's flag in an Olympic opening ceremony for the second time. He entered the arena and led the Swiss team around the stadium to their allotted space inside the parade track. No sooner had the Swiss reached their destination than a whole horde of other athletes descended on Federer, asking to have their photo taken with him. Federer obliged for as long as the structure of the ceremony allowed.

Two days later, he went to visit some friends in the Olympic village. In total, he spent 45 minutes signing autographs and being photographed. As one whose romance began in the Olympic village in Sydney eight years earlier, it had not been an easy decision to stay outside the village in Beijing, but for practical reasons it had proved to be totally justified.

In the tennis event, he was blessed with a reasonable draw; in fact, in his second-round match the greatest threat seemed to come from his opponent's name. He faced Rafael Arevalo, ranked 447, the first player of note to come from El Salvador. Arevalo's support team went out chanting, 'Come on, Rafa,' in the hope of unsettling Federer, but Arevalo was no Nadal, and Federer beat the Olympic wildcard 6–2, 6–4.

But then calamity struck. On day five of the eight-day tennis event, Federer came up against James Blake. Thunder, lightning and heavy rain had delayed the start of play for three and a half hours, and, when it did finally begin, Federer again looked diffident on the crucial points. Blake played a great match, but it was another of those that Federer would have won over the previous five years. Federer was ahead early in the second set tiebreak, but after squandering his advantage with a ridiculously tame volley that seemed to sum up his fragile confidence, he went on to lose 6–4, 7–6.

He was looking jinxed at the Olympics. His missed bronze in Sydney, his defeat to Berdych in Athens, and now this. Maybe Federer was fated never to get an Olympic medal, or so it seemed that Thursday night. But then the all-round skills of the man earned him the gold he had craved, and turned round his year.

It's a fact that few specialist doubles players like to admit, but most of them can only earn a living out of doubles because the leading singles players seldom play doubles. With the exception of a few quality pairs at the top of the game, notably the Bryan twins, top singles players who take to the doubles court in Davis Cup ties frequently beat high-ranking doubles players. And the Olympic doubles event is arguably the highest-quality doubles tournament in world tennis, simply because it attracts the top singles players (there were even three occasions in Beijing where a player pulled out of the singles to improve their chances of a doubles medal – something virtually unthinkable on the regular tour).

Federer had a choice of partners, between his former flatmate Yves Allegro and Stanislas Wawrinka. He had played with Allegro in Athens and in Davis Cup ties, but had played just twice with Wawrinka and lost in the first round on both occasions. But Wawrinka was enjoying the best year of his career and had given Switzerland two players in the men's top ten for the first time ever, and so Federer opted for 'Stan'.

After routine wins in the first two rounds, the competition suddenly got very stiff. The pair had to beat the Indians Mahesh Bhupathi and Leander Paes in the quarter-finals, and then the same day the Bryan brothers. In bright sunshine after lots of rain, they beat Bhupathi and Paes 6–2, 6–4, after which they indulged in a strange routine. Wawrinka lay down on his back, and Federer held his hands over him as if warming them over a hot fire. 'It's a private joke,' Wawrinka explained. 'It comes from cards, the story of fire, the story of being on fire. It developed naturally after we beat the world number-one pair.'

It actually developed after the Bhupathi–Paes victory, but there was no doubt both men were on fire against the top-ranked Bryan brothers. This was the match that would guarantee Federer a medal if the Swiss won, but would leave him still to win a play-off if they lost. And, when the Californian twins had break points in the opening game, it appeared that the opposition was going to be just too tough.

But that was the one chance the Bryans had. The Swiss came through, and were never broken after that, winning 7–6, 6–4, thanks to breaking Mike Bryan's serve in the seventh game of the second set, the only break of the match.

The danger then was to take the final too easily. In the bottom half of the draw, the fancied pairs had gradually tumbled, leaving the veteran Swedes Simon Aspelin and Thomas Johansson standing between Federer and gold. The score in the gold-medal match reads 6–3, 6–4, 6–7, 6–3, but, with no disrespect to the Swedes who had won the longest-ever three-set match at the Olympics to reach the final, there was only one pair in it, and Aspelin and Johansson did well to win the third set.

As Federer stood on the rostrum listening to the strains of the Swiss national anthem, while the white cross on its red background was raised, a gold medal round his neck, his year had been 'saved'. All the talk about his decline had suddenly been eclipsed, not because the decline was in some way fictitious – it was very real – but because he had filled one of the few remaining gaps in his impressive collection of titles.

'Right now this is quite a surreal moment,' he said after winning gold, his voice just starting to crack with emotion. 'The joy of sharing this victory with somebody else who I like very much, who we had a great two weeks with, it's quite different to anything I've ever gone through. I could only maybe compare it a little bit to some incredible Davis Cup victories I've ever had.'

That was the change in Federer. He had won his much-longed-for Olympic medal, and it had come not by himself but with the help of a partner. It had not been The Roger Federer Show with a little help from Stanislas Wawrinka; in fact, if anything Wawrinka had played better in the final, showing a confidence that betrayed no sense of being cowed by the presence of his more illustrious partner. And Federer seemed to appreciate that. 'I think I'm definitely going to play the [Davis Cup] first round next year,' he told the media after the doubles final, although other issues ultimately prevented him from playing the first-round tie the following year.

A team competition had helped 'save' Federer's year, and he promised to be a more committed team player after that.

Sport is full of turning points, and naturally the tennis world was keen to see whether Federer's gold medal would prove pivotal to his year. But it went a little deeper than that, and there seemed as much interest in whether Federer had changed as a person, and whether he would acknowledge that his slump had ended in a team environment – not just in doubles but as part of a wider team of athletes – and thus indicate a change in attitude to the wider team ethic.

Initial indications at the US Open suggested that nothing had changed for him as a singles player. In the second round he laboured to a 6–3, 7–5, 6–4 victory over the 137th-ranked Brazilian Thiago Alves. And his language after the match gave no indication that he had turned a corner. Asked about some easy shots he had missed, he replied, 'Well, I guess we're talking about it today and if I win the title you forget about it again. That's usually how it goes.'

Given that he did win the title, such comments are justified in hindsight, but, on the day itself, talk of winning the title seemed fanciful. In fact, there were numerous members of the tennis media family – including this one – who were convinced on that Friday night that Federer was in denial. He was beginning to sound like a former champion trying to convince himself despite all evidence to the contrary that he could still win the major titles. With a third-round match against Radek Stepanek, one of the players to have beaten him earlier in the year, coming up, it seemed Federer was in for something of a reality check.

Perhaps the quality of the opponent helped focus Federer's mind. Whatever his public utterances, he must have known he could not have got past Stepanek with the quality of play he showed against Alves. Whatever went on in his mind and his camp, he came out against the talented Czech with a new sense of purpose. Not only did he win 6–3, 6–3, 6–2, but the whole performance was that of a reborn man. Where in recent months his forehand had broken down on him, this time it worked to perfection, and, while previously he had shuffled around his backhand to hit the big forehand, this time he danced boxer-like, creating the impression of a man allowing his talent to overwhelm his opponent. Federer was back.

Not that he breezed through the rest of the tournament. He needed five sets in windy conditions to beat Igor Andreev, an immensely likeable Russian with a massive forehand, and there was only one break of serve in his straight-sets win over Gilles Müller. That took him into a semi-final line-up that reflected the new elite in men's tennis – Federer facing Novak Djokovic in the bottom half of the draw, with Nadal facing the rising Andy Murray in the top half. All looked set for the first Federer–Nadal final on hard courts in a Grand Slam event.

Federer did his bit. On a day when the imminent arrival of a hurricane forced an uncharacteristically prompt start of play at Flushing Meadows, Federer gained revenge for his Australian Open defeat against Djokovic by beating the Serb in four sets. It was a popular win; Djokovic had been booed off court following his win over Andy Roddick in the quarter-finals after receiving treatment for an injury. Then Murray did much of Federer's spadework for him, beating Nadal in four sets to reach his first Grand Slam final.

If Murray had beaten Nadal, he was surely a match for Federer. But not this time. While Murray would go on to beat Federer in lesser matches, this was a Grand Slam final, and Federer, in his 17th, would make Murray pay for his lack of experience. But, even more than that, Nadal's game provides problems for Federer, in particular the left-hander's use of the full width of the court and the heavy topspin that Federer finds hard to counter. Murray, while no easy player, is more within Federer's reach, and the Swiss was suddenly a red-hot favourite.

Using the dancing footwork to crunch his big forehand, Federer made his statement early, opening with an ace and breaking Murray in the sixth and eighth games. A little lucky with some line calls in the second set, Federer again knew when to press home his advantage, breaking in the 12th game for a two-set lead and, with it, effectively the match. His 13th Grand Slam title was achieved with a 6–2, 7–5, 6–2 scoreline and his celebration at the end smacked of vindication following eight months of people writing him off.

He was quick to acknowledge the role his Olympic gold medal had played in his US Open triumph. 'I think that's what really made the big difference,' he said after beating Murray. 'If I wouldn't have played doubles at the Olympics, I would have come here with three tough losses. But with the Olympic gold in doubles, it really sort of made me forget about it, and just come in here and enjoy this tournament.' He also said he felt the Andreev five-setter was the key to the tournament. Although that may be how it felt to him, to the watching tennis world, it was the Stepanek match which got him back on track, as it sent out a signal to the world that the old Federer was back.

But was it the old Federer? The US Open title was certainly a vindication, but was it a total rehabilitation? Well, of sorts, yes. But events four months later were to suggest that Nadal had moved on to a different level.

The fact that Federer won just one more tournament in the rest of 2008 to finish the year with four – his lowest total since 2002 – should not be seen as having too much significance. After winning a third successive title in Basel, he finished the year on two defeats to the increasingly impressive Andy Murray, the first of them in Madrid when Federer was fully fit, the second in Shanghai when he was fighting off a back strain that was to dog him into 2009. Both went deep into final sets, and the results suggested that Murray was catching Federer as the Scot's level improved and Federer's remained largely static. It was hard to fully assess Murray's wins, including three more at the start of 2009, as Federer's motivation is at its highest in the Grand Slams, where they had played just once (in the US Open final), but the threat posed by Murray certainly seemed to be reaching a similar level to that of Nadal.

As Pete Sampras frequently said in the twilight years of his career when his 'only' title of note was Wimbledon, 'Any year in which I win a major has to be a good year.' Federer had not only won a major, but he had also won it against the grain of a growing feeling that he might have peaked. And he had the gold medal too – if that was a bad year, there are many players, world number ones even, who would gladly have settled for it. It is only the magnitude of Federer's achievements in 2004–07 that allows for the question of why a year involving a Grand Slam title, an Olympic gold medal, two Slam finals and a Slam semi-final should be in any way 'bad'. It is all relative.

And yet, even allowing for relativity (Albert Einstein was after all Swiss!), there was a clear dip in success rate for Roger Federer in the first eight months of 2008, and it is more than just idle tennis gossip to wonder why. There seem to be four plausible theories.

The first is that his level did not dip at all, but that his greatness spawned the absolute best of Rafael Nadal. The Swiss former player, coach and broadcaster Heinz Günthardt subscribes to this theory – that Nadal reached a level that was just so phenomenal that no one in tennis history would have been able to live with him in 2008. In 2009, it became apparent that the stress Nadal puts on his body was starting to wear him down; he suffered severe patella tendinitis in both knees and his comeback was slowed by an abdominal strain that took longer to diagnose then originally expected. With Nadal having suffered a recurrence of his knee problem at the start of 2010, it remains to be seen how long he can keep up such a punishing style of play, and history may well record that he peaked in 2008-09. But even if it does, the Spaniard took speed around a tennis court to new levels, and, with his superb blend of strength, fitness and tactical awareness, Nadal fully deserved to take over the number-one ranking.

Taking nothing away from Nadal, there are many who believe Federer was slower in 2008 than in previous years. The obvious explanation for this – and the second theory – is his glandular fever. While he denied he felt in any way weak during the French Open/Wimbledon/Olympics period, he may well have still been suffering from the after-effects of an illness that in most cases leaves its traces for several months, if not a couple of years. And, if the glandular fever was indeed having an influence, however mild, his achievements in reaching the Australian Open semi-final, the Monte Carlo, Hamburg, French Open and Wimbledon finals and winning the titles in

Estoril and Halle must count as a remarkable body of work that can only serve to enhance the Federer legend. Asked what allowed him to regain his best form in 2009 and shine so brightly at the 2010 Australian Open, Federer said the key was regaining his movement, which suggests that his take on his relative slump in 2008 was because he wasn't physically as sharp as in previous years.

The third theory is that his success in the previous four years meant he simply lost the bite, the degree of competitive edge he had had up to then and was thus a little slower around the court and less confident in his big forehand. This could have been an unconscious thing, and raising it as a possibility is not a criticism of Federer. Which of us would be able to keep up the same level of hunger after such success? It's even possible Federer needed a handful of unexpected defeats in 2008 to put the hunger back up to its previous level.

The fourth possibility is that he got a little too distracted by other things. At the end of a tiring 2007, he dipped into his off-season to play three exhibition matches against Pete Sampras in Asia. While it would be wrong to attack the principle of exhibition matches per se – as they give players the chance of a somewhat competitive match with the knowledge that the number of matches is predefined and thus a victory will not lead to an overcrowded schedule – it does seem a little ill-advised for Federer to interrupt his quiet season for three exhibitions in which he had nothing to gain tennis-wise, however much he was financially remunerated.

It would be easy to blame his marketing company IMG for these distractions, and for Federer's increasing appearances with the glamorous set, but to do so would be to misjudge the control Federer exerts over his own affairs. For whatever reason, he accepted these invitations and would not want to pretend he was in any way persuaded. He even accepted another three exhibitions at the end of 2008, two against James Blake in Asia, the third partnering Björn Borg in a doubles.

There was also a lot of speculation as to whether something might be awry in his private life that was costing him energy and focus in 2008. Much of this speculation centred on his relationship with Mirka Vavrinec – the theory went that this was a relationship Federer had got into at nineteen, and that they might be starting to have different priorities in life. The fact that they guard their privacy jealously and those who belong to Federer's inner circle don't speak to the media only fuelled such speculation. But it was publicly quashed in March 2009 when they announced they were expecting their first child and got married on 11 April in a small and (well-kept) secret wedding in Basel. Federer also spoke in touching tones about how much it meant to him to be able to call Mirka his wife, and she now wishes to be known as 'Mirka Federer' for private and public purposes. Those who observe them in player lounges say there is seldom an open disagreement between them and they are often very lovey-dovey with each other. Perhaps those who have observed that Roger appears more socially gregarious when Mirka is not around were merely jumping to a wrong conclusion, and that all of us react a little differently when our partner is not present. Whatever the reality behind the closed doors of Mr and Mrs Federer's private life, the idea that there were problems there that contributed to his loss of form in 2008 can safely be dismissed.

Ultimately, his victory at the 2008 US Open and the historic wins at Roland Garros and Wimbledon in 2009 defused such speculation, as the dip in form in 2008 was clearly that – a dip and not the start of a permanent decline. As such, the most likely explanation was a mixture of the second and third theories – Federer being a little slower and more sluggish in his movement combined with the loss of a little of his competitiveness. Both were to come back in 2009, but not instantly.

Seldom have expectations at a Grand Slam tournament centred on a quartet of players as much as they did at the 2009 Australian Open. At an event notorious for producing an unexpected finalist, if not champion, almost all serious tipping for the men's singles title centred on Nadal, Federer, Djokovic and Murray. If anything, Murray was the favourite after a sparkling second half of 2008 and victory in two events at the start of January 2009: the Qatar Open and an exhibition event in Abu Dhabi, both of which featured Nadal and Federer.

But Murray fell in the fourth round in Melbourne to the breakthrough player of the fortnight, Fernando Verdasco, while Djokovic lost in the quarter-finals to Andy Roddick, a result which owed as much to Djokovic's physical frailties (or perhaps an over-awareness of them) as to Roddick's revival in form. Meanwhile, Federer was outstanding against Marat Safin in the third round, merciless against Juan-Martin del Potro in the quarter-finals, and just too good for Roddick in the semis. En route to the final, he wavered only in dropping the first two sets against Tomas Berdych in the fourth round, but came back to post his fourth win from two sets down in his career.

With Nadal looking every bit the world number one in the

top half of the draw, the great rivals had set up their first match since the epic Wimbledon final seven months earlier and casual polling of players, ex-players and journalists showed that a clear majority expected Federer to win. The tournament was desperate for a good contest after a women's final that proved as disappointing in the 6–0, 6–3 scoreline with which Serena Williams beat Dinara Safina as it was in its paltry duration of 59 minutes.

Nadal and Federer certainly made up for the women's final in both time and quality of play, but the result was a crushing blow for Federer. It may be no disgrace to lose a five-set match, especially to a player of Nadal's quality, but it was the way in which Federer lost that was so damaging. He was 4–2 up in the first set but lost two of his next three service games to lose the set. He had six break points in successive Nadal service games at 4–4 and 5–5 in the third set but, just as in past finals, he simply couldn't convert them into service breaks. And, after rallying back in the second and fourth sets, he crumbled in the fifth, his backhand deserting him as Nadal won the four-hour and twenty-three-minute match 7–5, 3–6, 7–6, 3–6, 6–2.

His assessment that he 'had many chances but missed them' and 'didn't serve particularly well' is fair. But the psychological damage to Federer came in the fact that the dice were loaded so favourably for him. His previous two matches had been straight-sets affairs, while Nadal's semi-final on the Friday night had been a record-breaking five-hour and fourteen-minute battle against Verdasco. And yet Nadal always looked the stronger player, with Federer's best chance appearing to be that the Spaniard might run out of gas having played so much tennis in the previous two days.

Nadal played a good match, but it wasn't his best tennis and he could have played better too.

The following morning, the Melbourne daily *The Age*'s front page declared: 'The king no longer holds court. Long live the king'. And another Australian daily, *The Australian*, continued the metaphor in its front-page story, which included the line 'Federer's kingdom, slowly but surely, is crumbling.'

Commentators on radio and television were similarly dismissive, using phrases such as 'the Federer era is over' and 'it seems like Federer's best chance of beating Nadal is if Nadal falls over and breaks his ankle'.

Needless to say, journalists and commentators are prone to hyperbole, and historical analysis is never at its best in the heat of the moment; after all, if Federer could take the world number one to five sets in his fourth consecutive Grand Slam singles final, it was hardly a sign that he was finished. But what the 2009 Australian Open had shown was that Federer was clearly the world number two – undoubtedly still ahead of the chasing pack led by Djokovic and Murray, but just as unmistakably behind the undisputed best in the world, Rafael Nadal.

Although he didn't mention it at the time, Federer was also bothered by his back. The problem he'd had in Shanghai had largely cleared up, but it was still in his mind. 'I don't actually remember whether the back was really bothering me,' he said a year later, 'but I was worried that it could come back, so I was playing with a bit of doubt.'

As Federer stepped up on to the Rod Laver arena's podium to receive his runner-up salver, there was another outbreak of what the Australians – with characteristic wit and very little sympathy – call 'the waterworks'. As the warmth of the ovation for him showed no signs of dying down, he stammered into the microphone, 'God, this is killing me,' and was ushered away in tears by the master of ceremonies to 'settle down' before speaking again a few minutes later.

As was the case three years earlier when he had cried on the podium, what caused the emotions to flow is not entirely clear. The presence of five of the legends of the game might have had something to do with it. On the 40th anniversary of Rod Laver's 'open' Grand Slam, Tennis Australia had invited Laver plus the four men he had beaten in the 1969 finals (Andres Gimeno, Ken Rosewall, John Newcombe and Tony Roche) to attend the final, and Federer is always moved by the presence of tennis's great names. The warmth of the ovation may also have contributed, as could the fact that Federer has always had a soft spot for Australia which could be traceable to Peter Carter's role in his life, as could the fact that Federer puts so much discipline into his tennis that his emotions do occasionally seep out when he least intends them to.

Later in the year, Federer made light of the tears, and on the first anniversary, it was he who was consoling a tearful Andy Murray who felt he had let down the over-expectant British public after losing to Federer in the 2010 final. 'I've been crying after losing matches since I was five years old,' Federer said, 'so to cry after the loss of a Grand Slam final was normal for me, but there was this big fuss that I didn't understand. The thing that was killing me was having to talk while crying. What I meant was "I wish I could stop crying and could talk normally and give Rafa the stage he deserves". The last thing I wanted was for people to feel bad for me. I wish I would have won, but I had to accept – and did accept without a problem – that Rafa was better on that day.' Federer also explained that the atmosphere at the Australian Open is more likely to bring out tears because there is less noise during the ceremonies than at other events, so it creates a more reverential environment.

All that makes sense with hindsight, but there may have been another reason for the tears – a tiny fear that his era of domination might now be over. His defeat to Nadal in the Wimbledon final could have been put down to his poor start to the year and the mononucleosis, and he had redeemed himself in the US Open final. But here was apparently conclusive proof that Federer had been surpassed by his greatest rival, that his best was no longer good enough to beat whoever was on the other side of the net. And the possibility of him being left stranded on thirteen Grand Slam titles, one short of Pete Sampras's record of fourteen, was becoming a real one.

While one should never read too much into Federer's tour form, as his priority has for several years been the majors and the number one ranking, there was considerable interest in how he would bounce back after his Australian Open defeat. He used the back as his reason for pulling out of his next two commitments, the Dubai tournament and his much-vaunted return to the Davis Cup first round, when the primary reason was concern about Mirka's pregnancy. (There are some who choose to believe Federer never intended to play those events, and had the events concerned been the French Open and Wimbledon, his attitude might have been very different. But the first thirteen weeks of a pregnancy throw up all sorts of genuine concerns, and backs can be strange things – they can be fine one moment and agony the next.) However troublesome the back issue really was, the five-week delay meant he was fully fit by the time he returned to the tour in Indian Wells in early March.

He reached the semi-finals there, and at the subsequent Masters Series event in Miami. Having lost to Andy Murray in Indian Wells, he faced Djokovic in Miami, with the winner to play Murray in the final. After winning the first set, Federer lost his way in the second, and as the third set began, it seemed a crucial moment to the tennis world. It was no doubt highly charged for Federer too, for after dropping serve early in the third set, he smashed his racket tempestuously on the concrete court in full view of all spectators and the world's television. It made headlines for its rarity value, and the incident became one of the most popular YouTube videos for several weeks.

Federer refused to engage in discussion about the incident after the match, a contest he lost 3–6, 6–2, 6–3 thanks to that one break in the final set. He said only that he broke his racket 'and felt good about it', a slightly odd way to dismiss a matter that was so out of character. He seemed to want to dismiss it as a minor aberration, but the tennis world read more into it than that. Taken in the context of the hold Nadal had on him, it was easy to see it as another step in a slow but inexorable decline in his on-court fortunes.

The Greek dramatist Euripides observed that 'whom the gods would destroy, they first make mad'. The tennis gods, it seemed, were making Federer mad by leaving him stranded on thirteen Grand Slam singles titles as his powers began to wane.

THE GREATEST **5**

15

A ND YET THE TENNIS gods had another twist in the tale. Instead of destroying him, they reprieved him.

As Federer arrived for the 2009 French Open, he seemed as vulnerable as ever. He had beaten Rafael Nadal in the final of the Madrid Masters (only his second win over Nadal on clay), but the biggest story from that tournament had yet to come out. Had it been known, the first week of the 2009 French Open could have been very different.

Nadal had followed his usual clay season routine by winning in Monte Carlo, Barcelona and Rome. But after beating Novak Djokovic in the Rome final to leave him with just one set dropped in 15 matches, Nadal returned home with increasing pain in his kneecaps. He was diagnosed as suffering from patella tendinitis in both knees and was advised to rest. The problem with top-level sports stars is that they invariably have an insatiable appetite for competition, and with the next event on the calendar being the Madrid

Masters, to be played for the first time in the Spanish capital's brand new state-of-the-art *Caja Magica* ('Magic Box') tennis centre, Spain's tennis icon felt he just couldn't pull out. So he showed up, and played arguably the match of the year in the semi-finals to beat Djokovic 3–6, 7–6, 7–6. But that left him with little in the tank when he faced Federer in the final the following day.

Federer's 6–4, 6–4 win announced that he was still capable of beating Nadal on clay, but no-one took it particularly seriously as a result – Nadal at Roland Garros would be a different proposition. Only it wouldn't be. His knees were even worse at the end of the Madrid week than at the beginning, and he was able to do very little court work in the remaining week before the tennis world gathered in Paris. It's just that the world didn't know it, so Nadal was as strong a favourite for the French Open as he had ever been.

Federer went to Paris to play his first Grand Slam tournament as a married man. He and Mirka had announced in March that they were expecting their first child, and when they married on 11 April in Basel in a ceremony attended by thirty-nine people sworn to secrecy, plenty of tennis watchers wondered whether Federer's priorities were now shifting to the domestic arena and away from tennis. Ivan Lendl once quipped, 'You can get married and still win Grand Slam titles, but you can't have children and still win Grand Slam titles.' According to that logic, Federer had two Slams left before the baby was due to arrive between Wimbledon and the US Open.

Everyone assumed it would be 'baby' – singular. Roger and Mirka knew as early as the end of January that it was twins, but such is the leak-proof nature of Team Federer that only when Mirka delivered Charlene Riva and Myla Rose on 23 July was the secret out. Federer actually learned that it was twins on the day he played Juan Martin del Potro in the Australian Open quarter-finals, and promptly went out and beat him for the loss of just three games in a magnificent display of tennis. If people had known at the time that he could play like that after receiving such life-changing news, they might have feared less for his chances as a parent. The only crisis in Mirka's pregnancy came shortly after that, and was part of the reason for Federer missing the Davis Cup first-round tie against the USA that he had promised to play after winning his Olympic gold medal. Again showing a remarkable ability to keep the lid on information about his private life, he kept quiet about the pregnancy and blamed his Davis Cup absence on his back.

The French Open didn't really get going until the middle Sunday. Nadal, parading a striking pink shirt, won his first three rounds confidently, leaving his fitness unquestioned. But then on the last day of May, he came up against Robin Söderling in a match that was to change his fortunes – and Federer's too.

Söderling had been a promising Swede who, like many promising youngsters, had never known how to make the transition from player of great tennis to great tennis player. Now aged 24, he began to see that his career wasn't infinite, and if he was going to make something of his ability, he had to start soon. He came out crunching his big forehand, and his relative height – he is 1.93 metres or six foot four – meant Nadal's heavily topspun shots came into his optimum hitting zone. After Nadal won the second set on a nervy tiebreak to level the match, Söderling's challenge could have collapsed, but the combination of his determination to seize the moment and Nadal's knee problem allowed Söderling to reassert himself in the third set. And when he won the fourth to defeat the champion, he had inflicted Nadal's first-ever defeat at Roland Garros.

Nadal was typically gracious in defeat. Asked about an injury he neither denied it, nor blamed his defeat on it. But the medical advice he received after he left Paris was unequivocal – he would not do himself any good playing on through patella tendinitis. He quickly pulled out of the following week's tournament at London's Queen's Club, and while it took him another two weeks to withdraw from Wimbledon, that decision hardly came as a surprise.

Suddenly the way was open for Federer. His nemesis had been felled and the gods were smiling on the Swiss once more. The number two seed became the new tournament favourite – only Nadal had stopped him in the previous four years. But it very nearly went wrong the following day.

Federer has subsequently admitted that he was desperately nervous when he came out to play Tommy Haas, the German enjoying an Indian summer at the age of 31 with three shoulder operations behind him. The fact that Nadal's defeat had removed his only insurmountable obstacle was preying on his mind. 'That was the only time in my life I think I went out feeling the pressure,' he said several months later. 'It had a huge effect on me when Rafa lost at the French, just knowing the opportunities I had and being already occupied with my own game and opponents.' When Haas led by two sets and 4–3 in the fourth against a strangely subdued Federer, the German had a break point on Federer's serve – he was just five points from victory, and only one from serving for the match. But a moment of genius (or was it luck? The line separating the two can be very fine) turned the match around. Federer played an in-to-out forehand that just clipped Haas' sideline, he went on to hold serve, and that was the first of nine straight games that put Federer back in charge. He won the final set 6–2 to complete his fifth comeback from two sets down.

Not that the draw got any easier after that. In the quarter-finals he faced Gaël Monfils, the flamboyant Frenchman he had beaten in the previous year's semis, and then Juan Martin del Potro took Federer to five sets in the semis. But by then it was a somewhat different Federer, and it had little to do with Nadal. He had added a new weapon to his armoury, the drop shot. For years he had largely shunned the shot, thinking of it as little more than a joke option, but four defeats to Nadal had woken him up to the potential of the well-disguised short ball, especially on clay where the bounce is lower than on hard courts.

The drop shot played an important part in all Federer's matches, but it deserted him a little in his win over del Potro, in which he started slowly and was twice a set down. Federer admitted he got a little lucky as del Potro ran out of gas in the fourth and fifth sets, though those watching the match felt he won it on a greater sense of belief, and del Potro was not to make the same mistake when the two men met in the US Open final three months later.

So, for the fourth year running, Federer walked out onto the Court Philippe Chatrier looking to complete his set of major titles. If some people had been saying in 2006 that victory then would have made him the greatest-ever tennis player, surely victory in his fourth successive French Open final would guarantee him that unofficial epithet? But it wasn't going to be easy on a day when rain was forecast.

Federer profited from a desperately nervous start from Söderling, who won just one game in the first set. The Swede got his game together in the second, a set characterised by an intruder who ran onto the court in the fourth game and approached Federer – it was not the Roland Garros security guards' finest moment. As the rain got heavier, Söderling got stronger, but the rain eased and the set went into the tiebreak. Despite the heavy conditions, Federer served perfectly, racking up four aces as he took the tiebreak 7–1.

The momentum of that tiebreak allowed Federer to break in the opening game of the third set. The title was in Federer's own control, albeit with another five games to serve out. Söderling's level picked up. He had a break point at 1–2 but missed it. At 5–4, Federer was serving for his moment of glory – but then the nerves set in big-time.

The forehand he hit to go 15–30 down was a howler, as the great man looked visibly nervous for the first time in years. Söderling then had a second break point at 30–40. Was it all going to go horribly wrong on the verge of triumph? No it wasn't. Söderling missed his break point chance, and two points later his backhand return went into the net on Federer's first match point. Federer's light blue shirt was suddenly at one with the clashing orange-red clay, as he collapsed with the relief of victory amid tears of joy.

He told the crowd it was his 'greatest victory', though he also admitted he had been hugely nervous. But then the stakes were as high as they could possibly be – this was his best chance, perhaps his last realistic chance, of completing his set of major titles, an achievement completed by only six other men in the history of tennis. He received the Coupe de Mousquetaires from the fifth man to achieve the full set, Andre Agassi, who had been asked to present the trophy on the tenth anniversary of his own accomplishment. The skies thundered, the rain really did get heavier after being incredibly kind to the players, but tennis history had been made under the grey Parisian skies.

The word Federer used several times in the subsequent months to describe his French Open triumph was 'relief'. Seven months later, in front of 15,000 spectators in Melbourne's Rod Laver Arena, he was asked for his highlight of 2009. Despite having won Wimbledon several weeks after Paris, he put his triumph at the home of clay at the top of his list.

'It feels a relief to be able to go back to Paris knowing they won't be asking me if I'll ever do it,' he said, a rich seam of truth hidden in a slightly jocular answer. It had been the last monkey off his back – all that was left to achieve was one more Grand Slam title to take him past Sampras's mark of fourteen.

Despite the contract tying him to play in Halle, no-one in the tennis world – even in northern Germany – seriously expected the newly crowned French Open champion to head to eastern Westfalia for a warm-up tournament he knew he didn't need for Wimbledon. His message of withdrawal was genuine: 'I sincerely apologise to the tournament organisers, my competitors, and my fans in Germany,' he said. 'I only hope they will understand that I still feel emotionally overwhelmed and exhausted by the incredible events of the past few days.' Pretty much everyone did, and though the Halle organisers wouldn't want this said too loudly, the tennis world knew that playing Halle would do nothing to enhance his chances of a sixth Wimbledon title.

With the defending champion Nadal absent nursing his sore knees, there was the question of who would be asked to open the first day's programme on the Centre Court, which boasted a new retractable roof. With Federer and Lleyton Hewitt the only former champions in the draw, the question barely needed answering, and for the sixth year running, Federer had the champion's slot – even if he wasn't the champion. He also continued a tradition of his own that his clothing supplier, Nike, was happy to fuel – the unveiling of a new Wimbledon fashion line.

Some like it, others don't. In the words of one of the British media's correspondents, 'He sauntered on to Centre Court, resembling a cross between a Sergeant Pepper figure and something out of *An Officer and a Gentleman*, before he put down his glittering kit bag, stripped off his embossed white jacket and started practising in a waistcoat ... Federer departed his second home two hours later, having proved conclusively that he has the game to carry off such preposterously dandy apparel.'

Once the waistcoat – really a cardigan – had been safely packed away, Federer beat Hewitt, Söderling and Haas en route to a final that the British had hoped would be against Andy Murray. It was against an Andy, but not the one the home fans wanted. Murray had been out-thought in his first Wimbledon semi-final by Andy Roddick, who was displaying the fruits of his coaching relationship with Larry Stefanki, the wily American coach with whom he had been working since the start of the year. Roddick's four-sets win over Murray was arguably the single best tactical performance of his career, certainly since winning the US Open in 2003, and this still prickly character had the considerable class and sensitivity to mouth the words 'I'm sorry' to the crowd after acknowledging the applause, recognising he had spoiled the home nation's party.

But could Roddick overcome Federer, the man who had defeated him in his two previous finals? He proved that he could, but he let his fish off the hook. Playing in a crowd that featured Rod Laver, Björn Borg and Pete Sampras, Roddick broke in the twelfth game of the match to take the first set 7–5; when he led the second set tiebreak 6–2 he had Federer on the ropes. But at 6–5, a moment of indecision cost Roddick the set and probably the match. Having driven Federer into his forehand corner, Federer threw up a lob over Roddick's backhand side. It was a good shot, yet Roddick still had time to guide the ball into the open court and claim the set. But his first thought was that the ball was going out, and when he realised he had to play it, he was too late, and put the volley wide. It was the let-off Federer needed, and he took the tiebreak 8–6 with six points on the run.

Roddick wasn't going to lie down, but the significance of the second set tiebreak was that from then he was chasing the game. Federer took the third set on the tiebreak, but Roddick bounced back to take the fourth. For the third year running the Wimbledon final was into a fifth set.

Statistically, the final set in 2009 reads more spectacularly than its equivalent a year earlier, but in truth it lacked the drama of Nadal's victory. Roddick maintained his level as 4–4 became 5–5, and 6–6 became 7–7. But he was always serving second, and while his serve kept up, he never got close to breaking Federer. For his part, Federer was happy to play a waiting game. As 8–8 became 9–9, 10–10 became 11–11, there was never the sense that he was looking to put his foot on the gas pedal, only to slice his backhand into the last half-metre of Roddick's court and wait for his opponent to play a lax game. He had to wait a long time, as 12–12 became 13–13, and then 14–14. Eventually the moment came. Serving for the eleventh time to stay in the final, Roddick mishit a forehand, the ball went into the stands, and Federer had won his fifteenth Grand Slam title in four hours sixteen minutes, the 95-minute fifth set notching up a new record for a Wimbledon final.

In the space of four weeks, Federer had equalled and overtaken Pete Sampras's record of fourteen Grand Slam titles, and he was able to pose for photographs alongside the three other greats whose achievements he had largely surpassed. Nadal's absence from Paris and Wimbledon had made it a little easier for him, but no-one wanted to hold that against the Swiss. On the tennis tour, it was widely acknowledged that Nadal's ability to match and out-do Federer was based on his phenomenally energy-intensive game, that would eventually take its toll on the Spaniard's body. By keeping his level and staying in great shape, Federer had bided his time and been in the ideal position to cash in when Nadal's body rebelled. Federer had made it to twenty Grand Slam singles finals, and won fifteen. The other five had all been won by Nadal. That speaks as much for Nadal as for Federer – he will go down as the only man able to regularly beat the greatest player of all time at his peak.

The Federers had not only kept the fact that Mirka was expecting twins secret; they had also jealously guarded the due date. Boris Becker was thought to have let the cat out of the bag when he said while commentating on British television that the baby (singular, and male) was due in the first week of August. But maybe that was just a bluff. Federer himself had talked about 'the baby'.

The twin girls (non-identical) arrived on 23 July in the Bethanien private hospital in Zurich. Although born sixteen days before their father's birthday, like him they are also Leos in the Zodiac star sign system, and one British bookmaker was offering somewhat gimmicky odds of 100-1 that, with such impressive genetic inheritance from father and mother, the girls would make it as professional tennis players. They were named Charlene Riva and Myla Rose – Myla is a Czech name derived from the diminutive of Ludmilla which in ancient Slav means 'the precious' or 'the lovely one', while Charlene is one of several female versions of Charles and is popular in South Africa. In a statement issued on his website, Federer said he and Mirka felt this was 'the best day of our lives'.

Much is made of the difficulty of winning tennis tournaments when a parent. The difficulty is self-evident for women who have put their bodies through the rigours of pregnancy, but very few men win the leading tournaments when they have the next generation in tow. No doubt many a night's sleep is disrupted by a crying baby, and in a close match the following day, such deprivation could make a difference. But it's largely a statistical thing – most men on the tennis tour don't become dads until they're well past their playing peak, and those dads who have won majors, the likes of Federer, Andre Agassi and Jimmy Connors, had earned enough money to afford a team of nannies to protect their beauty sleep.

Nonetheless, the tennis world was not quite sure what to make of Federer's first defeat as a father. In the quarter-finals of the Montreal Masters, Federer led Jo-Wilfried Tsonga 5–1 final set having taken eleven of the previous thirteen games, only to crumble to a 7–6, 1–6, 7–6 defeat. Having won his three previous tournaments in Madrid, Roland Garros and Wimbledon, the defeat deprived him of another chance to win back-to-back tournaments on three different surfaces. But the following week he beat Murray and Djokovic to win in Cincinnati. Much was made of him winning the Australian Open as a father five months later, but by then he was used to being a dad – his victory in 'Cincy' was the one that really meant something to him because the girls were still just a few weeks old. 'That was very special,' he says, 'because it was right off the bat, it was fresh.'

Ironically, the US Open in 2009 was won by a mother but not by a father. Like Federer, Kim Clijsters was playing her third tournament since becoming a parent, but in her case it followed a 'retirement' of twenty-seven months. Her triumph created the news story of the year in the women's game, especially as it involved Serena Williams being disqualified in the semi-finals for delivering a torrent of abuse at a line judge who had foot-faulted her. How Federer didn't join Clijsters in making it a first mother-and-father double in the open era is still baffling.

After wins over Söderling and Djokovic, Federer faced Juan Martin del Potro. Federer had won all their previous six matches, and if Federer could beat the tall Argentinian on clay, surely he would beat him on hard courts – so the logic went. And so it should have been, as Federer moved to within two points of victory in the fourth set.

Yet there was something edgy about Federer during that US Open. No-one is quite sure why, and he himself denies he was in any way irritable, but he came across that way, both behind the scenes and in another five-set Grand Slam final. With Federer serving at 5–4 in the second set for a two-sets lead, del Potro took a long time to request a challenge. When the challenge led to an overrule and del Potro then broke for 5–5, it began to rankle with Federer. Later in the match when del Potro was again slow to challenge, Federer let the umpire, Jake Garner, know exactly what he thought, using the F-word within clear range of the television effects microphones and refusing to admit anything Garner said in response. There are many people in the tennis world who agree that Federer has a point over challenges – if an umpire can only overrule if he or she instantly sees an error, why should a player be allowed to wander across the court to see a mark, glance up to their coach, and then challenge several seconds after the ball has landed? It's a legitimate point that the officiating branch of the sport has yet to get a grip on. Yet it was uncharacteristic for Federer to be so high-handed and abusive about it. He was later awarded a rare fine – $1500, which will hardly have troubled his accountant – and he went on to lose the match.

He should still have won it in the fourth set, but once del

Potro had taken the final into a decider, Federer looked a spent force, and del Potro won 3–6, 7–6, 4–6, 7–6, 6–2 in four hours and six minutes. In sets, it was a mirror image of Federer's victory in the French Open semi-finals.

In his post-match remarks, he seemed almost a little fatalistic. 'That's the way it goes sometimes,' he said. Perhaps he had a sense that this final just wasn't meant to go his way. He has been equally fatalistic about the Wimbledon final he lost to Nadal, saying 'I believe things happen for a reason, and maybe that sixth Wimbledon in 2008 was not meant to be.' But despite his otherwise great year, this was one that got away, and del Potro became the first player other than Nadal to beat Federer in a Grand Slam final.

Like most players who beat Federer, del Potro found it easy to be magnanimous. 'I had two dreams this week,' he said at the trophy ceremony, glancing towards his beaten opponent. 'One was to win the US Open, and the other was to be like Roger. One is done, but I need to improve a lot to be like you.'

It had been a remarkable turnaround. Federer had begun the Grand Slam year with his game disintegrating for him to lose the final set of the Australian Open 6–2. It ended with his game disintegrating again for him to lose the final set of the US Open 6–2. But he had once again reached the finals of all four majors, and had won two of them. Even in his moment of defeat in New York, he could see the big picture. 'I was two points from the match today, but I've had an unbelievable run this year, being in all major finals and winning two of those. Sure I would have loved to win those two as well, but the year has been amazing already –

got married and had kids, don't know how much more I could want.'

And, in reality, he didn't want much more. He reluctantly travelled to Genoa for Switzerland's Davis Cup play-off round against Italy; he played in Basel, losing the final to Djokovic; he lost the first round at the Paris Masters and he lost in the semi-finals of the ATP World Tour Finals in London after beating Murray and del Potro in the group stage. It would be wrong to say he didn't take those matches seriously – such was his wish to remain at the top of the rankings at least until 7 June 2010, when he would surpass Pete Sampras's record of 286 weeks in the number one slot, that he was keen to pick up ranking points wherever possible. But Grand Slams clearly meant more to him than tour events, and it was only when the Australian Open came around at the start of 2010 that his level really picked up.

Six days before the Australian Open began, a massive earthquake hit the central American state of Haiti. Already very poor and ravaged by decades of questionable government, the country suffered a humanitarian catastrophe on a scale few people had ever seen. The United Nations described it as the worst disaster it had ever had to deal with.

On the Saturday morning, two days before the start of the tournament, Roger Federer phoned Craig Tiley, the Australian Open's tournament director, and asked whether he and a group of other top players could play a charity match to raise money for Haiti. 'My initial reaction was to say no,' Tiley says, 'because it would be a logistical and safety nightmare.' But he agreed to explore the idea, while Federer went off to sound out his top-level colleagues about their willingness.

At five o'clock that afternoon, barely seven hours after his call to Tiley, Federer gave a pre-tournament press conference in which he announced the 'Hit for Haiti'. He had secured Lleyton Hewitt, Rafael Nadal, Andy Roddick, Novak Djokovic, Serena Williams, Kim Clijsters and Australia's top women's player Samantha Stosur to play a mixed doubles in which substitutions were allowed and all players would play with a headset-microphone so the crowd would hear everything they said. For his part, Tiley had mobilised the massed ranks of the Melbourne Park temporary staff, notably security and catering, to work an extra day, in some cases for free.

In explaining the rationale, Federer used the term 'the tennis family', a phrase often used by administrators trying to get various warring factions to pull in the same direction. 'I think it's something as a tennis family that we're very happy to do,' he said. 'In know it's on the eve of the first Grand Slam of the season, so it's for some not so easy to separate mentally, but I think it's a great initiative. I'm happy we can go through with it, we hope to have some fun tomorrow, maybe also make it a nice day for families to come and see some top players play.'

Less than thirty hours after his initial phone call to Craig Tiley, Federer and the other seven players stepped out onto the Rod Laver Arena for what was to prove a magical experience. Charity days on the eve of the French and US Opens are now commonplace, but it was new in Australia. A briefing sheet handed out on the morning of the event to staff and some broadcasters said a crowd of between two and five thousand was expected. That was to be a hopeless underestimate of Federer's pulling power. The 15,000-seater stadium was full, and many Melburnians who had queued couldn't get in and had to make do with watching the event on the big screen in Garden Square, Melbourne Park's equivalent to Henman Hill at Wimbledon. Everyone paid ten Australian dollars admission (children under twelve were allowed in for free but many parents paid for them), and bucket collections went from row to row. Even journalists had to pay the entry fee if they wanted to watch the event from the stands. Nearly A$200,000 was raised, a sum that was quadrupled thanks to contributions from the ATP, WTA Tour, ITF, Grand Slam Committee and individual players.

But it was more than just an exercise in raising money for a humanitarian disaster. It showed the public a different side to the players. If Federer always has his 'game face' on when he plays matches, this was a chance for the joking personality to shine through. All players entered into the spirit, and the result was ninety minutes of wonderful artistry and great fun. Roddick captured the spirit of the occasion when he told a line judge who had foot-faulted him that he ought to be careful as Serena Williams was on his team – after Williams's outburst at the US Open, it was a wonderful way of defusing tension, and Serena roared with laughter at the joke at her expense.

It was a great success all round, and it also showed the role Federer plays as a statesman and de facto leader of today's tennis players. He spoke to the crowd after the event, he held a couple of extra press conferences, and took a commanding role. There will be many in Haiti who have reason to be grateful to him, even though most will not know who he is.

There was one other act of statesmanship that Federer was required to perform at that tournament.

On the first Thursday, Melbourne received a visit from Prince William, the second-in-line to the British throne and son of the late Princess Diana, who had been a great tennis fan and frequent visitor to Wimbledon. The prince was in Melbourne to meet survivors of some horrendous bush fires that had ravaged the state of Victoria eleven months earlier, and his evening entertainment at the Australian Open had been kept out of the public domain until he took his seat during Federer's match against Victor Hanescu.

Federer had, however, been privately briefed. The briefing included informing him about the way he should address someone of Prince William's status. When told that the correct way to address him was 'Your Royal Highness', Federer at first thought this was a joke. When told that it wasn't, he is said to have replied 'All right, I'll call him "Your Royal Highness" if he calls me "king of the court"!'

All that was behind closed doors and no doubt meant as a harmless private joke. When Federer had beaten Hanescu, he did his on-court interview with the former world No 1 Jim Courier, at the end of which Courier invited Federer to formally welcome the prince. Federer took the microphone and uttered the words, 'Your Royal Highness, welcome to the world of tennis – thanks for coming!' But he did so with a barely suppressed giggle that betrayed his apparent belief that having to address a twenty-seven-year-old spectator as 'Your Royal Highness' was all rather silly. As a genuine fan of England and the

English, Federer can easily be allowed his snigger at the pomposity of British royal protocol.

If one dismisses the first part of Federer's opening match of the 2010 Australian Open against Igor Andreev, there is a case to be made that his sixteenth Grand Slam title was the one in which he played his best tennis ever. 'I think this has been one of my finest performances,' he said after beating Andy Murray in the final, 'certainly in a long time, maybe for ever.'

It had seemed such an open Open. Federer was the bookmakers' favourite, but it was plausible to see any one of about eight players lifting the Norman Brookes trophy. In hindsight, perhaps the greatest threat to Federer was Nikolay Davydenko, who came to Melbourne having won the ATP World Tour Finals at the end of 2009 and who won the biggest tour event before the Australian Open, the Qatar Open in Doha. And it was Davydenko who gave Federer his greatest test.

For an hour of their quarter-final, Davydenko seemed destined for a major upset. In a match starting late because of two long previous matches, Federer seemed bothered by the setting sun that caused a two-tone effect on the court. Rallies were frequently played with one player in the sun and the other in the shade, the ball passing between the two. It happens at a lot of tournaments, but the combination of Davydenko's precision hitting and Federer allowing himself to become unsettled by the tricky light led to an hour of total dominance by the Russian. Federer even admitted he took his time over a bathroom break at the end of the first set, to allow the sun a little longer to disappear behind the roof of the arena.

Yet there is a pattern to many of Federer's matches that challengers need to be aware of. They can frequently work themselves into a commanding position, but if they then don't seize their opportunity, they can find the full force of Federer's talent unleashed upon them. So it proved with Davydenko. When the Russian led 6–2, 3–1 and had Federer at 15–40, the top seed was looking so frail that some wondered if he was ill. But then at 30–40, Davydenko dumped a fairly simple backhand into the net. That was the let-off that Federer had wanted, and he surged into a run of twelve successive games that effectively won him the match.

The Australian and British media were convinced Federer engaged in a form of psychological warfare before the final against Andy Murray. After beating Jo-Wilfried Tsonga emphatically in the semi-finals, Federer joked with Jim Courier in an on-court post-match interview that poor Murray was carrying the pressure that the British hadn't had a Grand Slam champion 'for 150,000 years or whatever it is'. He also mentioned in his post-match press conference that Murray had yet to win his first Grand Slam title, and that the Scot was 'playing me who's won many Grand Slams and has won three times here'.

Federer and the Swiss press saw it very differently. When asked about the 'psychological warfare' in a question that specifically mentioned that term, Federer replied, 'It got exaggerated. You ask me a question, I'll give you a straight answer. That's what happened after the Tsonga match. It's not an easy thing to win your first Grand Slam. That's not mental, trying to screw with his head. It's just a tough thing.'

It would be disingenuous for Federer to claim he always

gives straight answers – there are always nuances in what he says that indicate to those who can read the runes what he thinks about someone. But it is fair to say that the media are often so keenly on the lookout for a different news angle that they can read more into something than was ever intended, and miss an unloaded straight answer.

Whatever Federer may or may not have intended, he let his tennis win the war in a final that saw him outclass Murray. The Briton's consistent play from the baseline wears down most opponents, but against an aggressive and creative player at the top of his form, it was never going to be enough, and Federer notched up his sixteenth Grand Slam title with a 6–3, 6–4, 7–6 win. The tiebreak had lots of drama, before eventually going to Federer 13–11, but there was always a sense that, even if Murray had converted one of his five set points, Federer would have bounced back to take the fourth set. And let's face it, if you've got the greatest player of all time playing pretty much at his peak, it would take a very special performance to beat him.

A year earlier, it had been Federer in tears on the podium – this time it was Murray. And the normally taciturn Scotsman came out with one of the quotes of the tournament when he composed himself to utter, 'I can cry as well as Roger, it's just a shame I can't play as well as him.'

But then with the form he showed at the 2010 Australian Open, who could play as well as Roger? Federer had raised his level to a new degree of sublimity, spurred on by the new generation of players who hit powerfully and seldom miss. 'When I came on the tour, matches were played very differently,' he said. 'It was more of a bluff game – guys served well, but there was always a weakness you could go to. Today that doesn't exist any more, and that's thanks to guys like Murray. They've made me a better player.'

As the competition got hotter, the best got better, and the greatest was becoming even greater. In an ominous postscript to the Australian Open, Federer said, 'I believe I can always improve.'

16

UNTIL ROGER FEDERER came along, the idea that you could work out who was the greatest tennis player of all time seemed fanciful. Not only were you dealing with different eras of tennis, but also, for a good thirty years the world's leading players didn't all compete in the leading tournaments – so it's mightily difficult to assess the meaning of greatness on a level playing field, even for some multiple Grand Slam champions.

From the 1930s until tennis went 'open' in 1968, the sport was divided into amateur and professional circuits. It meant the greatest players of an era remained amateurs until they had won two or three of the Grand Slam titles, which then made them sufficiently marketable on the professional circuits for them to turn pro and make a living out of tennis, playing never-ending series of exhibition matches in a motley collection of arenas. Many of the amateurs weren't truly amateur anyway – tales abounded of under-the-table payments from national associations who wanted to collect more major titles, and the word 'shamateurism' came into use, and is still used to describe this less than glorious period of tennis's history.

So how can one say how good Fred Perry was in the 1930s? He may have won eight major titles, but by then the big-serving Ellsworth Vines and the wily Bill Tilden had turned professional so were out of Perry's way. Similarly, would Donald Budge have done the first pure Grand Slam in 1938 if Perry and others had been in the starting line-up? And what of the great Aussies of the 1960s? Would Rod Laver have won a pure Grand Slam in 1962 if Ken Rosewall, Lew Hoad, Ashley Cooper, Pancho Gonzalez and others had been in all four draws? Would Roy Emerson have won twelve Grand Slam titles if Laver hadn't turned pro after his Slam year of 1962? All impossible to answer.

There's another element that makes defining the greatest tennis player hazardous. For years, the sport was the preserve of a certain affluent social elite, and only in the past thirty years or so has it become more accessible to a wider social spectrum (albeit still often very dependent on affluent and committed parents who can ferry their talented offspring to practice and tournaments). As such, fewer people played tennis in earlier eras, so the strength and depth of competition among the top one hundred or so players was nowhere near as great as it is today.

It's therefore possible to make the case that any one of Bill Tilden, Don Budge, Jack Kramer, Lew Hoad, Ken Rosewall, Rod Laver, Björn Borg, John McEnroe, Pete Sampras, Andre Agassi and Roger Federer are the greatest of all time. It certainly makes for good discussion, especially when you take into consideration factors such as Hoad regularly beating Laver on the professional circuit. All were men who, like Federer, combined immense natural talent with a work ethic that is frequently missing in the intensely gifted.

The one way of slicing through the inability to compare one great champion with another was always going to be if a player emerged who was just so good and so dominant that he elevated himself above all the variables in the equation. Has Federer done that?

By winning the French Open to complete his set of majors, and then beating Pete Sampras's record of fourteen Grand Slam singles titles, Federer has, in the eyes of most tennis watchers, elevated himself to that position. There are still some doubters. It would of course be nice if he could one day win the Davis Cup (a competition he seems to be relegating rather than promoting in his priority list), and beat Nadal at Roland Garros. A return to full fitness by Nadal would help the Federer legend in general terms, as it's hard to escape the thought that Federer never fully mastered Nadal, and only returned to full confidence in 2009 after Nadal's knee injuries removed him from the tour. Another couple of Grand Slam titles to put clear water between himself and Sampras would also help to cement Federer's position as the greatest, as would an Olympic singles gold in 2012 to go with the doubles gold he won in 2008.

But in many ways, the Federer legend is made up of more than just the big titles. For many, the fact that he reached the semi-finals or better of every Grand Slam title from Wimbledon 2004 to the Australian Open 2010 (twenty-three and counting when this book went to press) speaks for a consistency that no-one in history can compete with. True, the 'shamateur' era meant that the likes of Perry, Budge,

Bobby Riggs, Jack Kramer and the Aussie greats never had the chance to play twenty-three consecutive Slams at their peak, but neither did they face the depth of competition Federer has faced. Another statistic that tells its own quiet story is the number of weeks Federer has been at the top of the world rankings. He began 2010 having occupied the top slot for 264 weeks, just twenty-two short of Sampras's record of 286 – assuming he overtakes that, it stakes another statistical claim for the Swiss's historical standing.

But there are other factors than just statistics that add to the argument that Federer is the greatest-ever.

An unquantifiable factor that sways opinion is that he has played with an elegance that attracts people sometimes ambivalent about tennis, and his eloquence in three languages gives him a statesmanlike quality that McEnroe, Agassi and Sampras could never approach. That shouldn't be held against those brought up without a workable second language, but there's no doubt Federer has a radiance that only McEnroe's volatility and Borg and Agassi's sex appeal could eclipse in the public consciousness, and that further adds weight to claims that he is the greatest ever.

The elegance with which Federer plays his tennis stems from the fact that his strokes are a modern version of the classic technique that evolved in the era of wooden rackets (he has described his own playing style as 'modern retro'), and it might well have protected his body from the punishment endured by some players with modern technique. While it's too early to be sure, the pounding that his hips and lower back take while playing his groundstrokes might well have been reduced by the much lesser degree of exaggerated body rotation that normally comes with the two-handed backhands and heavily topspun, wristy forehands that characterise modern top-level tennis. (On his backhand, he has been quoted as saying, 'Two-handed backhand for me? Utterly unthinkable. I couldn't do it. The ball would fly over the roof of the stadium. I wouldn't even be in the top 100.' Believe it if you will.)

And he also makes it look so easy. In *Moments '05*, the Swiss journalist Freddy Widmer writes, 'Federer's game makes it look as if his side of the court is smaller and the opponent's side is bigger, and that he has more time to play his shots than his opponent. You're almost tempted to tear up the rulebook and give the opponent two bounces of the ball to Federer's one, just to be fair. In many situations, Federer seems to know what his opponent should be doing well before his opponent realises this for himself.'

This broader mix of achievement, style and general demeanour was neatly encapsulated by John McEnroe, who for years said that Rod Laver was the greatest tennis player and that the era in which he, Borg and Connors played was the greatest. While much of what McEnroe says can carry a slightly self-serving element (when he and Borg were playing on the oldies' circuit, it suited him very well to push the line that their era was the golden one!), he has mellowed his view about tennis today compared with the late 1970s and early 1980s, and is increasingly effusive about Federer.

'Roger is just the greatest player of all time,' McEnroe said in an interview ahead of an ATP Champions Tour event in Zurich in early 2010. 'He is the most beautiful player I've ever seen and I don't ever get tired of watching him. Rod Laver is my idol, Pete Sampras is the greatest grass court player ever, but Roger is just the greatest player of all. I think we can all appreciate how incredible he is even more lately, because he's shown a bit more emotion on court, and he's become a father, so he seems a bit more human, more relatable. That makes what he's doing seem even more amazing.'

It is therefore statistically, stylistically and emotionally plausible to say Federer is the greatest tennis player in the history of the sport, if only because, on the complete package of all attributes, no-one can really match him.

So much for the tennis legend – what of the man himself?

There is a paradox with Roger Federer: he is very open with his emotions and enjoys chatting to people, but he guards his private life jealously. This makes an assessment of his character as it has evolved through his playing career somewhat tricky. In addition, some of his current personality traits may be temporary ones to protect himself from the constant threat of intrusion, a threat that may diminish when he is no longer so much in the public eye. But as he approaches the twilight of his career, Federer the man still stands in a very good light; his basic humanity remains intact despite the onslaught of intense scrutiny, demand for his time and fawning.

Essentially, he is a positive person. In his interview with Paul Kimmage for the *Sunday Times* in November 2009, he explained that when he and Tiger Woods came to do an advert for their clothing provider, the script involved the lines 'I love winning' and 'I hate losing'. Roger said he was keen to take the 'I love winning' line – and said Tiger was happy to take 'I hate losing' – because he (Federer) felt his love of winning characterised him much more than a fear of losing. 'I'm a positive person, a very positive thinker,' he said. 'To me, to hate losing is a bit negative. I dreamed about doing what I'm doing now, but it's so difficult to keep winning and to keep your love for the game because of all the travelling and the sacrifices. So I just said "I'm not going to let that happen to me. I'm going to take a positive approach that travelling is great and that I'm going to see different cultures and places I would never see if I wasn't a tennis player". My wife loves it, I love it, so let's have a good time because it's not going to last until I'm seventy.'

Part of this positive approach is an awareness about his responsibilities to the sport in general. 'I try to be good for the game,' he says, 'to leave it better off than when I arrived, even though that's hard. I'm very thankful to the legends of the game who created this great platform for us. Of course the Grand Slams are important, but I try to respect every tournament that invites me. There are the fans who pay for tickets, and I want to live up to my expectations too.'

Also part of the positivity is his enjoyment of interacting with others, and he has a good rapport with most of those he deals with. The one exception to this is tennis umpires, with whom his relationship seems to buck the trend – at least during matches. He is not a saint, and when his buttons get pressed, he can react in ways that show that the tempestuous youth may have been mastered, but not eliminated; and the situations in which his buttons get pressed often involve umpires. He seldom looks at umpires when talking to them, and was uncharacteristically rude to Jake Garner during the US Open final of 2009. His dislike of electronic review of line calls is legitimate, but the way he expresses it manifests itself in a reaction that comes across as arrogance. It probably isn't arrogance – it's more likely to be that he doesn't like a situation but doesn't quite know and how to handle it – but it doesn't look good. It would be more Federer-like if he were to look up to the umpire and say 'Challenge please' rather than muffle 'Challenge' into his beard or even just half-raise his left hand dismissively as if summoning a waiter in colonial times. Given his belief in the importance of being polite to everyone, his relationship with umpires still feels like a work in progress.

Despite his riches – or perhaps because of them – he remains very much a man who understands what is important in life and what isn't. His work with the Roger Federer Foundation could be dismissed as good PR or just fashionable, but this would be unfair as his links with Africa in general and South Africa in particular mean he knows what suffering there is, and his response to other humanitarian crises suggests he knows what really counts in the big picture. This has also helped make him into a tennis statesman par excellence, and the sport may have good reason to look back in years to come at how lucky it was in the second half of the past decade to have two guys at the top of the game – Federer and Nadal – who genuinely understand how tennis fits into the world and what the obligations of the top players are.

This is important, as it goes beyond the comprehension of the average tennis fan. The role of 'world number one' is thought of as just a statistic, a number to signify the person whose results have been the best over the previous twelve months. But there's more to it than that. It is a genuine role, albeit an indefinable one. Whether they are aware of it or not, world number ones set the tone of the locker room and player lounges. When Steffi Graf was the women's world number one, the women's players' areas were quieter, more subdued, less sociable places than they became when Martina Hingis succeeded her in 1997. The difference was that, while Graf was a shy person who came alive on court but retreated into herself in social situations (except for radio and television interviews, for which she developed a broadcast persona), Hingis was outgoing, gregarious and socially interactive. In an environment where implicit hierarchies play a big role in the social pecking order, the tone set by the top player(s) resonates throughout the entire players' area.

When Federer became world number one in early 2004, the tone he set was an outgoing but responsible and respectful one. While he has to turn down many interview and representative requests, he does as many as he feels able, he is always very helpful, and is exemplary in the way he deals with questions from non-regular tennis journalists who don't know his world as well as some, and who can sometimes ask some pretty bizarre things. He has the politician's knack of putting people at their ease by establishing immediate rapport, something often called for, as plenty of people he meets in formal situations go weak at the knees in the presence of such a well-known world figure.

This was also the tone Rafael Nadal adopted in his three years as world number two, and forty-six weeks as number one. Nadal was brought up to believe that children in Africa and other parts of the world would love to have just one of his rackets, so in no way should he abuse his racket on court. As a result, he seldom if ever does. Nadal is also scrupulously polite, thanking journalists at the end of interviews even if he may have felt the interview was a pain he could happily have done without. And there is the story from September 2008 of Nadal eating a meal on a café terrace in Madrid with his Davis Cup colleagues when the sound of a boy's voice came down from a balcony above: 'Rafa, can I have your autograph?' it said.

'Come down here and I'll give it to you,' replied Nadal.

'OK, but it may take a few minutes because I'm in a wheelchair,' came the boy's voice.

At which point, Nadal shouted, 'Wait there', then scaled the outside of the building, climbed up the balcony, gave the boy his autograph and sat chatting with him for ten minutes.

The shorthand for such an attitude is that Federer and Nadal 'get it'; they understand their responsibilities as well as their rights and privileges, and there are signs that the tone they are setting as tennis statesmen is filtering through to the next generation. The leading aspirants to their thrones – players like Juan Martin del Potro, Andy Murray and Marin Cilic – have grown up with Federer's and Nadal's ethos, and in 2008 there were signs that it was influencing del Potro in a positive way. The tall Argentinian always looked up to his country's number one and Davis Cup talisman David Nalbandian, but, in some increasingly bitter negotiations surrounding the 2008 Davis Cup final, it seems del Potro favoured the ethos of Federer and Nadal over the somewhat more self-centred approach of Nalbandian. This could be an important legacy bequeathed by Federer.

The innate sense of fairness that characterised Federer's junior days still remains with him. Julian Tatum, the invigilator of Federer's press conferences at Wimbledon, recalls one occasion when Federer felt the French press had not had a fair crack of the whip after a press conference, so offered to speak separately with French journalists. 'Admirable though that sentiment was, it can sometimes be a delicate balance to give everyone a fair hearing,' Tatum says, 'because organising the players' exposure to the press and fitting in with live TV feeds after matches is an operation that requires military precision. Yet you have to admire him for appreciating that he is an entertainer as well as a tennis player, and that he feels this sort of thing is expected of him. I do know the French appreciated it.'

The Swiss press often complain that they do not get the access to Federer that they should, given that they helped build him up before he was a world name. There may be something in that, but he receives dozens of requests every match for interviews, a good part of most of his press conferences is conducted in Swiss-German, and he does create time on occasions throughout the year to talk exclusively to the Swiss press. Taken together with such incidents as Julian Tatum recounts, it is hard to make a convincing case that Federer has abandoned any of his core media responsibilities.

A fact that the Swiss and international communities don't always appreciate is that Federer comes across somewhat differently in Switzerland than abroad; or more specifically, he comes over differently when speaking Swiss German than when speaking English, French or High German. It's not really the comfort of his mother tongue, as there's nothing he can't say in any of his learned languages, but rather that he's more the unaffected boy-next-door when speaking his Basel German, compared with the international ambassador in the other three languages. This was particularly apparent when, a week after winning the French Open in 2009, he went on a live sports talk show with the experienced Swiss television interviewer Matthias Hüppi. In tennis terms, it wasn't the greatest interview ever, but by catching Federer back on home soil and in his mother tongue, Hüppi extracted more of the personality of Roger Federer than emerges from many a dignified international interview.

Something remarkable about Federer is that he has remained popular throughout his career. Players who reach the top normally become the villains, not necessarily because of anything they have done, but because they are the big names that all the little fish want to beat – and the public wants them to beat. Yet Federer always receives a rapturous reception, and in close matches crowds frequently want him to win when they would normally favour the underdog. Even after five Wimbledon titles when the British could have been forgiven for wanting a change of champion, Federer still had the bulk of the support in the 2008 Wimbledon final, despite no one having any tangible reason to object to the pretender, Rafael Nadal. Julian Tatum says, 'One of the things that characterised people's reactions to that final in the days afterwards was that many people were saying to me, "What a great final, and wasn't it a shame that Federer lost." It would appear that there was a genuine sadness among those I spoke to that he hadn't won a sixth title.'

He has also impressed many of his fellow players with his role as president of the ATP Player Council. He decided to run for election because he felt the players' voice wasn't being sufficiently heard, but he was also not averse to countering the prevailing view of his fellow competitors if he felt it was not in the best interests of the sport. At a general players' meeting in Melbourne in 2009, players expressed their horror at a decision by the World Anti-Doping Agency (Wada) to introduce what became known as the 'whereabouts rule'. Wada insisted that, to allow it to randomly test athletes without warning, it required players to give their whereabouts for one hour every day up to three months in advance. Because no-one can say for certain where they will be three months hence, there was scope for players to update the information they had given, but the players were still in a severe state of uproar, with one after another standing up and voicing their disgust. What should have been a ninety-minute meeting lasted for nearly four hours, and experienced players said the level of indignation was pretty much unprecedented.

Eventually Federer stood up and calmly said that while the indignation was understandable, everyone wanted a clean sport and this was the price they would have to pay. He suggested they all fill in '5am player hotel or home' for the next three months and make amendments as their plans changed. The doubles player Ashley Fisher, who himself later served on the Player Council, said, 'To me, this showed what a class act and practical guy Roger Federer is. In the back of the room one player after another ranked 30-100 in the world was arguing, yet the guy who probably gets tested the most and has less time than anyone was able to calmly rationalise the actions of Wada. I found it inspirational, and it was one of the factors that made me agree to join the council when a vacancy came up shortly after that meeting.'

Federer is universally thought of as a nice guy, and the reputation has a lot of substance. There is scarcely a person who has encountered him who has a bad word about him, and even those whose requests for his time he has turned down generally come away with little or no sense of resentment.

Three people who have known him since his junior days are Madeleine Bärlocher, Roger Brennwald and Yves Allegro. Bärlocher, who ran the junior programme at the Old Boys tennis club in Basel, describes him as 'a thoroughly nice guy. He's never looked down his nose at people. He's not made any big story, not tried to make himself popular. He's generous, and he has remained Roger.'

Allegro says Federer 'is not playing a role. It's not a game he's playing – it's just the way he is. He looks relaxed because he is relaxed. That's just him.'

Brennwald, who first met Federer when asked to present the twelve-year-old with a prize for the most talented sports boy in Switzerland, agrees, 'People are always looking for the hair in the soup, but there isn't one. He tries to be polite, and he is. Most people wouldn't handle the fame and riches the way he has, but he has an awful lot to be grateful to his family for – but then, you deserve the people you have around you. He is a highly intelligent lad, who has the right feeling for the right moment, and there are very few people who in the right moment find the right thing to do. He is one of them.'

Handling fame and riches is a big part of the Federer story, and any assessment of his personality must keep in mind what the economists call 'the business as usual scenario' – a comparison with what would have happened if nothing had changed. This is important, because, while Federer is not quite the same affable, easy-going character he was when he first won Wimbledon, who wouldn't be in some way affected by the strange cocktail he has to deal with in his everyday life? It's a mixture of athletic rigour, public pressure, large sums of money and massive adulation, adoration and fawning of those with whom he comes into contact – it's a cocktail that would influence the character of a saint, and would drive many of us to despotism. While it has now become somewhat easier – perhaps thankfully – to find the not-so-positive attributes of his personality, there are surprisingly few, and any realistic assessment of Roger Federer the person comes out very favourably.

He seems to inspire remarkable loyalty in those immediately around him: the group of friends, family and service providers known loosely as Team Federer. One could argue this is pure self-interest – after all, when you have a mate who's earning millions and is happy to provide a bedroom for you in his luxury apartment in Dubai, you're unlikely to do anything to rock the boat. Yet by modern media standards, the good ship Federer is phenomenally leak-proof. All thirty-nine people invited to Roger and Mirka's wedding in April 2009 kept the secret to the point where the press only heard about it after the event, and no-one spilled the beans about Mirka expecting twins.

Perhaps in some respects the art of remaining the nice guy lies in keeping your own nose clean while all around are dirtying theirs. In 2008, Federer appeared in a television commercial for Gillette razors alongside two other clean-cut sporting heroes, the golfer Tiger Woods and the French footballer Thierry Henry. By the end of 2009, both Woods' and Henry's reputations were in tatters, Woods' after the revelation of a series of affairs, Henry's following a double-handball that allowed France unfairly into the 2010 soccer world cup finals. Simply by doing nothing, Federer's stock had risen.

He is not into alcohol or fast cars, preferring instead to play cards or computer games. He's willing to try out new things, though isn't a great risk-taker – he's scared of bungee jumping and sky diving, and says he was only able to play on the helipad of the Burj al-Arab hotel in Dubai 'because it wasn't moving'. He enjoys spending time with his mates, and has a natural knack of finding the right level of conversation whenever he finds himself talking with someone new.

An attribute that goes hand-in-hand with his affable

personality is a strong sense of fairness and responsibility. He himself has said, 'I think there's a lot of fair play involved when I play the game, respect for the game, respect for the opponent, being polite to everyone you meet. I think those are key things my parents have taught me.' His sense of responsibility has led to him getting more involved in tennis politics, in particular running for the presidency of the ATP Player Council in 2008, and for a while he had to battle to ensure he wasn't getting too involved in extraneous matters to the detriment of his tennis. 'He always wants to be involved in decisions,' says Thomas Wirz of the Basler Zeitung newspaper. 'He's a very profound person who finds any incorrectnesses or unfairnesses hard to deal with, whether consciously or unconsciously, and thus, if anything isn't quite right, he can lose his thread, because he's basically a perfectionist.'

He's not massively materialistic, at least not ostentatiously so. The Swiss tennis journalist René Stauffer tells a delightful story about how Federer's aspirations as a teenager were different to those of many aspiring tennis players, and how people hear what they want or expect to hear rather than what is actually said. In an interview for a youth magazine, Federer was asked what he would buy when he received his first prize-money cheque. When Lynette read the published article, she was surprised to see her son quoted as saying he'd buy a Mercedes. After further reflection, she was so sure this was a mistake that she called the magazine's office and asked to listen to the recording of the interview. It transpired that Federer had said 'mehr CDs', the German for 'more CDs' which is pronounced almost identically to the German pronunciation of the luxury car.

Federer himself hasn't changed much in this respect and his own materialism has remained very low-key. His move from Oberwil to Wollerau in early 2008 may or may not have been influenced by financial considerations. Of course, the odd percentage point of the tax rate makes a fair bit of difference when you're earning several million dollars a year, but one could argue that the people who are earning several million dollars a year have enough coming in that they shouldn't need to be concerned about a higher tax level. It would be wrong to condemn Federer for wanting to keep more of his money – many of us would want to reduce our tax liability to its minimum but the fact that he seeks to maximise his earning potential must be taken into account when assessing this apect of his character. It would be fairer to say that he is not very materialistic than that he isn't materialistic at all.

The executives at IMG appear to have done their job of maximising his potential. They have supervised three major deals that will define Federer for the rest of his playing career, and probably beyond: his racket and clothing contracts, and a deal for his wrist watch.

The racket contract with Wilson Sporting Goods was secured in early 2006. This is a lifetime deal, which means we will never see Federer with another company's racket in his hand – in fact if he turned up at an event without a racket and someone asked him to hit a few balls, he would be contractually obliged to decline unless the racket was a Wilson. Federer's racket has been re-branded and is now called the '[K] Six.One 95'. But it is essentially the same one he has used all his career, and what people buy in the shops under that name is something that looks the same but will play slightly differently.

Although his deal with Nike, signed in 2007, is not a lifetime one, it is hard to see him wearing any other clothing during his playing days. Nike has had a habit of letting some of its top players go – Andre Agassi finished his career with Adidas after spending a lifetime as a Nike icon, so his emotional US Open final of 2005 was played in Adidas clothing, and Amélie Mauresmo's best results came after Nike dropped her after a decade of sponsorship. With Nadal also with Nike, it's not impossible that Federer might one day seek another name, but Nike targets various markets, and he is as important to the Oregon company in attracting the 'clean-cut tennis player' sector as Nadal is in attracting the more brash sector.

In 2004, Federer signed a five-year deal with a Swiss luxury watch maker, Maurice Lacroix, following the end of a contract with another Swiss watch maker, Rolex. After switching back to IMG's representation in 2005, Rolex brought back Federer in 2006 by buying him out of his Lacroix contract. The noises that came out of Lacroix were remarkably conciliatory – perhaps some of that was a brave face, but executives talked about having got the maximum benefit out of Switzerland's greatest ambassador, and that they couldn't see themselves getting as much out of the remaining three years of the deal as they had got out of the first two. Federer is now very much associated with the Rolex brand, which has a neat tie-up with Wimbledon, where Rolex sponsors the on-court clocks.

The amount of money he earns from these deals is never made public, and when amounts are bandied about in the media, they have to be taken with a pinch of salt as most deals have lots of variables in them that depend on performance, number of tournaments played, etc. But in the 2008 sports rich list published by the American magazine

Forbes, Federer was the top-earning tennis player in third place with £24.1 million, behind the American basketball stars Kobe Bryant (£26.8m) and LeBron James (£26.1m). The next-best tennis player was Maria Sharapova in fourth place (£17.9m), with the Williams sisters fifth and sixth (£9.6m and £8.9m). If he is not maximising his earning potential, then Federer is not far from it.

But perhaps his desire to maximise his full monetary worth, in which IMG plays a prominent and proficient role, has also led him into some situations which don't seem naturally his own.

He inevitably moves in circles that lead him to rub shoulders with some prominent personalities, including the pop singer and tennis nut Gavin Rossdale, and, through that friendship, Federer came into contact with Rossdale's high-profile pop singer wife Gwen Stefani. Stefani and Rossdale were in Federer's box during Wimbledon 2008 and for a couple of days attracted as many questions in his post-match press conferences as his matches had done. Yet those who know Roger say mixing with leading members of the glitterati just isn't him – he is much more at home having fun with his mates than being photographed with glamorous celebrities.

Some of the people interviewed for this book expressed the concern that Federer doesn't exhibit much interest in the world beyond tennis. When lauding those who have built tennis to the global multi-million-dollar spectacle it is today, he frequently lists the high levels of prize money as one of the major benefits, seemingly oblivious to the fact that high levels of prize money don't impress everyone in the tennis world, especially those with an awareness of wealth inequalities in the world at large.

His former school head teacher, Theresa Fischbacher, defends Federer from suggestions that he is less informed than he perhaps ought to be. 'There's no doubt that Roger is a highly intelligent young man!' she said. 'Nobody thinks about asking a prominent scientist to explain the word "deuce", because his main concern is his special field of sciences, and an active tennis player's main concern must be tennis.'

On a personal note, I recall being pleasantly struck by Federer's composure as a teenager with issues he didn't feel competent to comment on. In June 2001, I conducted a lengthy interview with him in Halle for an article for a British newspaper and, after I'd asked my main questions, the interview developed partly into a casual chat. At one stage, the topic got onto South Africa and, in the course of the conversation, I asked him what he thought about the political situation there. He stopped in his tracks and said that, at nineteen, he couldn't be expected to make judgements about the politics of South Africa. For me, the most interesting aspect of that brief exchange wasn't that he didn't know enough about the subject to have an opinion (to admit you don't know something can be as much a sign of strength as of ignorance), but that I'd assumed he would have an opinion. Something about the assurance with which he talked about the country of his mother's childhood made me feel it was entirely logical to ask him about the political situation there. Maybe he is just waiting until he feels secure enough in his arguments before offering any opinions on matters of global importance. From my brief exchange with him, I suspect it won't be difficult for him to take an intelligent interest in something more meaningful than tennis when he decides to put his mind to it.

People close to Federer say he will never fundamentally change, that his basic humanity is strong enough to withstand any temptation. That will probably only be tested when his playing days are over and he returns to a lower-profile existence. He himself has said it would be unrealistic for anyone to expect him to have remained unchanged by his achievements. In an interview in June 2004 in the run-up to Wimbledon, when he was the defending champion for the first time and still a relatively new world number one, he said, 'I feel like I had to change – or adapt to the situation, I'd rather call it. There are a lot of demands from press, media, veryimportant people I've met in the past, and it's a different life I'm living now. It has changed me a little bit because I'm more careful, but at the same time, now that I've reached my dreams, it's more of an enjoyment playing on the tour.'

Perhaps the bigger change in Federer came before he began winning things. If one talks to those who knew him as a junior, the picture painted is one of a fun-loving, happy, joking person who was always into practical jokes. While the happiness is clearly still there, the figure Federer cuts on a tennis court is much more dour now. He has curbed his natural exuberance in pursuit of success, and deserves credit for that, especially when compared with the millions of highly talented tennis players who could never blend their innate ability with the discipline required to make the most of it. But has curtailing his natural exuberance come at a price?

It's possible he may have suppressed more of his natural spirit than was strictly necessary, though he wouldn't be alone in that, and he's not scared to let the tears flow in public when the emotion of a moment catches up with him.

He has a stubborn streak, but few champions in any sport

don't. He clearly revels in match situations, having the rare ability to play much better in matches than in practice (for most players, it's the opposite). And he seems to thrive without a formal coach, although it would be unfair to overlook the important role Severin Lüthi plays for him as a travelling confidant and hitting partner.

It will be an interesting test of Federer's personality to see how he handles his declining years. Understandably, a number of names from sport and the arts find it hard to keep their dignity when their star begins to wane, with many struggling to deal with their status as potentially vulnerable prey, and the need to adjust goals as the body is no longer able to cope with the rigours it could take in its stride a couple of years earlier. If Federer is able to handle his declining years with a dignity coupled with a feistiness that sees him fight to beat players increasingly fancied to beat him, it can only add lustre to his legend.

Although his status and legacy are well established, the end of Federer's playing career appears to be a long way off. His victory at the 2010 Australian Open suggests that being a father will not be a problem. He seems to take great delight in having the twins with him, but has enough practical support for him to have enough time and space to continue playing at the highest level.

Of course there is the question of how long his motivation will last, but again this may well not be a problem. When asked about his motivation, he cites 'my love of the game', and he is a genuine tennis fan. When away from a tournament, he frequently watches matches, not to scout them for possible future opponents but for the enjoyment of watching one guy trying to work out how to beat the other guy. 'I just like to see a good tennis match,' he says, 'see how they battle it out and see the intensity of both players. I obviously liked watching the net rushers back then like Rafter and Henman, but I just watch because I like tennis.'

As for his own motivation, it was never really about money, and these days he has and earns more than he's ever likely to spend. His marketing people could do more deals for him, but he's happy with what he has. He often talks about 'my dream to play on the biggest stages around the world, especially Wimbledon', and while that dream has long since been fulfilled, he seems able to connect with it again and again, so it still has its pulling power. He has rightly observed that he very seldom plays a bad tennis match, which keeps the opportunities for others to beat him to a minimum; and he says he wants the twins to see him playing, which suggests he will continue for another four or five years. So when people ask how long will Roger Federer go on playing tennis, the answer appears to be: as long as he can.

If he is the greatest in tennis, where does that leave him in the wider sporting world, and indeed the wider world in general?

There is no question that he is recognised as one of the sporting greats of our time. The fact that he has been nominated so often – and won – the Laureus Sportsman of the Year award confirms his standing among his sporting peers. The Laureus awards have been criticised for having too strong a tennis bias, and there is some truth in that. But, even allowing for any bias, it's still hard to think who could have a greater claim to the top award than Federer. His obvious contemporary rivals would be Lance Armstrong, Tiger Woods, Michael Schumacher and possibly Michael Jordan (one might include individuals in a given year, such as Usain Bolt or Michael Phelps in 2008, but we are talking here mainly of enduring presence at the top). Armstrong had the emotional appeal of having been told he had less than a fifty-fifty chance of surviving advanced testicular cancer that had spread to his brain and lungs, before coming back to win the Tour de France seven times; and Jordan captured the imagination of a sporting nation with his ability to apparently hang bird-like in the air. Federer can't match either of those attributes, but does it make Armstrong and Jordan greater sportsmen? Greater sports personalities perhaps, but that is a slightly different matter.

And, as for comparison with Woods and Jordan, James Blake offered this assessment after losing to Federer in the quarter-finals of the 2006 US Open: 'I heard something on television about two weeks ago saying Tiger Woods is going to pass Michael Jordan as the best athlete of our time. I think that's a joke. I'd make a case for Roger Federer being the best athlete of our time. Not tennis player, athlete. No offence to Tiger, he's an incredible golfer, but his record in matchplay events, the events where you're out if you have a bad day, isn't particularly impressive. We tennis players have that every single week. Roger wins every Grand Slam title except the French Open, and he wins every Masters Series tournament. That means he can't allow himself a single bad day. That's incredible.'

Where Federer scores less well than some of the great names in sport is on personality. That doesn't mean he is dull – tennis fans are well aware of his personality, even if it is often hidden behind a very focused calm exterior until a match is won. But, as a sports personality, he cannot be said to have transcended the boundaries of sport as much as some have done.

Martina Navratilova was known beyond both tennis and sport thanks to her forthright social views, in particular those on matters of sexual orientation and the environment. It made her a household name, even in households whose members knew little or nothing about tennis. The same went for John McEnroe at the height of his volatility in the early 1980s. At that time, the British satirical television programme *Not the Nine O'Clock News* performed a sketch that seemed to sum up McEnroe, then at the height of his playing career. Entitled 'Breakfast in the McEnroe house-hold', it portrayed McEnroe coming down to breakfast, hyperactively gulping down some orange juice, and being ticked off by his mother for slurping. 'What did I do?' pleaded the McEnroe character incredulously, thereby triggering a domestic row that mirrored his rages at umpires. Even the contemporary dancer Wayne Sleep had a routine that portrayed McEnroe's anger in balletic form.

Such instances reflect players becoming bigger than just the tennis or sporting world in which they have made their name, and so far there have been few of them associated with Federer. The opinions he has expressed publicly are generally within the realms of tennis, such as on electronic review of line calls, the round-robin format and the demotion from Masters Series status of the Hamburg tournament. It is very much his style to keep his opinions low-key, a character trait that works against building up a high profile in a celebrity-driven world. Perhaps in the future he might venture an opinion on, say, the unacceptability of severe poverty in the twenty-first century, based on the work in Africa undertaken by his foundation. That could raise his broader profile, and might lead to some diplomatic role as a quiet but persuasive voice for social justice in the developing world.

His standing in Switzerland is a little different. Obviously he is a household name there, having become an unofficial ambassador for the country and carried the Swiss flag at two successive Olympic Games. Yet the Swiss don't go overboard about him, and non-Swiss sports fans who have been in Switzerland when Federer is winning Grand Slam titles testify to a people pleased with his success but a long way from ecstatic about it.

A lot of this may be to do with the Swiss as a land-locked people with no raw materials, a combination of economic circumstances that has spawned a powerful land-based work ethic that underlies all Switzerland's big exports (from cuckoo clocks and luxury watches to cheese and chocolate). Against that background, a player achieving fame and fortune through sporting prowess doesn't cut as much ice as in other countries, and his decision to move from his home to a canton with a lower tax level has not pleased everyone. (On the other hand, many will see his decision to stay in Switzerland as a positive move, when he could have joined the band of a couple of hundred tennis players registered as living in Monaco for tax reasons.)

'There isn't the adulation and adoration for him here,' says his former primary-school head teacher, Theresa Fischbacher. 'Perhaps that's why he can still afford to live in Switzerland.'

The Basel journalist Thomas Wirz goes further: 'The Swiss don't like top stars. When the first Roger Federer fan club was opened in Allschwil [a suburb of Basel], I thought there would be a storm of fans but it was very intimate. I think it has less to do with Basel and more to do with Switzerland.'

There are certainly no plaques around Federer's old childhood haunts, and it wasn't until he'd won three Grand Slam titles that the Old Boys club put up a portrait of him in the clubhouse and renamed Court 1 the Roger Federer court. 'It hangs together with the reticence of the Swiss to respect people who make their living from sport,' says Niki von Vary, a former teammate of Federer's at Old Boys who is now a political adviser. 'You saw it with Marc Rosset. Whatever you may think of him, he won an Olympic gold medal, but there's no monument or plaque to him. The same with [top-level skier] Bernhard Russi. However much sportsmen and -women achieve at the highest level, they don't earn the same reputation that they do in America or Australia or other European nations. It'll certainly come, but it'll take at least a decade. And it's hard to imagine a cult like that of David Beckham. The typical Swiss citizen is so grounded, so connected to the land, he doesn't want to stand out from the crowd; he just wants to come through life without creating a scene. That's the history of Switzerland. It's always been that way and, to a large extent, will always be that way. You see it in politics, with Switzerland's attitude to the EU. We don't have a star culture and as a result we haven't had a boom like Boris Becker created in Germany. The Swiss are probably too low-key for that.'

All the coaches interviewed for this book were asked if they thought the Federer factor had increased interest in tennis in the Basel area. All could point to the enthusiasm that many youngsters there today have for Federer and their wish to play like him, but few have much evidence that youngsters gifted in several sports are being attracted to tennis because of the inspiration of Roger Federer. Even Christopher Eymann, a councillor who chairs the Basel education committee, says there has been 'no discernable Basel tennis boom'.

'For us Swiss, only the best is good enough,' says the radio journalist Marco Mordasini. 'Whether it's in sport, in the economy, in politics – when someone begins something, they're interesting, but, once people realise there's a consistency of performance, people lose interest. That's why it has become hard for me to get radio stations interested in Federer before the quarter-finals of tournaments, but then we had the same problem with Hingis once she got to the top. Roger is inevitably going to polarise people, anyone who's that successful is going to create some envy. But he will remain a symbol for Switzerland even twenty or thirty years after he stops playing.'

As one of three Swiss gold medallists at the 2008 Beijing Olympics, Federer did enhance his reputation at home, but short of winning the Davis Cup for his country, it's hard to see what he can do that will further enhance his status among the majority of his compatriots.

Whatever he goes on to achieve as a tennis player, Roger Federer will be a dream catch for whoever he goes on to work for and with. He is unlikely ever to *need* to work again, but it's hard to see how such a bundle of energy could survive in the long term without some form of physical occupation.

He is happy to admit that there are more important things than tennis, and that will no doubt help him make the transition to his post-playing career when that moment comes. He may well find what others have found – that he is mentally and physically exhausted at some point in his early thirties, announces his retirement, but then finds a couple of years later that the rest and recuperation have given him new appetite. Whether that would lead to a full comeback or merely joining the oldies' tour remains to be seen. He would be a fantastic catch for the seniors tour, both as a legend in his own right and for what he could offer on-court. With results on the seniors tour mattering less than the entertainment value, he could unleash the full range of his arsenal, and become a successor to the Iranian player-turned-entertainer Mansour Bahrami. Then again, would someone who has been so dominant at the top of the game get much satisfaction out of the seniors tour? Only time will tell.

One possible future job is as a television pundit, as he can talk sufficiently lucidly and has a good broadcast voice. He's an obvious Davis Cup captain for Switzerland, although probably not until a good five years after he's played his last match. He'd also be a valuable asset for any business looking for a global figure to front up a publicity campaign, and if he ever develops an interest in world affairs he could carve out a political role for himself, be it party-political, ambassadorial or for a non-governmental organisation (in the 1970s the US president Jimmy Carter asked the former world heavyweight boxing champion Muhammad Ali to be a one-time envoy to Africa, and it would be easy to see Federer doing something similar).

The Basel sports impresario Roger Brennwald says, 'He won't be lost to the tennis world, he'll play some sort of role in tennis, but let's not burden him with this issue now – let him play another five years or so of top-level tennis.'

One aspect of being an elite sports star that isn't readily appreciated by the public at large is that the star reaches the age of thirty with the realisation that, with more than half their life left, they have already reached their peak. For most people in traditional career jobs, the 'peak' comes around fifty or sixty, but, for most athletes, their whole childhood is devoted to sporting excellence and the task has been completed (or not) by their early thirties, and some handle this better than others. With his innate humanity and ability to get on with people, Roger Federer will no doubt handle it very well, but it will be a challenge for him nonetheless.

Through this chapter, and indeed throughout this book, I've tried to identify the flaws in Federer's personality in order to paint a realistic picture of him. In truth, there are precious few, and there's no doubt he's a remarkable man and a great benefit to his sport. He exudes a calmness both on and off the court that gives the impression of wisdom beyond his years, almost of an old soul who has an innate sense of what's really important and what can be discarded. And while the journalist Marco Mordasini might be correct in saying, 'You can't be as success-ful as he is without creating some envy,' it's astonishing how little envy Federer has created and how few enemies he has.

When I asked Seppli Kacovski, Federer's first coach and a man who's seen his fair share of real life and suffering, what he thought Federer's less attractive attributes might be, he replied, 'He must have his shadow sides, but I don't know them. I think he has everything he needs. He needs to be physical and competitive, so tennis gives him that. He has a sense of fun, and that is satisfied by people around him. He likes to make contact with people, so he gets them talking. He is basically fulfilled, and that is why he's the man he is.'

BIBLIOGRAPHY

THIS BOOK IS A development of two earlier editions of *Fantastic Federer* and one edition of *Roger Federer – Spirit of a Champion*. At the time the first *Fantastic Federer* was published in May 2006, it was the first full-length biography of Roger Federer and, as such, there was no obvious bibliography or recommendation for further reading. Much of the information for both *Fantastic Federer* editions, *Spirit of a Champion* and this book has come from my own personal experience, articles I have written for various publications, and recordings of interviews and press conferences. Obviously, I cannot be everywhere so a lot of other information has come from newspaper cuttings, especially those of fellow tennis journalists I have worked with and respect. I have tried to credit them at least once within the text.

Since the first edition of *Fantastic Federer* came out, there has been another full-length biography, written by the Swiss tennis journalist, René Stauffer. It is titled *Das Tennisgenie*, and it was published in German in 2006 by the Swiss publishing house Pendo. The title translates as 'The Tennis

Genius', but when it came out in English published by the American firm New Chapter Press in 2007, it was under the name *Quest for Perfection: The Roger Federer Story*. That book was written under the same circumstances as this one, namely without the direct co-operation of Roger but with no serious obstacles put in the way. As a result, it covers similar ground to this one. It is stronger than this book in some ways and weaker in others; as the tennis correspondent of the *Tagesanzeiger* newspaper of Zurich, René has been at more Federer events than I have, though inevitably I have been at some he was not at. As a result, his book is more Swiss and mine more international.

I have tremendous respect for René, believing him to be the most knowledgeable of the Swiss tennis writers; I am pleased that his book now forms part of the database of public information from which a biography of Roger Federer can be drawn; and it's good that his work is available to the English-speaking world. I would, however, encourage anyone who has the ability to read German to opt for the original Stauffer book rather than *Quest for Perfection*. Translations never feel quite as authentic as the original, and René's smooth-flowing German prose hasn't always survived the journey into English with its meter intact!

The database of public information on Roger Federer also includes two short books that were of considerable help to me. Roger Jaunin's French-language book *Roger Federer* (Favre/Le Matin, 2004, updated 2006) was very useful, particularly for stories from the French-speaking part of Switzerland, while Freddy Widmer's *Moments '05: Augenblicke mit Roger Federer* (Basler Zeitung, 2005) provided some of the details about Federer's background in Basel.